THE SCORSESE PICTURE

THE
SCORSESE
PICTURE

THE ART AND LIFE OF MARTIN SCORSESE

BY DAVID EHRENSTEIN

A BIRCH LANE PRESS BOOK
PUBLISHED BY CAROL PUBLISHING GROUP

A Birch Lane Press Book
Published by Carol Publishing Group
Birch Lane press is a registered trademark of
Carol Communications, Inc.

Editorial Offices   Sales & Distribution Offices
600 Madison Avenue   120 Enterprise Avenue
New York, NY 10022   Secaucus, NJ 07094

In Canada: Canadian Manda Group
P.O. Box 920, Station U
Toronto, Ontario M8Z 5P9

Queries regarding rights and permissions
should be addressed to: Carol Publishing Group,
600 Madison Avenue, New York, NY 10022

Carol Publishing Group books are available at special discounts
for bulk purchases, for sales promotions, fund raising, or
educational purposes. Special editions can also be created to
specifications. For details contact: Special Sales Department,
Carol Publishing Group, 120 Enterprise Ave., Secaucus, NJ 07094

Manufactured in the United States of America
10 9 8 7 6 5 4 3 2 1

Design by Steven Brower

Library of Congress Cataloging-in-Publication Data

Ehrenstein, David.
        The Scorsese picture : the art and life of Martin Scorsese / by David Ehrenstein
                p. cm.
        "A Birch Lane Press book."
        Filmography : p.
        ISBN 1-55972-152-9 (cloth)
        1. Scorsese, Martin. 2. Motion picture producers and directors-
    -United States–Biography.   I. Title.
        PN1998.3.S39E35   1992
        791.43' 0233' 092–dc20   92-28650
                                                                  CIP

To the memory of Vito Russo

ACKNOWLEDGMENTS

For their invaluable advice, assistance, and encouragement, I should like to thank Eric Ashworth, Deana Avery, Marion Billings, Margaret Bodde, Sharon Butler, Robert Cohen, Raffaele Donato, Ann Edelstein, Bob Foster, Ann-Marie Harty, Julia Judge, Gail Kinn, Bill Reed, Richard Rouilard, Jonathan Rosenbaum, Thelma Schoonmaker, and Martin Scorsese.

CONTENTS

DAILY VARIETY

DAILY | DAILY

A Cahners Business Newspaper   **VOL. 231 No. 18**   Los Angeles, CA 90036, Monday, April 1, 1991   Newspaper Second Class P.O. Entry   16 Pages   75 Cents

SCORSESE, U EXTEND GOOD FELLASHIP

$10 MIL IN CLAIMS

Bankruptcy Petition Filed Against Troubled MGM-Pathe

By JUDY BRENNAN and AMY DAWES

MGM-Pathe's weeklong attempt to negotiate a creditors group's claims and block an involuntary bankruptcy collapsed Friday with a Chapter 7 petition filed against the company in U.S. Bankruptcy Court.

The filing culminates a two-month-old threat by some creditors (*Daily Variety*, Feb. 8), frustrated by the newly merged company's inability to pay its bills. The petitioners claim they are owed about $10.05 million of the estimated $50 million outstanding to vendors and creditors, outside of the company's bank notes.

Sources said other creditors not part of the petition may take similar action within the week.

Although MGM-Pathe officials said they had not read the filing, they said in a statement it was "unwarranted . . . would be vigorously resisted . . . and (the company) anticipates that the petition will be promptly dismissed."

For two months, MGM-Pathe's cochairman Giancarlo Parretti said he was expecting a $250 million infusion from Credit Lyonnais Bank Nederland. As of late Friday, the funds had yet to arrive, company insiders said.

In addition, a Superior Court judge has placed a lien against Pathe's theaters in Great Britain.

The Chapter 7 filing means the company is forced to liquidate its assets.

(Continued on Page 4, Column 3)

BV Wraps Syndie Pic Package

By ELIZABETH GUIDER

NEW YORK — In what is believed to be the first film output deal in syndication history, Buena Vista Television has sold a 50-title package to a consortium of independent and affiliate stations, including Tribune, Gaylord and Koplar Communications broadcast groups and Ted Turner's superstation WTBS.

The deal, which was anticipated (*Daily Variety*, March 12), includes 17 already released films — from "Who Framed Roger Rabbit" to "Pretty Woman" — and 33 yet-to-be-released pix, including "Billy Bathgate," "The Marrying Man"

and the sequel to "Honey, I Shrunk The Kids."

Some of the titles won't be available for broadcast tv until the late 1990s.

To date, more than 65 stations are involved in the deal, representing more than 70% of the country. Several of these broadcast station groups had joined forces last Summer in an informal consortium to reverse the trend whereby most major studio A titles had been going to cable outlets rather than to broadcast stations.

The stations joined together to establish a competitive bid for the so-called "Buena Vista I" package, effectively prenegotiating prices while BVTV toppers shopped the package to prospective cable buyers.

Both USA Network and Lifetime Cable apparently passed on the package. Official confirmation that the films would be going to syndication and not to cable came last week. There is also a 50-50 barter split on the Disney package.

BVTV president Bob Jacquemin says the deal represents a record fee per title. Sources estimate the price per film will hit $2.5 million, topping the last reported record of $2.2 million. That sum was paid by USA

(Continued on Page 15, Column 1)

New Cable Nets Feel Left Out In The Cold

By JOHN DEMPSEY

NEW ORLEANS — While cable operators are savoring the prospect of a bonanza of almost unlimited channel capacity in the next couple of years, fledgling basic-cable nets are fighting for their lives in the current channel drought.

There was euphoria at the National Cable Television Association confab last week as systems operators contemplated the vast channel expansion that digital compression technology has suddenly made cost-

(Continued on Page 10, Column 1)

ESZTERHAS BACK AS VERHOEVEN TRUSTS 'INSTINCT'

Ending a bitter feud that erupted seven months ago, screenwriter Joe Eszterhas and director Paul Verhoeven have resolved their creative differences over Carolco's "Basic Instinct" and will collaborate after all on the production, which rolls next Monday in San Francisco.

During their first and only meeting on the project Aug. 8 of last year, the two clashed over the dramatic structure and direction of the script, which Verhoeven now admits he "highly underestimated" and read initially "on too superficial a level."

Disagreements over plot points

(Continued on Page 6, Column 3)

'Quantum,' 'Law,' 'Doogie' Renewed

By BRIAN LOWRY

Three more primetime series have received pickups from their respective networks — with NBC ordering the Universal TV dramas "Quantum Leap" and "Law And Order" while ABC has admitted Steven Bochco Prods.' "Doogie Howser, M.D." for a third season.

"Law And Order" has been given a 22-episode pickup for next year, making it the only freshman series thus far to receive such an order. The show is currently on hiatus but is expected to return to 10 p.m. Tuesday with repeats this Summer and hang on to the slot next season.

Dick Wolf is exec producer of "Law," which stars Michael Moriarty, Richard Brooks and Chris-

(Continued on Page 15, Column 3)

Five Radio, 17 Tv Nods Top Peabodys

By RICHARD HUFF

NEW YORK — Cable News Network's wall-to-wall coverage of the Persian Gulf crisis has earned the service a 1990 George Foster Peabody Broadcasting Award.

Joining CNN in receiving the prestigious award are ABC for the premiere episode of "Twin Peaks," NBC's "Saturday Night Live" and The Disney Channel's "Mother Goose Rock 'N' Rhyme."

All totaled, the panel selected five awards in radio, 17 for televi-

(Continued on Page 14, Column 1)

Studio Signs Oscar Nominee To Exclusive Six-Year Pact Covering Producing, Directing

By CLAUDIA ELLER

Martin Scorsese

Martin Scorsese has entered into a rare exclusive six-year motion picture producing and directing deal with Universal Pictures, the studio for which he just completed "Cape Fear" and previously directed the controversial pic "The Last Temptation Of Christ."

With the exception of only two projects that the filmmaker can direct for outside companies — including the previously announced "Age Of Innocence" for 20th Century Fox and another yet to be decided — Scorsese's services as director and producer are exclusive to Universal for the entire term of the deal.

As Universal officials explained it, other preexisting projects Scor-

(Continued on Page 12, Column 1)

DELAYED RELEASES

Spring Pix In Holding Pattern

By LAWRENCE COHN

NEW YORK — Distributors have postponed first and second-quarter releases left and right, as indies fall short of p&a cash and as blockbusters and sleeper hits from last year refuse to leave theaters.

Some new pix are being put off just until April or May, but others are bouncing from Spring berths to late Summer or Fall, hoping to come up for air after the flood of big Summer releases.

Meanwhile, new feature films released domestically in the first quarter dipped to 1989 levels, with 105 pictures opening.

The shortfall was strictly in the independent sector, as major suppliers remained solid.

Chart on page 14 displays the steady nature of the majors' output, except for 1987 when distribs stockpiled films in anticipation of a strike.

But the majors have also been holding back plenty of product this quarter:

Orion has twice postponed its sequel "FX 2," from March 15 to April 5 to May 10, which results in probably a stronger positioning for this film's launch just ahead of the Summer big guns. Distrib's strong legs for both "Dances With

Wolves" and "The Silence Of The Lambs" makes this a logical delay.

MGM, like Orion in the midst of financial problems, reshuffled its schedule several times so that now the distrib has five films to choose from for May release. Yet that company's schedule is a blank for the four months following its Jan. 11 launch of "Not Without My Daughter."

Disney has delayed its Sylvester Stallone comedy, "Oscar," for five weeks after its initially planned

(Continued on Page 14, Column 4)

Disney Pix Names Fink Prod'n Veepee

Charles Fink is moving from the world of animation into live-action production with new duties as v.p. of production for Walt Disney Pictures, effective today.

Fink was v.p. of creative affairs for Disney theatrical animation since August 1989, previously serving as a director in the department.

According to Disney/Touchstone prexy David Hoberman, Fink's appointment is timed with an expansion of activities under the Disney

(Continued on Page 10, Column 3)

MARTIN SCORSESE (ABOVE) AND ROBERT DE NIRO
(BELOW) AT THE AMERICAN CINÉMATHÈQUE TRIBUTE TO
SCORSESE MARCH 22, 1991.

SCORSESE AT THE AMERICAN CINÉMATHÈQUE TRIBUTE. THE MOST RESPECTED AMERICAN DIRECTOR OF HIS GENERATION IS FETED IN THE GRAND BALLROOM OF THE CENTURY PLAZA HOTEL IN LOS ANGELES.

DE NIRO, SCORSESE, AND FILM INDUSTRY LAWYER PETER DEKOM AT THE CINÉMATHÈQUE TRIBUTE.

[Top] Robert De Niro. [Center] Nick Nolte and Rosanna Arquette. [Bottom] Michael Ovitz.

→6 →6A →7 →7A →8 →8A →9 →9A →10 →10A →11

→12 →12A →13 →13A →14 →14A →15 →15A →16 →16A →17

→18 →18A →19 →19A →20 →20A →21 →22 →22A →23

→24 →24A →25 →25A →26 →26A →27 →27A →28 →28A →29

→30 →30A →31 →31A →32 →32A →33 →33A →34 →34A

PROLOGUE: "I'M NOT QUITE SURE WHAT HAPPENED"

Halfway through *Taxi Driver,* director Martin Scorsese turns up in an acting role, playing a fare picked up by the film's cabbie hero, Travis Bickle. As the cab comes to a stop at a street corner, Scorsese is seen in the passenger seat — neatly dressed in a dark suit, with carefully groomed beard and mustache. It is very late at night.

"Put the meter back," he orders Travis sharply. "Let the numbers go on. I don't care what I have to pay. I'm not getting out. Pull over to the curb. We're gonna sit here." Closing his eyes, he sits calmly for a moment, then continues his speech: "You see that light up there? The woman on the second floor? See the woman in the window? That's my wife. But that's not my apartment."

He smiles broadly and chuckles to himself, almost gloating.

He continues, "You know who lives there? A nigger lives there. Now what d'you think of that? Don't answer. You don't have to answer everything. I'm gonna kill her with a .44 Magnum pistol. Did you ever see what a .44 Magnum could do to a woman's face? Just fuckin' destroy it. Blow it right apart."

Leaning forward in a slightly conspiratorial manner, he says, "Now, did you ever see what it could do to a woman's pussy? *That* you should see!"

He again pauses briefly and smiles broadly.

"You must think I'm pretty sick or something," he says to the silent cabbie. "Do you think I'm sick?"

We get no answer; the scene is over. Neither the man nor the woman he claims to be his wife nor the "nigger" with whom she's allegedly committing adultery are ever seen or heard from again. We don't need to see them because the scene has served its purpose. It has cast over the film a pall of sexual violence that is almost palpable.

To say the scene is disturbing doesn't begin to describe the effect. Within that disturbance lies a shock of recognition of the terrible truths the scene discloses about racism, sexism, misogyny, and violence in modern American culture. It is a shock of recognition absent from almost any other American film one could name.

While I was preparing this book, I was commissioned by a major newspaper to write a profile of Martin Scorsese on the occasion of the release of *GoodFellas*. In my conversations with the newspaper's editors, this scene from *Taxi Driver* was referred to again and again. Though none of them had met Scorsese, they were adamant about the scene's centrality to his life. His films are filled with violence, aren't they? He's given to wild mood swings, isn't he? Hasn't he been married four times? Hasn't he had tumultuous love affairs? Hasn't he had drug problems? And why stop there? Could there be some *actual* Mafia connections? In short, When did he *stop* beating his wife?

Pointing out that the borderline psychotic they were describing would be constitutionally incapable of directing a movie, I managed to get the editors to admit that they had perhaps gone a bit overboard. Did they really believe that Martin Scorsese *was* the character billed as "passenger watching silhouette"? Of course not. But a picture of this kind makes better copy than a discussion of the issues the scene raises, or an examination of the hard work that went into its making.

It's difficult not to "go overboard" when talking about a filmmaker who so often does so himself. Visual extravagance, extremes of emotional and physical violence, and an overall indifference to the traditions of the "well-made" dominate Scorsese pictures: *Taxi Driver*, *Raging Bull*, *The King of Comedy*, *The Last Temptation of Christ*, and *GoodFellas*. Playing a pivotal character like the "passenger watching silhouette" would be out of character for Steven Spielberg or Francis Coppola, but it's almost expected of Martin Scorsese. His commitment to his work has always been total — out front and white hot. It's tempting to want to erase the line that separates art from life. But in order to make any sense of Scorsese that line must remain in place.

Martin Scorsese wasn't bedeviled by interracial adultery during *Taxi Driver*. He was trying to execute a complex, risky project under trying, underbudgeted circumstances while battling a studio hostile to his ideas. *Raging Bull* emerged from a period of intense self-doubt and struggle, in part brought on by what Scorsese has admitted was "a serious bout with drugs." Yet the film examines the problems of its deeply troubled boxer hero with an almost serene lucidity, refusing to justify his brutal behavior in any way. Most remarkable of all is *The King of Comedy*, directed by Scorsese while his marriage to Isabella Rossellini was coming to end. During production the filmmaker was hospitalized, near death from physical complications due to chronic asthma. A devastating critique of show business, the film is the

wittiest and most psychologically incisive picture Scorsese has made. But it doesn't bear a trace of the personal turmoil that went on during its making.

Obviously, there is a relationship between Scorsese's life and certain of his films. His studies of New York's Little Italy, *Who's That Knocking at My Door?* and *Mean Streets,* are plainly drawn from a world Scorsese knew. But to deal with his works as if they were nothing more than raw material for discovering the "truth" about the man standing behind them is grotesque. It reduces Scorsese's life to tabloid caricature and virtually ignores what the films themselves have to say. What the films have to say — about our time and about ourselves — is so upsetting that the temptation many feel to want to "blame the messenger" is perfectly understandable.

Martin Scorsese is the American commercial cinema's most controversial director. Critics and audiences are deeply divided in their feelings about his work. For every movie lover who passionately supports Scorsese, there's another just as angered by him. Often as not, violence is the principal objection.

The fantasy shoot-'em-ups of Stallone and Schwarzenegger may sport a higher body count, but the violence in Scorsese's films disturbs audiences as no other director's work has since Sam Peckinpah. But *Taxi Driver*, with its famous blood-splattered finale, may be among Scorsese's least disturbing films. In that study of the gradual mental disintegration of a lonely New Yorker, viewers are at least granted a form of catharsis. But while *Raging Bull* has a zero mortality rate, there's no escaping the physical brutality that runs throughout. And in *The King of Comedy*, where no punches land, the threat of violence is such a constant that the character's ostensibly humorous antics are unrelievedly tense.

In 1988, *The Last Temptation of Christ*, Scorsese's adaptation of Nikos Kazantzakis's existential version of the New Testament, inspired worldwide protests. Without having seen the film, leaders of the radical religious right claimed grave spiritual offense and mounted a campaign to ban *Last Temptation*. In spite of well-organized demonstrations and several incidents of violence (there were firebombings at European theaters playing the film), the protests did not stop the film from being shown. However, the controversy led to Hollywood's increasing turn toward "inoffensive" movie subjects.

Making a controversial film is one thing; changing the course of history is another. Some observers feel Scorsese came frighteningly close to doing just that in March 1981. John W. Hinckley, Jr., the black sheep son of an upper-middle-class Republican family, attempted the assassination of President Ronald Reagan — seriously injuring Reagan press secretary James Brady in the process. Hinckley was obsessed with *Taxi Driver* and its star, Jodie Foster. Could it be that Scorsese pictures weren't simply contentious, but downright *dangerous* as well?

In 1989, polls conducted by *Premiere* and *American Film* magazines, disclosed that, by an overwhelming margin, film critics here and abroad considered *Raging Bull* to be the best motion picture of the decade. In light of the mixed-to-hostile notices the film received on its 1980 release, this was a remarkable critical turnaround. More striking still was the fact that, in the *American Film* poll, *The King of Comedy*, a 1982 box office disaster that opened to some of the most scathing notices of Scorsese's career, made the Top Ten of the decade's best.

These poll results underscore the most important thing about the films of Martin Scorsese — the lasting effect. The same critics who initially found the works disturbing, later discovered that they couldn't get them out of their minds. Scorsese's imagery was too powerful, his examination of character too deep, his storytelling methods too rich. They discovered that Martin Scorsese made pictures that *last*.

On the evening of March 22, 1991, twelve hundred people representing the highest levels of the American motion picture industry attended the American Cinematheque's "Sixth Annual Moving Picture Ball." The key fund-raising event for this organization devoted to the presentation and preservation of classic films, the "Moving Picture Ball" pays tribute to the career of a high-profile Hollywood notable. Previous tributes were staged for Eddie Murphy, Bette Midler, Robin Williams, Steven Spielberg, and Ron Howard. This time the spotlight was on Martin Scorsese.

The Scorsese salute was long overdue. He has been the industry's most vocal champion of classic film preservation and exhibition. In 1980 he launched a successful campaign to encourage the Eastman Kodak company to produce a longer-lasting film stock. Over the years he has lent his assistance to the reconstruction and re-release of such diverse films as *Peeping Tom*, *Rocco and His Brothers*, *Once Upon a Time in the West*, *The Golden Coach*, *Lawrence of Arabia*, *Spartacus*, and *Earth Entranced*.

Lavish fund-raisers are a way of life in Los Angeles, and the Scorsese event was much like any other. The army of reporters, paparazzi, and autograph hounds outside the hotel were the same as those at any splashy movie premiere. The Ball also provided ample numbers of stars and celebrities: Robin Williams, Robert De Niro, Jodie Foster, Nick Nolte, Barbara Hershey, Rosanna Arquette, David Bowie, Giorgio Armani, Sydney Pollack, and Michael Ovitz among them.

Still there was an air of expectancy to this particular evening. The Academy Awards were three nights away, and Scorsese's *GoodFellas* was in the running for six Oscars, including Best Picture, Best Director, and Best Screenplay. Having won 1990's Best Picture and Best Director prize from the three major American critical bodies (the New York Film Critics Association, the Los Angeles Film Critics Association, and the National Society of Film Critics), the film's chance of winning the Oscar as well was one of the two prime topics of conversation. The other was Michael Ovitz.

Ovitz, the president of Creative Artists Agency, whose client list includes Robert Redford, Kevin Costner, and Jane Fonda, Madonna, Michael Jackson, and the Coca-Cola company, is by consensus the most powerful man in Hollywood. The embodiment of the bottom line — fixated, high-pressure deal-making that rules present-day film production, he is the town's most controversial figure as well. His hard-nosed business practices are discussed with admiration by some and likened to petty thuggery by others. In 1987 Ovitz added Scorsese, one of commercial moviemaking's most famous mavericks, to his roster of clients. Scorsese has yet to make the $100 million-plus box office blockbuster that is Hollywood's measure of success. Still, to most industry observers his alliance with Scorsese is not without its logic. As Katharine Hepburn reportedly said of Fred Astaire and Ginger Rogers — "She gives him sex, and he gives her class" — Scorsese gives Ovitz class, Ovitz gives Scorsese *clout*.

Scorsese first met Ovitz in 1986 while making *The Color of Money*. Its stars, Paul Newman and Tom Cruise, are major Ovitz clients. Still reeling from Paramount Pictures's last-minute cancellation of *The Last Temptation of Christ* in 1984, Scorsese was determined to revive the project. After signing with Ovitz (at the completion of *The Color of Money*) Scorsese found he was able to do so. Universal Pictures agreed to back *The Last Temptation of Christ*. Ovitz was the reason this otherwise cautious studio was willing to go where Paramount feared to tread.

Many industry observers wondered if *The Color of Money* was the price Scorsese had to pay to make *Last Temptation*. Was he simply trying for a "mainstream" hit? Or was it a case of wanting to work with Paul Newman, the star of one of his all-time favorite biblical spectaculars *The Silver Chalice?*

And what about the work that Scorsese has been doing since signing with Ovitz? The hard-edged *GoodFellas* is followed by a mass market thriller, *Cape Fear*. Then Scorsese started *The Age of Innocence*, a period romance without a trace of sex or violence. Is he alternating "one for them" and "one for me?" Hardly, for

he has never shied away from mainstream filmmaking.

Martin Scorsese has been consistently vocal about his love of Hollywood. Moreover, while his topics and techniques may be far off the beaten path, his attitudes haven't been uncommercial. Scorsese seriously considered directing *Dick Tracy* (which eventually fell to Warren Beatty) and even wanted to do the musical *Little Shop of Horrors* (directed by Frank Oz) in 3-D. So it should be no surprise that Scorsese would want to make *Cape Fear*. He is doing exactly what he wants. The only difference in his moviemaking is that he now has Michael Ovitz in his corner.

SCORSESE: It's the oddest thing. *Everything* changed at the beginning of 1987 when I signed with CAA and Mike Ovitz. To this day I'm not quite sure what happened. I try to stay out of that. I live in New York. I'm not part of that Hollywood world. All I know is someone says they're going to try to do something for me and they come through. Ovitz is a very supportive man.

But the support of Michael Ovitz, and of the actors, technicians, and other collaborators who sang Scorsese's praises at the Moving Picture Ball is one thing. Hollywood's highest honor is another. Three days later, at the Academy Awards, *GoodFellas*, while winning a Best Supporting Actor Oscar for Joe Pesci, lost Best Picture and Director to neo-conservative heart-throb Kevin Costner and *Dances With Wolves*.

Oscar 1990 was a virtual replay of Oscar 1980, when Scorsese lost to Robert Redford — another matinee idol making his directorial debut. *Ordinary People*, Redford's plea for parent-child understanding among upper- middle-class WASPS, beat out *Raging Bull* for Best Picture. Redford's film didn't figure in either the *American Film* or *Premiere* polls of the decade's best. It was a film of its moment, and that moment had passed. *Dances With Wolves*, Kevin Costner's plea for understanding between nature-loving Native Americans and virtuous white cavalrymen, is also a film of its moment. When that moment passes, *GoodFellas* will be recognized as less a gangster melodrama than an indictment of Reagan-Bush America, where brute force and conspicuous consumption have completely subsumed identity and ethics. In short, *GoodFellas,* like *Raging Bull,* is not the stuff of which Oscars are made.

"We knew we weren't going to win," Scorsese's film editor, Thelma Schoonmaker, said of the Oscars. "What we should have done was to send telegrams to all our friends — 'We know we're not winning!'"

Yet Scorsese won something that in the long run may prove to be more valuable. A week after the Oscars, the trade press announced that Universal Pictures had signed him to a six-year pact for his future projects as both a director (as with *Cape Fear*) and a producer (as with *Mad Dog and Glory*, a Scorsese production directed by John McNaughton). Under the terms, he will also be able to continue to work on projects previously announced for other studios, including *The Age of Innocence*, for 20th Century Fox.

The Universal deal is reminiscent of a pact the studio struck with director Alfred Hitchcock. From 1962 to his death in 1980, the master of suspense called Universal his home, making films as he saw fit. But in the increasingly competitive and financially distressed world of big-time filmmaking, it's going to be different for "Marty" than it was for "Hitch."

SCORSESE: I hadn't anticipated, and I was even surprised — pleasantly surprised — that the signing of the deal prompted headlines in *Variety*. So when people ask "What does Hollywood think of you?" I really don't know. Judging from the wonderful tribute that the Cinematheque gave, I think genuinely a lot of people like me. I also think a lot of other people remember me from the seventies, think I'm crazy, and don't want to have anything to do with me.

These are the people still stuck with the image of Scorsese sitting in Travis Bickle's cab. They have the Scorsese they want, and no other is likely to satisfy them — even when it's offered by Scorsese himself.

"Films are my life," Martin Scorsese has repeated in interview after interview. Not sex, not violence, not religion, not even being an Italian-American; films are the most important thing in the world to him.

Scorsese: "Films are my life."

It's time to take Martin Scorsese at his word.

THE WORLDS OF MARTIN SCORSESE — THE DIRECTOR ON THE SET OF (CLOCKWISE FROM TOP LEFT) MEAN STREETS, THE KING OF COMEDY, RAGING BULL, AND TAXI DRIVER.

TAXI DRIVER: "ARE YOU TALKING TO ME?"

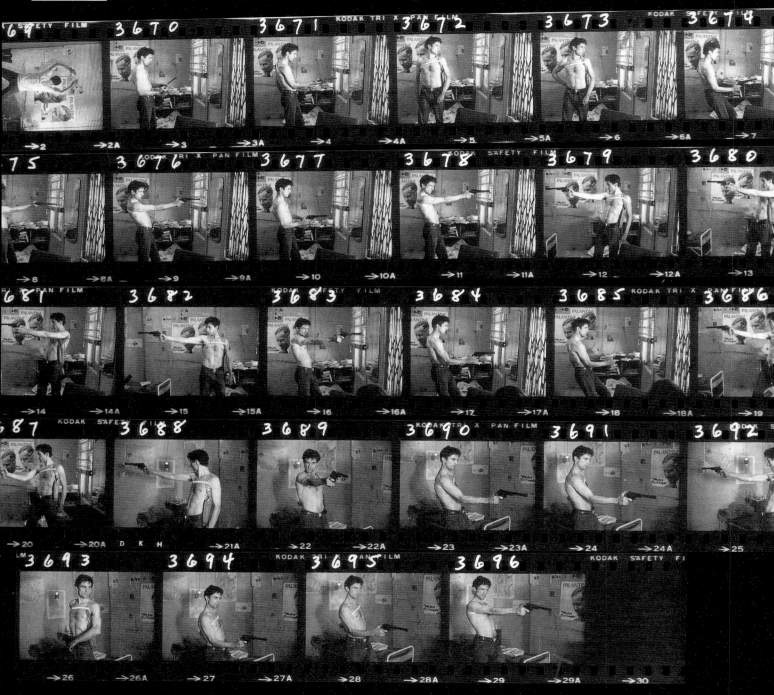

RAGING BULL: "HIT ME IN THE FACE!"

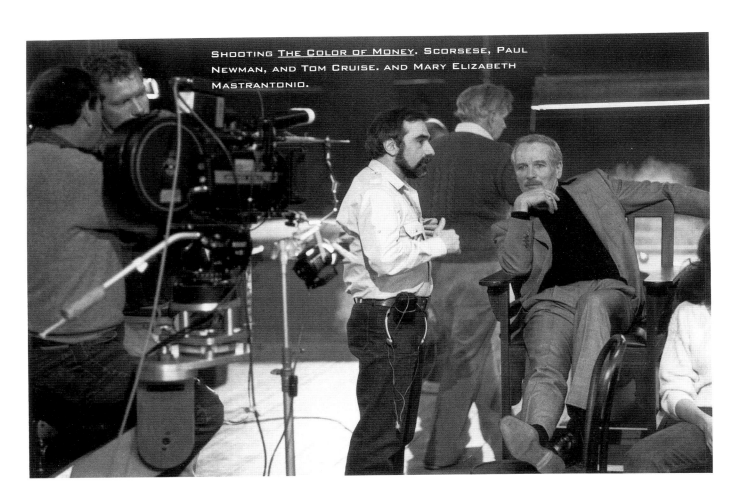

SHOOTING <u>THE COLOR OF MONEY</u>. SCORSESE, PAUL NEWMAN, AND TOM CRUISE. AND MARY ELIZABETH MASTRANTONIO.

Deep inside the "underworld" — GoodFellas.

Shooting the wedding scene in GoodFellas — Lorraine Bracco, Scorsese, and Ray Liotta.

A scene from GoodFellas — Tommy (Joe Pesci) moments before getting "wacked." Charles Scorsese (left) and Frank Dileo are the assassins.

The relationship between mobster James Conway (Robert De Niro) and small-time hood Henry Hill (Ray Liotta) reaches a turning point in this scene from GoodFellas.

Karen (Lorraine Bracco) confronts an imprisoned Henry (Ray Liotta) in GoodFellas.

SEQUENCE FROM <u>GoodFellas</u> — KAREN (LORRAINE BRACCO) NEARLY GETS "WACKED." JIMMY (ROBERT DE NIRO) TELLS HER TO GO DOWN THE STREET AND PICK OUT A DRESS FROM A NEWLY STOLEN SHIPMENT. SUDDENLY SHE BEGINS TO SENSE THERE'S SOMETHING WRONG.

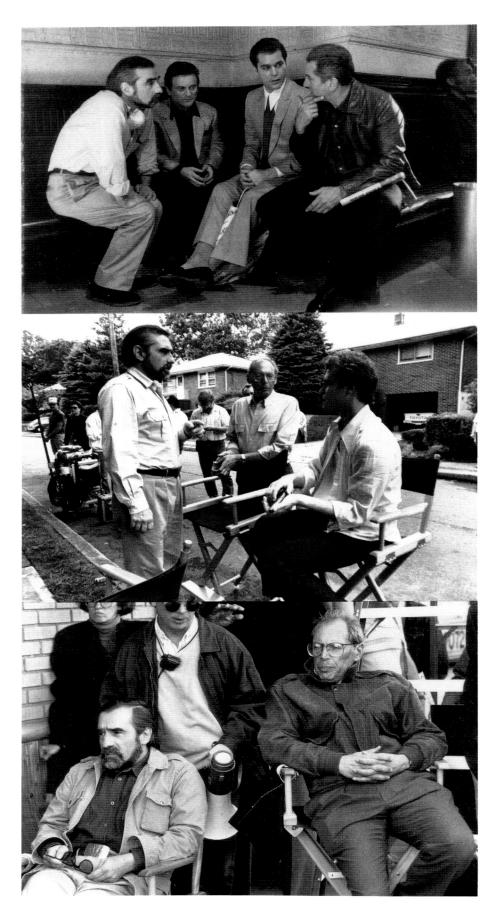

SCORSESE SHOOTS <u>GOODFELLAS</u>. (TOP) WITH HIS
THREE LEADING PLAYERS. (CENTER) WITH RAY LIOTTA.
(BOTTOM) WITH PRODUCER IRWIN WINKLER.

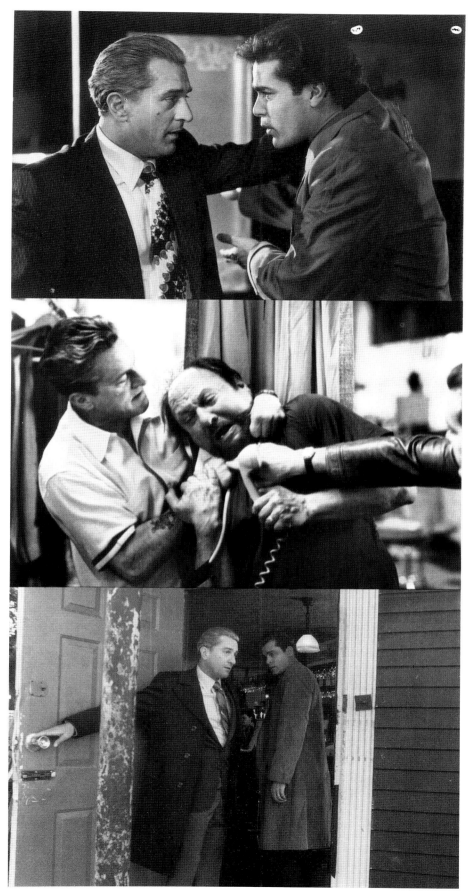

GOODFELLAS — THE COOL VIOLENCE OF JAMES CONWAY (ROBERT DE NIRO).

ONE: "EVERYTHING WENT INTO FILM"

"I was born in Queens in 1942. Both of my parents worked in the garment industry. My father pressed clothes, and my mother was a seamstress. We first lived in Corona, near my aunts and uncles. I remember we had a two-family house with a yard in the back that had a tree in it. I first contracted asthma around that time, and when I had my tonsils taken out there were all kinds of complications. I was kind of sickly. I didn't go out of the house very much. Then in 1949 we had to move back to the Lower East Side because my father had some problems with the landlord. I've never found out what it was all about, exactly, but basically, we couldn't afford to live in Corona anymore.

"The whole idea, when my parents got married in 1933, was, like all their other brothers and sisters, to move to Long Island to places like Corona or Sunnyside — to get out of the tenements. But we had to move back to the city to the block my father was born on. Until we found the three rooms that we eventually settled in, we lived with my grandmother and grandfather at 241 Elizabeth Street. We shared four rooms — my grandparents, my father, my mother, and me and my brother Frank— for six months. You can imagine the shock of moving from Queens to the Lower East Side, where you looked out the window and saw kids running down the street playing with garbage pails."

— SCORSESE

There is a shot near the beginning of Martin Scorsese's first feature, *Who's That Knocking at My Door?*, that starts with a view of the window of a butcher's shop taken from a high angle. We briefly see a butcher chopping meat, then the camera pulls back and slowly pans to the right, up the street on which the shop is located. At the corner of the street the panning movement stops. The camera then zooms in on two young men as they come around the corner and follows them down the street toward the butcher shop.

This zoom-and-pan represents a good example of Scorsese's technical filmmaking skill. In one simple shot, he sets a scene and introduces two important characters at the same time. But there is another level of meaning involved. The scene is set on Elizabeth street, and Scorsese's camera is on the roof of Scorsese's grandmother's apartment building. What we're seeing is roughly what we would view from his grandmother's window.

The zoom-and-pan approximates a scanning motion of the eyes — Martin Scorsese's eyes. The boy too sick to be "running down the street playing with garbage pails" was able to watch everything that went

33

on outside from this apartment perch. This sense of participatory distance — being at it once an insider and an... outsider— rapidly became an important feature of Scorsese's work. But in order to conceive and execute this visual/dramatic idea, Scorsese needed something more than the inspiration of his grandmother's window view.

Scorsese's parents knew the asthmatic child couldn't be kept housebound indefinitely. He desperately needed some form of escape. Moviegoing was the simplest and safest means of providing it, they discovered.

It was the early 1950s, the golden era of the Hollywood biblical spectacular. To recapture the public that had begun to abandon movies for television, the studios produced lavish, lascivious epics in widescreen processes like Cinemascope, VistaVision, and Todd-AO. Critics dismissed the films as vulgar trash, but to the young Scorsese *Samson and Delilah, Quo Vadis?, The Robe, Demetrius and the Gladiators, The Ten Commandments,* and *The Silver Chalice* were nothing of the sort. They complemented a religious iconography with which he was already familiar. The holy statuary in old St. Patrick's Church, which Scorsese attended every Sunday, were just as garishly colored. And what were the Stations of the Cross that decorated the church's walls but a storyboard for a film scene? Soon the boy began to plan religious epics of his own. He made fresco-like drawings of Roman soldiers and Christian martyrs — sketches for imaginary "Marsco Productions" to be shot in fabulous "Marsco Color."

In addition to biblical spectaculars, Scorsese was exposed to movies in which heavenly choirs and pious poses played no part. *Giant, Duel in the Sun, Land of the Pharaohs, I Shot Jesse James, Night and the City,* and *Abbott and Costello Go to Mars* were among his favorites. But the film that left the most lasting impression on the young Scorsese was a British musical drama set in the world of international ballet, *The Red Shoes.*

Nothing could have been further from Scorsese's world than this tale of a steel-willed impresario obsessed with a beautiful ballerina. The film displayed a visual inventiveness unlike anything he'd seen in Hollywood movies. The screen was constantly filled with eye-catching details and startling color combinations. The camera was rarely still. There didn't seem to be anywhere it couldn't go or anything it couldn't do. To the housebound boy, *The Red Shoes* proved the movies were a means of total escape.

But camera mobility wasn't all he saw. Tales of commitment and self-sacrifice were familiar to the boy from the sermons he'd heard in church. *The Red Shoes* dealt with the same themes from a radically different perspective. The film's ballerina heroine wasn't a saint dying for the love of God; she was a mortal woman dying for the love of Art. In films as different as *Raging Bull, The King of Comedy,* and *Life Lessons* Scorsese made this self-sacrificial theme his own. But at the time he first encountered it in *The Red Shoes,* the future filmmaker's main arbiter of ethics and aesthestics was still the Catholic Church.

SCORSESE: I'm a lapsed Catholic. But I *am* a Roman Catholic — there's no way out of it. Remember when it was a mortal sin to eat meat on Friday, and then they changed the law and said you could? My parents never changed — they always ate fish on Friday, because it had become the custom. But just imagine: a *mortal* sin to eat meat! The worst possible sin for something like that! And then all of a sudden you *can* eat meat, and it's not a sin anymore. I can't begin to tell you the effect something like that can have on you. It's all dogma, of course, but you believe it, and the effect of it stays with you.

I'm not a theologian, but I do follow some of what goes on in the Catholic Church. And there's an enormous difference between the role played by the Church in this country and what it does in the rest of the world. You can argue all you want about policy issues and moral issues, but Pope John Paul still did an enormous amount of good in helping the situation in Poland. Here, on the other hand, you have people like Cardinal O'Connor making veiled threats of excommunication to politicians if they vote for freedom of choice for women who want abortions. So my feelings about the Church are very mixed.

When I went to church as a kid, they would from time to time have these things they called a "Mission." Priests and nuns who had worked as missionaries in places all over the world would come and tell their stories. They would bring these giant crucifixes and stand right in front of the altar and talk — scary hellfire-and-brimstone stuff. What they were doing was really *theater*. It was a holdover from the medieval period, when the church would have miracle plays that told about the lives of the saints, and dramatized tales from the Bible. Eventually these plays got a little bawdy, and had to be done outside of the Church. Everybody enjoyed watching Noah get drunk and his wife beat him with a broom instead of paying attention to the religious implications of the story. But for me the important thing has always been this notion of theater — and, by extension, film — stemming from something being done in front of the altar.

Scorsese's films are filled with references to religious ritual. In *Who's That Knocking at My Door?* and *Mean Streets* there are scenes in which characters are shown putting on street clothes in the ceremonial manner of a priest donning religious vestments. Both films also feature drinking scenes in which liquor is treated like the consecrated wine used in church services. On a more cryptic level, there are the overhead shots of a desk and a candy counter in *Taxi Driver* across which Travis Bickle passes his hand like a priest in the midst of the mass, and in *Raging Bull* the iconlike shots of the bloodied Jake splayed across the ropes like a Rouault Christ.

However, religion in Scorsese's work doesn't come into play on the visual level alone. In an early scene in *Mean Streets,* the film's hero, Charlie (played by Harvey Keitel), enters old St. Patrick's Church and kneels before the altar rail. On the sound track a voice (Scorsese's) intones, "Lord, I am not worthy to eat your flesh, to drink your blood." Almost immediately Charlie complains that the act of confession has little meaning for him. "You don't make up for your sins in church," he says. "You do it in the streets. You do it at home. The rest is bullshit and you know it."

Scorsese's insistence that the secular can't be separated from the spiritual sets him apart from other filmmakers who have dealt with spiritual matters, including Roberto Rossellini, Carl Th. Dreyer, and Robert Bresson. Rossellini's *Europe '51* and Dreyer's *Passion of Joan of Arc* are films about saints mistaken for sinners. Bresson's *Pickpocket* and *L'Argent* are films about sinners awaiting the moment of redemption that will transform them into saints. Scorsese's sinners may come to understand their faults, as do Charlie in *Mean Streets* and Jake in *Raging Bull,* but there's not a chance they'll achieve sainthood.

Scorsese doesn't sit in judgment of his characters. He sees their "good" and "bad" sides as simply *there* — everyday matters of fact. It's a viewpoint he acquired naturally. In the neighborhood in which Scorsese was raised, with its rich mixture of middle-class families, priests and shopkeepers, and petty crooks operating on the fringes of organized crime, the good and the bad are never mutually exclusive.

SCORSESE: People always ask me why I'm interested in characters like the ones in *Mean Streets.* The answer is I grew up with a lot of these people. Before I knew what it was that they did, I thought it was all normal. For example, they would disappear sometimes for a few days and come back with a load of shirts somebody got off a truck. Everybody in the neighborhood wore a shirt.

I had a little disagreement with Melvyn Bragg, the British television interviewer, about this. He thought my "nostalgia" was reprehensible. I said I couldn't see it that way at all. Like — this one guy. I loved him. You couldn't call him a "gangster" because he wasn't at all. He was just this *guy*. Today you'd say that he was involved in a certain lifestyle. It was pretty scary at times, but he was always at our house. He lived in the next apartment. He practically raised me! And there were a lot of people around just like him.

Because of this familiarity, it would be misleading to draw the conclusion that Scorsese had to make a conscious "choice" between church and "street." Asthma, and the physical limitations that accompanied it, made moot any question that "the street" would come to predominate in Scorsese's life. The Church failed to take hold for him — but for very different reasons.

SCORSESE: Originally I wanted to become a priest. When I was a teenager I really thought that that was what I was going to do in life — be a priest. People may think I didn't go through with it because of the rules about celibacy, but that's not really true. There was so much sexuality in the neighborhood, on the streets, I was facing it all the time. I didn't see it as that much of a problem, then. What really happened was, I studied at a seminary for a year, but was expelled because my grades were poor. I *still* wanted to become a priest. In fact, when I went to New York University, my thought was always that I'd graduate there, and *then* go back and study for the priesthood. But that all changed after I started college — *everything*

went into film.

The person most responsible for this change in Scorsese's thinking was Haig Manoogian, an associate professor of motion pictures at New York University and the director of that college's summer motion picture Workshop. Manoogian had served with the military as an information and education specialist during World War II, creating film, radio, and theatrical presentations modeled on the WPA's *Living Newspaper* revues of the 1930s. After the war he worked as a writer and producer for films made by the State of New York. He was also an independent producer of children's films. In the 1950s he turned to teaching filmmaking — both its history and its practice — creating at NYU a course of study remarkable for its thoroughness.

Manoogian's book *The Filmmaker's Art* (Basic Books, 1966) puts on paper what Scorsese studied in person. A distillation of Manoogian's lectures and course plans, the text offers a concise history of film and a reasoned assessment of aesthetic theory while arguing in favor of the works of such foreign directors as Bergman, Kurosawa, and Satyajit Ray over the output of Hollywood. Manoogian's "art film" bias is typical of postwar mainstream academic thinking about the movies. But there is one thing his work offers that like-minded film scholars of his generation did not: solid nuts-and-bolts information about how to actually make films.

Manoogian's insistence on wedding theory to practice, coupled with his frequently combative teaching style, immediately attracted Scorsese. For his part, Manoogian was excited to discover in Scorsese a student so responsive to his ideas and at the same time willing to challenge them. With Manoogian's help, Scorsese was able to make two short films at NYU — *What's a Nice Girl Like You Doing in a Place Like This?* and *It's Not Just You, Murray!* — and begin work on *Who's That Knocking at My Door?* Most students only managed to make a single short during their course of study.

SCORSESE: Haig had a class on the history of television, motion pictures, and radio.

That was the first year — two credits, about four hours a week. He would show you a film or a television program, and then give you a history lesson. You'd have to write a paper — that was all. It was a very large class, up to three hundred kids, and it was in a little auditorium. He would get up on stage and say, "There are a lot of you here today, but at the end of the course there won't be." He would weed out those students who were just using the class to spend the afternoon looking at movies. He was very tough. He would start by just rattling off facts as fast as he could, and go through the history of film so quickly that in an hour and a half, if you'd been writing it all down, you would have everything you really needed to know. By the second year he had you taking introductory production courses, where you learned what a camera is, what a lens is, and so forth. But he had gotten rid of so many of the students from the first year, by then, that the course would really work.

I was very, very lucky to have Haig as my teacher, but it was more than that. What was great about Haig was that he had such *passion*. Incredible arguments would come up between him and the class. But there was a reason for them. He cared so much about it. *We* cared so much about it. I was really blessed in meeting someone who inspires you to "stay true to what you know. Do that — don't do anything else." That was *very* important in helping me make films like *Who's That Knocking at My Door?* and *Mean Streets*.

Of course, I couldn't agree with him about everything. That would have been impossible. For example, my major paper for one of his classes was on *The Third Man*. He gave me a B for it and wrote on the margin, "Remember, it's just a thriller." Now Haig wasn't a snob. He loved musicals. But he loved Italian neorealism much more. *Bicycle Thief* he adored. I was becoming increasingly interested in genre movies. Haig wasn't that way, so we'd always argue. To try to even *intimate* that a western — except for *High Noon* or *The Oxbow Incident* — was any good, was unheard of. *Buchanan Rides Alone?* "How dare you?" To bring up Budd Boetticher's name, or Andre DeToth's or some upstart named Sam Peckinpah — "outrageous!"

By this time, Scorsese *had* dared to love Boetticher, DeToth, Peckinpah, and a host of other directors considered culturally disreputable by establishment critics. For he had become part of New York City's film-buff circuit, a community whose tastes leaned not only toward this trio of western-film directors, but also looked upon such genres as the thriller, the gangster melodrama, and the horror film with complete seriousness.

In the days before the videocassette recorder made agoraphobes of us all, moviegoing — particularly in New York — was something of an urban sport. The truly dedicated could rise at dawn and catch a double feature of westerns or action flicks at one of the score of theaters on Forty-second Street between Seventh and Eighth avenues. In the afternoon the scene moved to the Museum of Modern Art for silent films or Hollywood movies of the thirties and forties that weren't yet regarded as classics. In the early evening, the place to be was the Upper Westside for an obscure independent American film at the New Yorker or an equally obscure foreign picture at the Thalia. Those with the energy could finish the night in Greenwich Village with a late show of *Hiroshima Mon Amour* at the Bleecker St. Cinema or an underground film at the Charles.

In perpetual moviegoing motion, the hardy band of nomads that moved across this landscape were a curious lot. Some were budding filmmakers like Scorsese. Others were movie critics in the making. The rest might best be described as cracked utopians — people determined to rid the real world of its flaws by virtually replacing it with the perfect imaginary world of the silver screen. Nothing if not partisan in their likes and dislikes, the buffs disagreed about everything except the importance of a lengthy article by critic Andrew Sarris published in *Film Culture* magazine (no. 28, Spring 1963).

Simply titled "The American Cinema," Sarris' article consisted of filmographies of Hollywood directors, ranked in order of importance, followed by brief commentaries explaining the ranking. Scorsese was amazed to see such Manoogian-approved masters as Fred Zinnemann and William Wyler referred to as "Fallen Idols," while Howard Hawks and the past-master of the "just a thriller," Alfred Hitchcock, were included in a pantheon of American filmmaking's all-time greats. Nevertheless, like all the other buffs, Scorsese found himself using "The American Cinema" as a guide to moviegoing, and his opinions about films and filmmakers quickly changed as a result.

When it first appeared, "The American Cinema" was attacked by critic Pauline Kael and ridiculed by mainstream academics. But this opposition didn't stop the article (which was expanded into a book published by E. P. Dutton in 1968) from having a profound effect on American film culture. Like Scorsese, others discovered that Sarris's views were a part of something larger having to do not just with film taste, but film practice. What Sarris called the "*auteur* theory" was his adaptation of a critical trend that first appeared in the pages of the French film magazine *Cahiers du Cinema* in the early 1950s. The *Cahiers* critics — François Truffaut, Jean-Luc Godard, Eric Rohmer, and Claude Chabrol — in revolt against a French filmmaking system in which studied adaptations of literary classics were predominant, declared that Hollywood's genre-oriented directors set an example that should be followed. They proved their point when they became filmmakers themselves. The fruits of their labors, including *Breathless, Shoot the Piano Player*, and *The Cousins*, arrived on American screens just before the Sarris article appeared.

Much as the French were inspired by the speed and energy of American films, Scorsese now found himself responding to the wit and visual excitement of the French "new wave," incorporating many of its editing techniques into his student shorts. At the same time, "The American Cinema" encouraged Scorsese to feel that there was a place for someone like him in Hollywood. Personal expression, the *auteur* theory argued, was possible even within the confines of the studios. Deeply involved with Manoogian's aesthetic principles (in 1980 he dedicated *Raging Bull* to his recently deceased teacher "with love and resolution"), Scorsese still couldn't help but be impressed that the films his teacher liked least often were the most influential on him as a director-in-the-making. For Manoogian, the cinema was divided into greater and lesser genres. Scorsese had come to see things in more pragmatic terms. Seth Holt's lurid melodrama *Station Six-Sahara* had as much to teach him about film technique as a classroom classic like David Lean's *Great Expectations*. As with the church and the street, coexistence was possible.

There was something else Scorsese needed to learn before his evolution from film student to filmmaker was complete, and neither Haig Manoogian nor Andrew Sarris could teach it to him.

As the 1970s began, Scorsese found himself at a turning point. Film was no longer just an enthusiasm, it was becoming a career. His problem was putting that career in focus.

By this time Scorsese had added another short film to his credit, the darkly comic *The Big Shave*. But his larger-scaled filmmaking plans weren't jelling. He was hired to direct a low-budget thriller called *The*

Honeymoon Killers, but its writer-producer, Leonard Kastle, took over as director after Scorsese had been on the project for only a few days. Working collectively with his class of NYU film students — ex-student Scorsese had now become a teacher — he supervised a documentary on the antiwar movement, *Street Scenes 1970*. He also began taking jobs as a film editor, making a name for himself with the seminal rock music spectacular *Woodstock*. Other editing jobs on *Medicine Ball Caravan*, *Elvis on Tour*, and *The Unholy Rollers* quickly followed.

What Scorsese desperately needed was to make a feature of his own. But the experience of *Who's That Knocking at My Door?*, begun in 1965 but not properly completed until 1969, had disillusioned him.

SCORSESE: We had such problems making that film. It had taken so long. Finally it was ready, and we were having problems getting it to open in theaters. Harry Ufland, who was my agent at William Morris then said "What do you expect? Here we are in the age of free love — total sexual expression — and here *you* come with a picture about a guy who claims to love a girl so much that he won't make love to her because he has too much respect for her." I was totally mortified by that — the realization that my way of life, the place I came from, was so small and self-contained that the rest of the world simply couldn't respond to it.

But in the end there was one person who made me feel really good about that film, and that was John Cassavetes. There were a lot of things about *Who's That Knocking at My Door?* that disappointed me, that I thought didn't really work. But John said the kiss at the end between Harvey Keitel and Zina Bethune was much more powerful than the one at the end of *Invasion of the Body Snatchers*, where Kevin McCarthy kisses Dana Wynter and discovers she's an alien. Of course I didn't agree with him. They were

entirely different kinds of films and, to me, *Invasion of the Body Snatchers* was so much more dramatic. But John made me understand that in *Who's That Knocking* I was *trying* to do something genuine, something that was authentic about certain types of people and a certain way of life. That was so important for me to hear then.

To anyone familiar with Cassavetes' career, his feelings about Scorsese's film come as no surprise. A promising young performer during 1950s television's Golden Age, Cassavetes went on to make an impact in such Hollywood films as *Crime in the Streets*, and *Edge of the City*. But just as he seemed to be settling down to a standard-issue career, the actor turned filmmaker.

In 1959, Cassavetes and a dedicated crew of actors and technicians scraped together $40,000 to make a 16mm film called *Shadows*. Released theatrically in 1961, this drama, shot in a loose, free-wheeling, documentary-like style, centered on a light-skinned African-American brother and sister and their dark-skinned half-brother. Compared to Hollywood movies, *Shadows* was messy, disorganized, even incoherent. Yet it explored race relations in America in a way no Hollywood film had before or since.

Critics throughout the world hailed *Shadows* as a breakthrough in film technique. Hollywood took notice and offered Cassavetes directing work. But studio interference on two Hollywood films, *Too Late Blues* and *A Child Is Waiting*, led the actor-director to go it alone once again. *Faces*, his independently made drama of a suburban couple in crisis, revived his reputation. It also brought sharp criticism of his "self-indulgent" techniques. The films that followed, *Husbands, Minnie and Moskowitz, A Woman Under the Influence, The Killing of a Chinese Bookie, Opening Night, Gloria*, and *Love Streams*, did nothing to change the minds of Cassavetes' detractors, but they brought him an ever-growing circle of supporters, Scorsese among them.

Shot on a shoestring in actual locations, favoring

character over plot, and raw emotion over conventionally contructed drama, *Who's That Knocking at My Door?* was clearly influenced by *Shadows. Mean Streets, Alice Doesn't Live Here Anymore,* and *New York, New York,* all bear traces of Cassavetes' ideas. But the most profound level of Cassavetes influence on Scorsese was a personal one.

SCORSESE: I met John through my friend Jay Cocks in 1970, around the time of *Husbands.* I remember we stood in the back of Cinema I in New York watching it, and certain actors we knew — I won't mention any names — started to walk out during the vomiting scene. It was hilarious. They couldn't take it because it was just so *real.*

John was an amazing man. He was the first person I met in the business to carry his sense of enthusiasm over to the people around him. He kept instilling a sense of security in me; that what I felt inside me was real and truthful and valid. However I wanted to express it was OK by him — as long as the truthfulness was there. That's why I would sometimes want to just go and *listen* to him. He'd go out to dinner, I'd follow him. He would go somewhere, I'd walk him home.

John was open to new people if he respected their work. And even though I hadn't made very much, he respected what I did. I remember the Sunday before I flew down to Arkansas to do *Boxcar Bertha* I went to his house and I stayed there the whole day. Sometimes he would have people over at his house reading scripts — and I would be one of the people reading with actors like Ben Gazzara! He *wanted* me to hang around, basically. I remember another time I went over to his house, just after *Medicine Ball Caravan.* I was living in Los Angeles then. My girlfriend at the time was with me and . . . she . . . well after a

short time — she left me! I was very upset. Immediately I wanted to move away from the house where I was at the time, because I'd been living there with her. I was very young then, about twenty-five or twenty-six, but I was still acting like I was thirteen. John let me stay on the set of *Minnie and Moskowitz,* which was the Elaine apartments on Highland Avenue. I stayed there just to get the other place out of my mind and find an apartment of my own. The thing was, this apartment was a set. There was a phone there, but you'd pick it up and there was a sticker with a little note that said "telephone." It was so weird!

John kind of took care of me in a way then. I was alone. I wanted to work, and I was finding it very difficult. So he had me do some sound effects editing for him on *Minnie and Moskowitz.* I really didn't do much, but he put me on salary. I was making $500 a week for a few weeks. I would watch him edit, and sometimes I would tease him about it. "Come on, John, get to the point of the scene and get it over with." He'd say, "Never! Never! Once you get to the point of the scene you have to undo it again!"

You know, he originally wrote *The Killing of a Chinese Bookie* for me to direct. He needed to do a picture, and he started walking around his office in Universal City, dictating to Elaine Ward, his assistant. He wrote like that — walking around dictating these beautiful speeches that never came to a point. So he started with, "It's this Chinese guy who's a bookie, and everybody owes him money, and it's called *I've Got a Yen For You!*" I've got the original two-page dictation.

He was a giant, and Hollywood knew it too. It was just like with Orson Welles. He got an Oscar nomination for acting once, for script once, and for directing once. He never won. I felt so badly after he passed away in 1989, because I saw him so seldom over the last few years. I remember especially when he came to see *Raging Bull*. He was very supportive of that film. But then I got married again and started to stay in New York more. I saw him less and less. But we talked. He wanted to do a film with me where he played the director and I played his assistant. The director has a nervous breakdown, and the assistant carries him through and becomes the person who really directs the film. He said, "Come on, we'll do it!" But I was doing *The King of Comedy* then. It was a great idea. He had the script written and everything. It would be nice to do it someday, but you'd need *him*.

John Cassavetes did more than offer Martin Scorsese moral support and part-time jobs; he gave him the most important advice of his career. After Scorsese directed *Boxcar Bertha*, a low-budget gangster melodrama made on assignment for producer Roger Corman, Cassavetes told him, "Now that you've made a piece of shit, why don't you make a movie about something you really care about?" And so, instead of accepting another assignment from Corman — a *Papillon* rip-off called *I Escaped From Devil's Island*, Scorsese made *Mean Streets*.

Set in Little Italy, this melodrama of youthful drifters on the fringes of crime was a return for Scorsese to a world he'd once dismissed as "too small and self-contained" for general interest. *Mean Streets* proved that wasn't the case. The film won him critical accolades, made a star of actor Robert De Niro, and finally lifted Scorsese's filmmaking career off the ground.

By staying true to his vision (as Cassavetes advised), Scorsese won the day. At the same time, he felt he had taken on a great responsibility; he was putting the lives of Italian-Americans on screen in an unprecedented way.

SCORSESE: Before *The Godfather* and *Mean Streets* came along, there were only a few Hollywood films about Italians that made sense. *House of Strangers* was accurate in terms of emotion — particularly in the character of the son played by Luther Adler. Richard Conte was great in that too. As for Edward G. Robinson, I love him as an actor, but there was a little too much of the old "Mustache Pete" Italian in his performance. Hawks's *Scarface* is a great film, but it's marred by that "Mama Mia!" school of Italian acting. Paul Muni was a great actor, but his performance in it is dated. George Raft and Ann Dvorak on the other hand were so good, so natural. Muni's scenes with his mother were embarrassing. No one talks that way.

Take *The Black Hand*, I don't think there were any Italians in the cast. Can you imagine? But it was still pretty good, and so was *Pay or Die!* even though it had a lot of "Mama Mia!" stuff. Ernest Borgnine and Zohra Lampert were great, and the story was just like a western — one man cleaning up the town. Someday somebody should redo that story because of John Petrozino and what he tried to do — get Italian-Americans to stand up for themselves. Actually I shouldn't even say Italian-Americans, they were just *Italians* then, because in the teens and twenties no Italian was going to deal with an "America" run by Irish cops. Petrozino showed them the American way — you don't have to pay off the extortionists here. In Sicily, yes — but not here!

Oh yes, another good film was *The Brotherhood*, Marty Ritt's film. I think the actors did a very good job, considering that *none* of them were Italian. There's an honesty to it, especially the scenes with — again! — Luther Adler!

Scorsese's next film had nothing to do with Italians. *Alice Doesn't Live Here Anymore*, a comedy-drama about a widow trying to make a life for herself and her son by reviving her career as a singer, only to end up working as a waitress in a coffee shop, was one of a number of intimate, small-scale productions the studios produced in the early seventies. *Alice* turned Scorsese from a promising talent into an important player. It was a commercial success and won for its star, Ellen Burstyn, an Academy Award for Best Actress.

SCORSESE: I got that picture through Francis Coppola. He was having dinner with Ellen Burstyn, and she told him she was looking for a young director because she had this script that Robert Getchell had written that she wanted to do. He'd just seen an answer print of *Mean Streets*. We took it to him right away to show him how great Bob De Niro was — that's how Bob got cast in *Godfather II*. Francis told Ellen about me, and John Calley of Warner Bros. sent me the script. I realized immediately that this was the thing I should try to do.

Now *Alice* was purely and simply a film made for a studio. I made it in order to learn how to make a studio picture. It was really a business proposition. But I tried to do something of my own with it at the same time. At one point John Calley called me into his office to talk about the film. He said, "I gotta tell you one thing. My boss, Ted Ashley, said he wants a happy ending. That's it. I can't help it." It was a given. I said OK. So I did a happy ending in spades with the marriage proposal in the cafe and everybody applauding. But there's a touch of uncertainty in the last shot with Alice and her son walking away. You see, the movie is really about the two of *them*.

Scorsese had now fully evolved as a film director. He had learned the basics from a master teacher, struggled as an independent, served his apprenticeship in the exploitation field, taken a chance — and won — with a personal project, and made a film

by the studio rules. In the films that followed — *Taxi Driver, New York, New York,* and *Raging Bull* — he took a further step, one that decisively shaped his career. Scorsese had ideas about the creation and presentation of film characters that radically broke with ideas — Cassavetes' included — that had gone before.

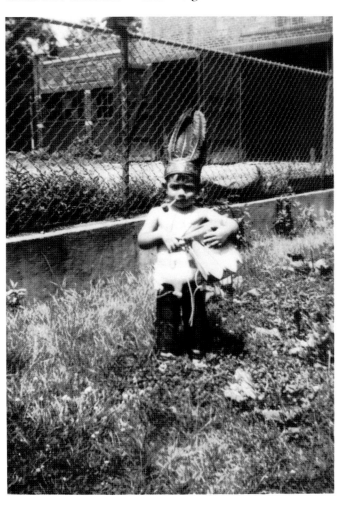

WHILE SCORSESE HAS YET TO DIRECT A WESTERN, HE SHOWS A FONDNESS FOR NATIVE AMERICANS IN THIS PHOTO TAKEN AT HIS HOME IN QUEENS, NEW YORK, CIRCA 1948.

MR. AND MRS. CHARLES SCORSESE FREQUENTLY MAKE
APPEARANCES IN THEIR SON'S PICTURES — AS DOES
SCORSESE'S DOG, ZOE.

INFLUENCES:

JAMES DEAN AS A BROODING LONER IN GEORGE STEVEN'S GIANT (1956)

FAVORITE SURREALISM OF ABBOTT AND COSTELLO GO TO MARS (1953)

IDA LUPINO IN RAOUL WALSH'S MUSICAL MELODRAMA, THE MAN I LOVE (1946)

FAVORITE WESTERN: SAM FULLER'S FORTY GUNS (1957)

ANNA MAGNANI IN JEAN RENOIR'S GOLDEN COACH (1952)

RENATO SALVATORI AND
ALAIN DELON IN LUCHINO
VISCONTI'S CLASSIC <u>ROCCO
AND HIS BROTHERS</u> (1960)

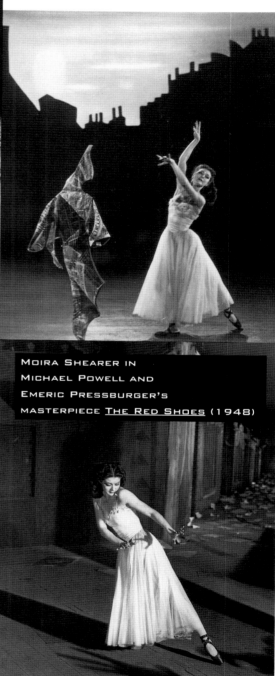

MOIRA SHEARER IN
MICHAEL POWELL AND
EMERIC PRESSBURGER'S
MASTERPIECE <u>THE RED SHOES</u> (1948)

JEAN ROUGEUL AND MARCELLO MASTROIANNI
IN FEDERICO FELLINI'S <u>8½</u> (1963),
A FAVORITE FILM OF COUNTLESS
DIRECTORS, SCORSESE BEING NO EXCEPTION.

JOSEPH COTTEN AND JENNIFER JONES IN
DAVID O. SELZNICK'S EROTIC WESTERN
<u>DUEL IN THE SUN</u>, DIRECTED BY KING VIDOR;
(1946)

SCORSESE DIRECTING HIS SECOND STUDENT FILM, IT'S NOT JUST YOU, MURRAY!

FILM STUDENT MARTIN SCORSESE AND HIS CREW SHOOTING HIS FIRST FILM, WHAT'S A NICE GIRL LIKE YOU DOING IN A PLACE LIKE THIS?

SCORSESE DIRECTS HARVEY KEITEL AND ZINA BETHUNE IN A ROMANTIC SCENE FROM WHO'S THAT KNOCKING AT MY DOOR?

WADLEIGH, SCORSESE, AND THELMA SCHOONMAKER
WORKING ON THE EDITING OF <u>WOODSTOCK</u> AS
HIPSTER ELDER AND W.C. FIELDS LOOKS ON.

Mat No. 103

"Abounds with vitality and cinematic invention. At parties, J.R. and his pals drink Vino, play with revolvers and have a good time with 'the broads'. Surpasses similar efforts in 'The Graduate' and 'Easy Rider.'"
—Time Magazine

"A highly original film of great worth and sensitivity. It is a very profound film in the way that 'Medium Cool' and 'Easy Rider' express and create ideas about a certain aspect of modern life."
—Parker, Newsday

ZINA BETHUNE
in Martin Scorsese's
WHO'S THAT KNOCKING AT MY DOOR
introducing HARVEY KEITEL
with LEONARD KURAS
A TRIMOD FILM PRESENTATION · A JOSEPH BRENNER ASSOCIATES RELEASE
Hear the hit song WHO'S THAT KNOCKING Sung by THE GENIES on EPIC LABEL

Mat No. 206

Mat No. 104

KURAS
RELEASE

t No. 501

PRAISE FROM EVERYWHERE

NEW YORK:

"More intense and sincere than most commercial releases. Scorsese is effective in isolating the moments of 'Marty'-like boredom that J. R. accepts as concomitants to life—a drunken beer party that almost turns into a gang bang."
—Canby, New York Times

"A highly original film of great worth and sensitivity. It is a very profound film in the way that 'Medium Cool' and 'Easy Rider' express and create ideas about a certain aspect of modern life."
—Parker, Newsday

"A fresh and very real experience. A gem in the worthy company of other gems made by such notable, realistic American film makers as Haskell Wexler ('Medium Cool'), Alan King ('Warrendale'), and Peter Fonda and Dennis Hopper ('Easy Rider')."

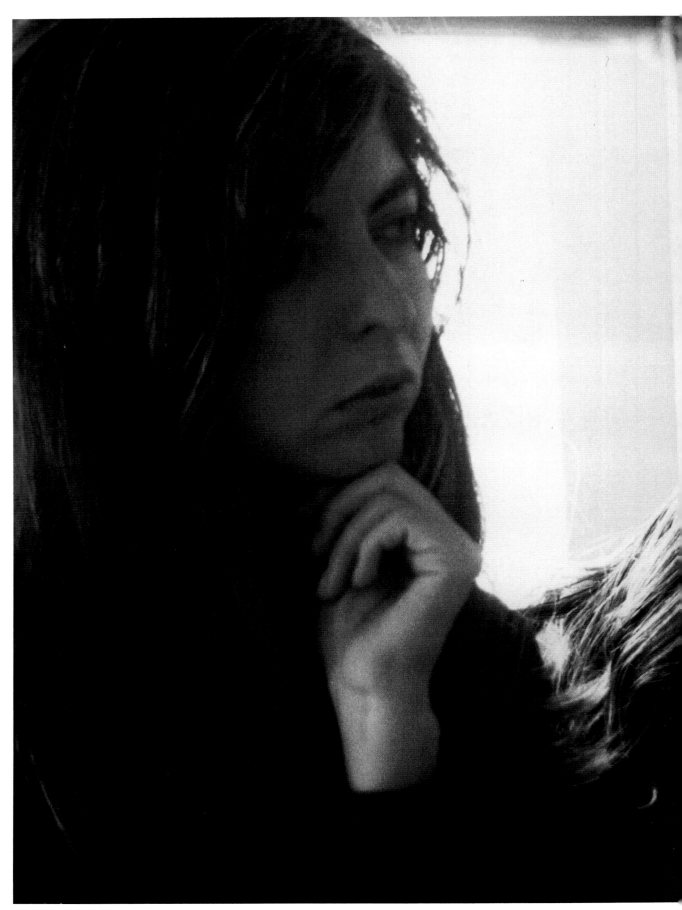

MARTIN SCORSESE AND FILM EDITOR THELMA SCHOONMAKER, CIRCA 1970:
THE BEGINNING OF A LONG AND FRUITFUL CREATIVE PARTNERSHIP.

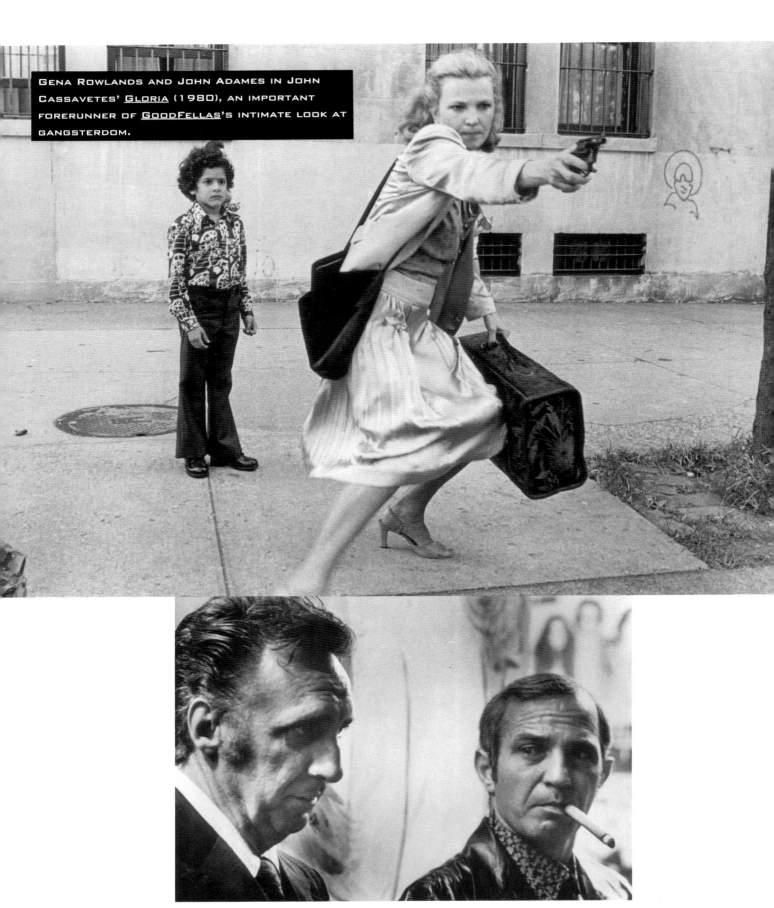

GENA ROWLANDS AND JOHN ADAMES IN JOHN
CASSAVETES' GLORIA (1980), AN IMPORTANT
FORERUNNER OF GOODFELLAS'S INTIMATE LOOK AT
GANGSTERDOM.

TIMOTHY CAREY AND BEN GAZZARA IN THE KILLING
OF A CHINESE BOOKIE (1978), JOHN
CASSAVETES' FILM WHICH HE HAD ORIGINALLY
WRITTEN WITH SCORSESE IN MIND TO DIRECT.

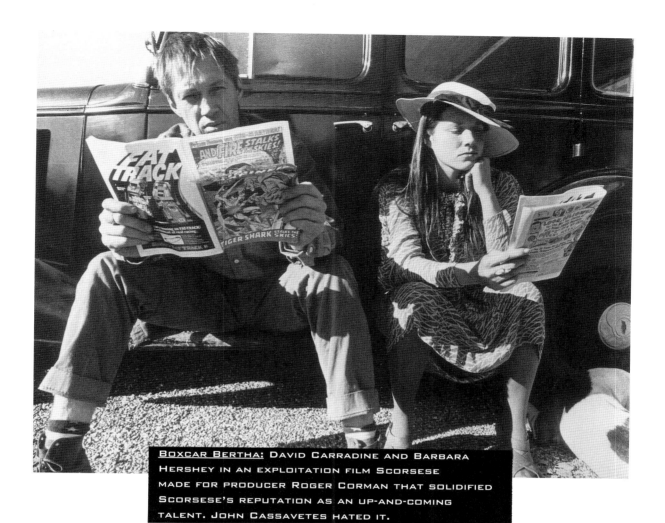

BOXCAR BERTHA: DAVID CARRADINE AND BARBARA
HERSHEY IN AN EXPLOITATION FILM SCORSESE
MADE FOR PRODUCER ROGER CORMAN THAT SOLIDIFIED
SCORSESE'S REPUTATION AS AN UP-AND-COMING
TALENT. JOHN CASSAVETES HATED IT.

UNHOLY IDOLS: (CLOCKWISE FROM TOP LEFT) A CHRIST-LIKE DE NIRO ON THE ROPES IN <u>RAGING BULL</u>; GREGORY PECK CLASPS HIS HANDS AS IF IN PRAYER ON THE SET OF <u>CAPE FEAR</u>; SCORSESE INSPECTS DE NIRO'S CRUCIFIXION TATTOOS FOR <u>CAPE FEAR</u>.

SCORSESE AT THE ALTAR RAIL WITH HARVEY KEITEL,
SETTING UP THE OPENING SCENE OF <u>MEAN STREETS</u>.

MEAN STREETS: ASSASSIN (ROBERT CARRADINE) AND
VICTIM (DAVID CARRADINE).

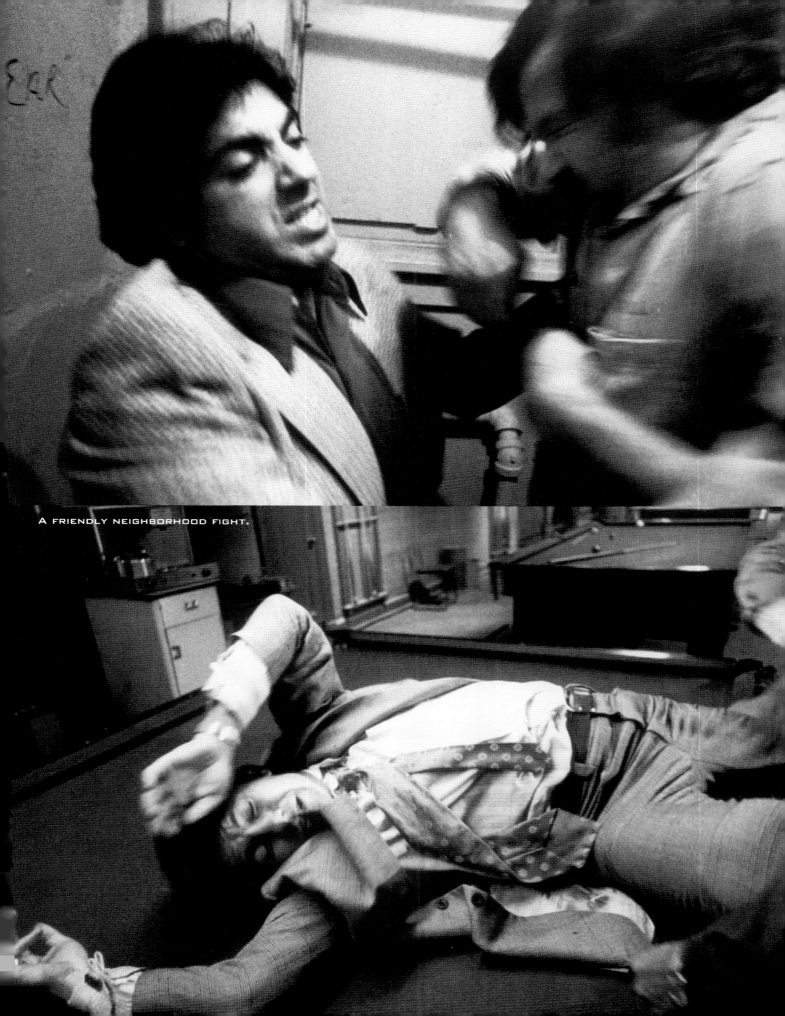

A FRIENDLY NEIGHBORHOOD FIGHT.

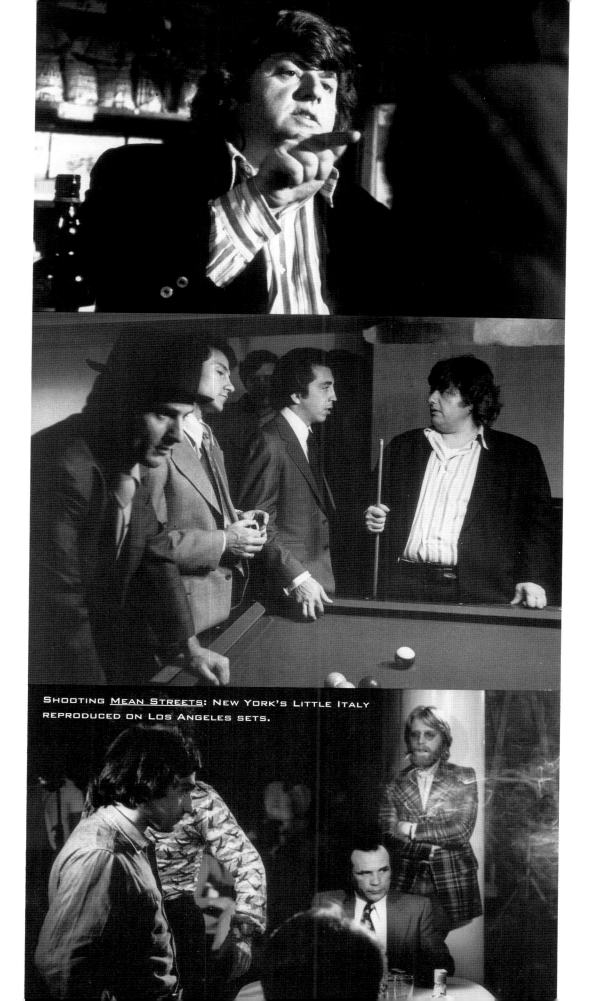

SHOOTING <u>MEAN STREETS</u>: NEW YORK'S LITTLE ITALY REPRODUCED ON LOS ANGELES SETS.

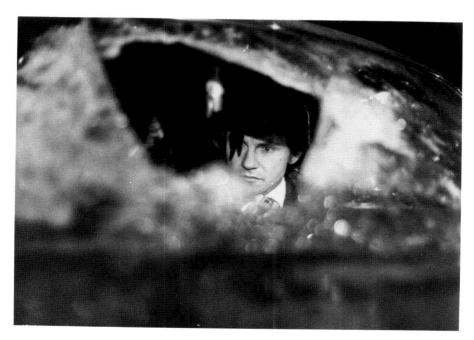

Scorsese's leading men: Robert De Niro and Harvey Keitel in <u>Mean Streets</u>.

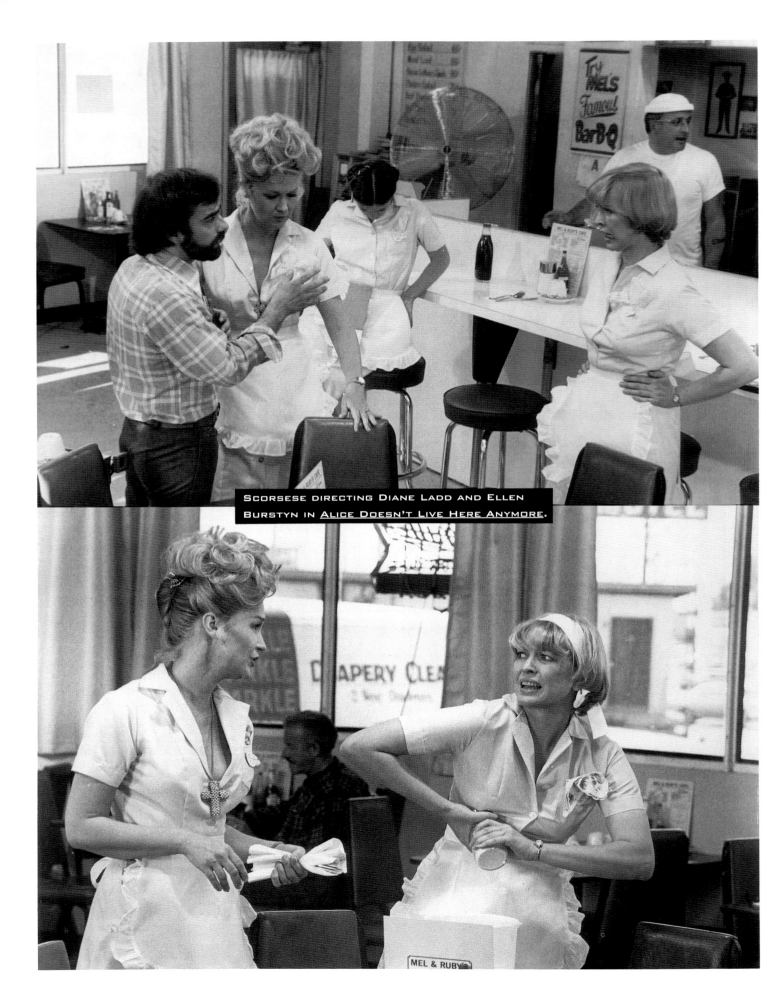

SCORSESE DIRECTING DIANE LADD AND ELLEN BURSTYN IN <u>ALICE DOESN'T LIVE HERE ANYMORE</u>.

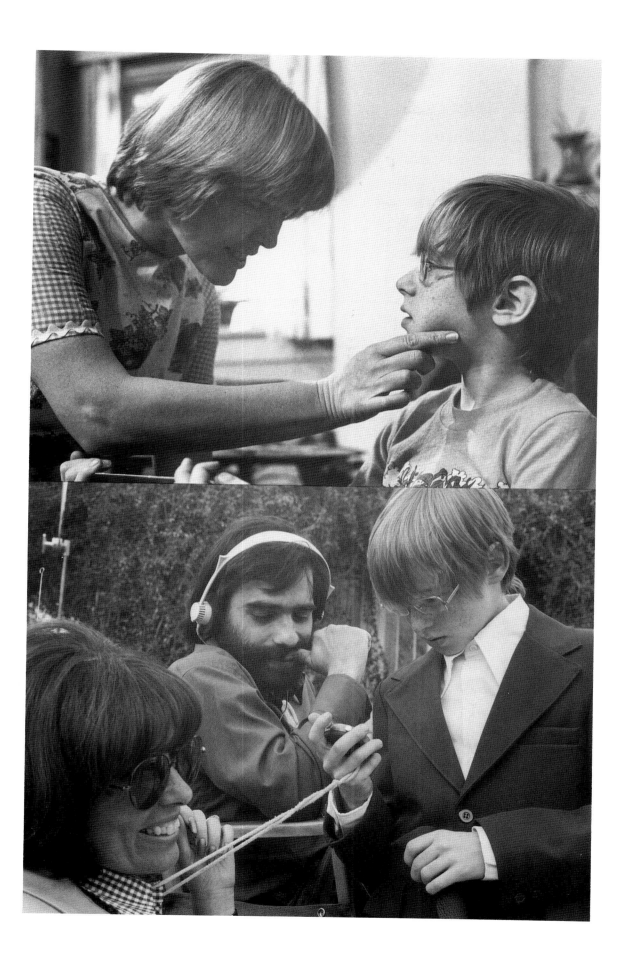

TWO: "I WANT TO PROVOKE THE AUDIENCE"

"What has always puzzled me," wrote critic Andrew Sarris in his *Village Voice* review of *Raging Bull,* "is why anyone would want to make a movie about Jake La Motta."

If you know anything at all about boxing, either in the ring or on the screen, Sarris's question is easy to understand. Jake La Motta was far from a fighting idol like Joe Louis, Muhammad Ali, or the man La Motta fought most often for the middleweight crown, Sugar Ray Robinson. In fact, there was never anyone quite like Jake La Motta ever associated with boxing.

The "Bronx Bull" wasn't noted for his technical skill, personal charm, or social consciousness. The only thing he appeared to have going for him was an ability to take — and dish out — brutal, punishing blows to the face and body. Seeing La Motta in the ring suggested he viewed boxing less as a public sporting challenge than as a private masochistic rite. Outside of his boxing victories, and his unsettling taste for abuse, the only other noteworthy aspect of La Motta's career is that two years before winning the championship away (from Marcel Cerdan in 1949), he was briefly barred from the ring for throwing a fight.

A major studio film about such a controversial figure is unusual, but *Raging Bull* moves into areas that are truly exceptional. Instead of attempting to justify La Motta's behavior, the film lets the ugly facts of his life, both in and out of the ring, speak for themselves. To audiences accustomed to feel-good fantasy, or uplifting biographies in the *Gandhi* mold, Scorsese's approach is deeply shocking.

Raging Bull depicts Jake La Motta as a bullying, paranoid wifebeater given to hysterically self-destructive rages. In one scene after another he picks ugly, petty fights with his wife, Vickie; brother, Joey; and almost anyone else who crosses his path. He channels this negative energy into his professional matches — taking blows, as if to punish himself for his venality, and giving them, as if to strike back against enemies real or imagined. This pattern of brutality comes to a climax in a scene in which Jake accuses Joey of sleeping with Vickie, effectively alienating the two people most willing and able to deal with him.

After his retirement from the ring, a different La Motta emerges — older, very fat, and less likely to hit first and ask questions later. Jake moves to Florida and opens a night club. But this new career comes to an abrupt end when he is arrested for allowing an underage prostitute to frequent his establishment. He is unable to raise bail, and is sent to prison. We next see Jake a few years later, reduced to working as an emcee at a seamy strip joint. It is the lowest point in his life, but things brighten when a chance meeting with Joey leads to their reconciliation. In the film's last scene we see La Motta on the verge of a comeback as a performer at a respectable night club, reciting Shakespeare, Tennessee Williams, and Budd Schulberg. However *Raging Bull* doesn't end with this scene of Jake, but with a quotation from the New English Bible, John IX: 24–26:

> So for the second time, [the Pharisees] summoned the man who had been blind and said: "Speak the truth before God. We know this fellow is a sinner." "Whether or not he is a sinner, I do not know," the man replied. "All I know is this: Once I was blind and now I can see."

This quote plainly implies a moral dimension to the life we've just seen. But in 1980, when *Raging Bull* was first released, many critics missed this point.

"One of the most repugnant characters in the history of the movies," declared Kathleen Carroll of the New York *Daily News*. She was mystified as to why the film "totally ignores [La Motta's] reform school background, offering no explanation as to his antisocial behavior."

"The movie doesn't throw up its hands in horror; it just looks on," Pauline Kael complained in her *New Yorker* magazine attack, upset that Scorsese "doesn't give us specific insights into La Motta."

"Martin Scorsese makes pictures about the kind of people you wouldn't want to know," Joseph McBride remarked in his *Daily Variety* review. He speculated that the film, filled with scenes "almost perversely chosen to alienate the audience," would "do well in class situations but may flounder in the mass market due to the off-putting character [of Jake]."

To these critics, Scorsese had broken some of the most important unwritten laws of commercial filmmaking. He had created an unsavory protagonist whose behavior he refused to justify in the accepted sociopsychological manner (i.e. "his reform school background"). Scorsese didn't condemn La Motta's misdeeds in the usual Hollywood fashion, by creating a contrasting "good" character to castigate Jake and provide a buffer between the troublesome hero and potentially offended viewers. Worse, Scorsese had failed to supply his film with a neatly resolved finale. Without some sort of catharsis — preferably one of the "life-affirming" variety — viewers were forced to take away unanswered questions and unresolved feelings. In short, *Raging Bull* was guilty of not being a standard-issue boxing movie.

Since the 1930s the image of the boxer in the movies has been as rigid as that of the gunslinger or the private eye. Films as superficially different as *Golden Boy, City for Conquest, Body and Soul,* and *Somebody Up There Likes Me* all tell essentially the same story. A lower-class youth, full of talent and enthusiasm, slugs his way to the top against incredible odds. He may have emotional problems or show a streak of self-destructiveness, but he is sure to be put back on course by a climactic dressing-down delivered by his ever-patient girlfriend or ever-loyal best friend and manager. This ritual verbal humiliation is quickly followed by the most important boxing match of the hero's life, which he, of course, wins.

In 1976 these same clichés were revived by *Rocky,* Sylvester Stallone's Oscar winner about a talented lower-class boxer who beats the odds with the help of his devoted manager and loving girlfriend. The only difference is that Stallone's fighter is a man of unblemished virtue. Dramatic conflict did not arise from the hero's attitude problem, but rather that of his boxing opponent, a cocky narcissist, plainly modeled on Muhammad Ali. The triumph of Stallone's Rocky offered white audiences, in fantasy, something they hadn't seen for years in reality — a white heavyweight boxing champion.

Stallone in *Rocky* is clearly meant to recall another movie boxer, Terry Malloy in *On the Waterfront.* Directed by Elia Kazan from a screenplay by

Budd Schulberg, this classic 1954 drama wasn't a boxing film per se. But as played by Marlon Brando, Malloy, a promising fighter-turned-dockworker, had much in common with the earlier cynical pugilists played by John Garfield and James Cagney. What was different about Terry was his manner — sullen and withdrawn one moment, expansively emotional the next. With his rolling gait and mumbling speech, Stallone in *Rocky* blatantly apes Brando.

But more than simple mimickry is involved. Terry Malloy, who "coulda been a contender" if he hadn't "taken a dive for the short-end money," left the ring and became "a bum." But like other movie fighters, he finally redeems himself with the help of a priest (filling in for the manager-pal role) and the traditional loyal girl. By contrast, *Rocky* offers the image of a Terry who actually *becomes* a contender. The "one-way ticket to Palookaville," spoken of in disgust in *On the Waterfront,* is transformed in *Rocky* through a hero whose "bum" exterior can't hide the fact that he's cast in the very image of comic-strip fighter Joe Palooka. The *Rocky* sequels continued to develop this Palooka paradigm along ever more unrealistic cartoonish lines, giving to the phrase a "one-way ticket to Palookaville" a literal meaning.

Raging Bull makes reference to *On the Waterfront* as well, but in a very different manner. In the film's last scene, Jake La Motta is seen rehearsing one of the bits he does in his club act, Brando's famous "I coulda been a contender" speech. Seated before his dressing room mirror, La Motta looks himself right in the eye and recites Schulberg's monologue. The irony of Jake doing Terry Malloy is rich: Jake became "a contender" precisely *because* he was willing to "take a dive for the short-end money."

In *On the Waterfront,* Malloy addressed his remarks to his brother Charlie, who he blamed for his plight: "You shoulda looked out for me. . . . It was *you,* Charlie." *Raging Bull* also centers on a fraternal conflict. But Joey's physical presence isn't needed for Jake to

deliver his lines, because by looking in the mirror, he's dealing with the real source of his problems — himself. The difficulty for viewers is dealing with that self, particularly in the manner Scorsese has chosen to present it.

Like John Cassavetes, Scorsese wants us to experience film on an immediate level — a series of audiovisual events unfolding in the white-hot here and now of the screen. A shot of Vickie languidly splashing her legs in a swimming pool as Jake's offscreen voice mumbles derisively about the gangsters who have been courting her, tells us about his possessiveness and his inability to deal with women. But on a more literal level, the shot is an evocation of summer in New York in the late 1940s — a lazy afternoon with the soothing sound of Frank Sinatra's crooning "All or Nothing at All" wafting through the air. Something similar is at work in the curious slow motion shot of Jake's first wife staring at him as she stands before the stove in their small New York apartment. She will soon explode in fury over Jake's behavior, but this frozen moment of peace allows an otherwise simply conceived character an intriguing trace of mystery. It's just a grace note, but it underscores Scorsese's insistence on creating films that at every moment possess as many levels of meaning as possible.

It's because of this multilevel approach that critics who reproach Scorsese for failing to "say" anything about his characters are so wildly off the mark. The boxing films of the thirties and forties featured heroes who, despite their lack of formal education, were somehow articulate and poetic. This conceit, though unrealistic, allowed the films to explore these characters' every thought throughout the action. *Raging Bull* deals with verbally inarticulate characters but doesn't try to disguise that fact. Instead, it gives us access to these characters' thoughts by other means.

In an early scene, Jake asks Joey to punch him in the face. Though fearful and embarrassed, Joey reluctantly complies, complaining all the while that the blows will reopen the cuts Jake received in the match the night before. Jake smiles at his brother's distress.

On one level the scene offers the audience its first glimpse of Jake's masochism. But its real meaning doesn't become clear until a short time later in a scene between Jake and Vickie.

The couple is alone in his bedroom, she in her nightgown, he in his undershorts. He embraces her and asks her to slip off her panties. She does so, then lies on top of him, slowly kissing his chest. "You told me not to get you excited," she says seductively as Jake, pleased that he has indeed become aroused, rises from the bed, goes to the bathroom, and pours a pitcher of ice water over his crotch.

In both scenes Jake thinks he's testing himself, seeing if he can "take" pleasure or pain. What is really involved is the way in which violence and sex — violence *as* sex — work in Jake's mind. Scorsese makes this sex/violence interface crystal clear in the final shot of the boxing scene that follows the bedroom tryst. Having lost a bout to Sugar Ray Robinson, Jake sits in his dressing room with his arm thrust into a pail of ice water. His fist, rigidly clenched inside the pail, has literally *become* his phallus. This visual metaphor is linked in turn to the dramatic thrust of another sequence, which highlights the sexuality of violence even more graphically.

When Vickie makes a casual remark about the fact that Tony Janiro, an opponent in an upcoming fight, is "good looking," Jake reacts as if the fighter, whom neither he nor Vickie has ever met, has become a rival for his wife's affections, a threat to their marriage. He comments to gangster cronies that Janiro's looks are such that he doesn't know "whether to fuck him or fight him." It's a joke, but a telling one. By imagining that Janiro is a sexual threat to himself and a rival for Vickie's affections, Jake psychs himself to win the boxing match all the more. In the bout, Jake hits Janiro in the face — just as he had asked Joey to do. The result is a blatantly orgasmic gush of blood, turning a scene nominally about

socially sanctioned violence into the most thoroughly sexual one of the entire film.

Yet for all of this, Scorsese refuses to present Jake as a simple psychosexual case history. He is a living breathing character, whose problems with masochism, misogyny, and latent homosexuality *Raging Bull* never tries to resolve. To do so would inhibit Scorsese's mission of rousing moviegoers from the torpor to which most commerical films have consigned them.

SCORSESE: My attitude as a film director has always been . . . provocation. I want to provoke the audience. Like in *GoodFellas*. What these people do is morally wrong, but the film doesn't *say* that. These guys are really just working stiffs. They understand that if you cross a certain line it's death. But that's "business." And it *is* business. In that world it's normal behavior. Their story covers fifteen years. It's like an epic. There are a lot of characters, and a lot of information to get across. So the way we do it is to have these simple shots with voice-over commentary, and every scene going by fast, fast, fast! That's what you have to do to show how these people lived, and make an audience really understand what they did.

Provocation has always been central to Martin Scorsese. From the sudden violence of a barroom murder in *Mean Streets,* to the eerie quiet finale of *New York, New York,* in which the hero and heroine go their separate ways, from the shot of an enormous Robert De Niro near the end of *Raging Bull,* his belly ballooning out of his shirt, to the mystifying scene in *The Last Temptation of Christ* in which Willem Dafoe's Christ pulls his heart out of his chest and displays it before his disciples, Scorsese has always endeavored to fill the screen with the out-of-the-ordinary. Yet Scorsese can't be put in the ranks of such "art film" experimenters as Michelangelo Antonioni, Pier Paolo Pasolini, or Jean-Luc

Godard. Unlike them, Scorsese has always worked within the confines of commercial film practice, generally framing his provocations against the backdrop of traditional film genres.

Despite its differences from sports films of the past, *Raging Bull* is still a relatively straightforward boxing drama. Similarly, *GoodFellas* is a gangster film; *New York, New York*, a musical; *The Last Temptation of Christ*, a biblical epic; and *Cape Fear*, a thriller. But in two of his most important films Scorsese left genre concerns by the wayside.

Taxi Driver, the film that transformed him from a promising young director to a major talent, has ties to the thriller genre, yet really isn't part of it. Paul Schrader's script is obviously indebted to Dostoyevski's *Notes From Underground*, with its alienated life-loathing hero, as well as to the modern religious parable films of Robert Bresson, particularly *Pickpocket*, whose title character roams Paris much as Travis Bickle drifts through New York. But while *Taxi Driver* ends in gunfire, it is outside the context of legalized violence of the Clint Eastwood action film in which policeman heros still embody governmental authority.

Scorsese never tries to disguise the fact that *Taxi Driver*'s hero is a psychopath. But the subtlety of Robert De Niro's performance and Scorsese's sensitivity in exploring the nuances of Schrader's script bring the viewer unusually close to this deeply troubling figure. Unlike the abrasive Jake La Motta, Travis's loneliness, longing for love, hatred of New York's corruption, and aching desire to make something of his life, involve emotions all viewers can share. While the violent route he takes to achieve his desires is one few would choose, we do sympathize with his frustration.

But what if someone were to make a film without literary or cinematic precedents of any sort, spotlighting a protagonist whose goals are less than noble, and whose emotional life is almost entirely hidden from view? That's what Scorsese risked with *The King of Comedy*, a film that cannot be categorized as either a comedy or a drama.

Scorsese's film based on an original screenplay by Paul Zimmerman, deals with Rupert Pupkin, an office messenger who has aspirations of becoming a stand-up comedian. This wouldn't be an unusual career goal, except Rupert has no intention of climbing the ladder of show business success. He wants to start at the top by appearing on the most popular late-night talk show on television, "The Jerry Langford Show."

Rescuing Langford from a mob of obsessed fans, Rupert manages to get his idol alone and make his pitch. Langford listens patiently and calmly, telling Rupert to call his production office. Rupert makes a tape of his routine and delivers it to Langford's secretary, who gives him a diplomatic brush-off. She suggests he come back after getting experience in a comedy club. But Rupert will have none of it. With the help of Masha, another obsessed fan, he kidnaps the star and demands an appearance on the show. His demands are met, but Pupkin goes straight from his television debut to prison for kidnapping. After serving his time, he finds he is a bigger media sensation than Langford ever was — with a show of his own to boot.

That is the film's plot; the actual effect of *The King of Comedy,* however, is another matter. Far from presenting a simple story with a cast of characters, Scorsese has created a series of provocations — frontal assaults on standard moviegoer expectations.

Instead of the visual pyrotechnics audiences have come to expect of Scorsese, *The King of Comedy* is filmed in a manner the director has described as "the style of 1909 — hermetically sealed frames." The camera seldom moves, close-ups are rarely used. Scorsese limits himself to medium two-shots, the simple *plan americaine* (medium shot) that *Cahiers du Cinema* critics so admired in the films of Howard Hawks.

While Hawks aimed for simplicity by placing the camera at a middle distance from the action, Scorsese is seeking something more complex. Just as the frenetic cuts and camera movement showed Jake La Motta's view in *Raging Bull,* the placid two-shots express Rupert Pupkin's guarded personality. The hermetically sealed style matches a hermetically sealed man.

With his wagging head and flapping arms, Pupkin more resembles a marionette than a human being. We know little about him except that he works as a messenger, that he lives with his mother (who is tellingly heard as an offscreen voice, but never seen), and that he's obsessed with his talk-show idol, Langford. Rupert works hard at creating an air of surface cheeriness and hail-fellow-well-met casualness. But there's a wellspring of aggressive resentment just beneath his smiling surface. He isn't willing to compromise on any level. We're not surprised when he resorts to kidnapping. Everything about him is a performance designed to achieve goals that can only be accomplished through force. Yet what those goals really mean to him is never disclosed. When Rita, the barmaid he claims to love (though we can't even really be sure of that), asks the only straightforward question of the entire film — "What do you *want*, Rupert?" — it remains unanswered.

As with his characters Travis Bickle and Jake La Motta, Scorsese has no interest in explaining why Rupert wants what he wants. He is intent on using Rupert as a device to investigate show business both as a profession and as a social construct with a stranglehold on the public's imagination.

Rupert's demand to enter Langford's world seems unreasonable, but he takes the talk-show host's easy banter as an open invitation to socialize with him. Likewise, Masha's determination to seduce Langford, which reaches a climax when the television star is forced to listen to her sing "Come Rain or Come Shine," has its logic. It is absurd on the surface, but no less so than the declarations of television personalities that they love each and every member of their audience. Rupert and Masha have simply taken them at their word.

Scorsese drives this point home most forcefully in sequences depicting Rupert's fantasies of success. He imagines Langford has become his bosom buddy, inviting him to his country estate, insisting he serve as guest host on the show, and even arranging to have Rupert marry his would-be girlfriend (Diahnne Abbott) Rita on television. Scorsese cuts directly to these fantasy scenes without indication (special photography or sound work) that they're any different from the film's other scenes. But, it's easy for viewers to understand (on plot and character information alone) that they're not to be taken as "real."

Still, for a moment or two, we may be fooled. We've taken that imaginative leap of faith that all films require to make their narratives viable. Scorsese asks us to make leaps of a different sort. For not only are stories and characters at stake, but separate worlds with their own rules and regulations to be either adhered to or broken.

It's for this reason that his desire to make a film of Edith Wharton's *Age of Innocence* shouldn't come as all that much of a surprise. Set in New York in the 1870s, Wharton's story tells of a fashionable man-about-town who, on the eve of his marriage to the most desirable woman of his social set, falls in love with his fiancée's cousin. Though deeply smitten, he stifles his romantic impulse and goes ahead with his marriage. All that remains is the regret that he failed to give himself over to passion, to risk everything for the love of his life.

SCORSESE: I know people are going to laugh at the idea of my doing a film like this. Edith Wharton — with shoot-outs in downtown New York, right? But you know, in a way it's just like *Taxi Driver*. Both of them have this thread running through them of a love that's so strong, yet the two people involved can't get together. There's that same yearning, that same sense of want, and the frustration that comes from the demands of society and the way people are forced to live in it. People are *really* going to laugh when I say this, but I find that Wharton's hero, Newland Archer, shares the same sense of isolation that Travis had for this image of Betsy, the character that Cybill Shepherd played. Of course, Travis is an outsider, and Newland's an insider. As an insider he's stuck. In both stories the love comes to naught. But in *Age of Innocence* Newland gets to make an adjustment. He marries. He stays with his wife. He has children. And it's not really that bad. It takes a certain maturity to accept and carry on the arrangement.

DE NIRO, SCORSESE, AND PRODUCERS IRWIN WINKLER AND ROBERT CHARTOFF ON THE SET OF RAGING BULL.

MARLON BRANDO IN ELIA KAZAN'S <u>ON THE WATERFRONT</u> (1954), ONE OF THE FIRST FILMS THAT SCORSESE SAW THAT REFLECTED SOMETHING OF THE LIFE HE KNEW GROWING UP ON THE STREETS OF NEW YORK. BRANDO'S FAMOUS "I COULDA BEEN A CONTENDER" SPEECH WAS USED BY BOXER JAKE LA MOTTA IN HIS NIGHTCLUB ACT, AND CONSEQUENTLY QUOTED IN <u>RAGING BULL</u>.

CATHY MORIARTY IN <u>RAGING BULL</u>.

Winkler Pro...

OPEN CALL FOR MAJOR MOTION PICTURE

A Chartoff-Winkler Production

Martin Scorsese Directing

Robert DeNiro Starring

in

"THE RAGING BULL"

Time 10AM - 3PM

Date:

Young woman to play 15-30 years old. Must be blond beauty with great figure. No regional accents except New York. Bring pictures and resumes. No telephone calls.

All personnel should park in the Montana and Overland parking lot next to MGM Lot #2, Culver City. A Studio Bus will provide transportation to and from Stage 24 at MGM.

MARTIN SCORSESE

LERMITAGE BVHL

WU INFOMASTER
ICS IPMBHLA BVHL   1-017084R092 04/02/81
ICZC 01022 (1-062533G092 0634) 04-02
TLX 698441 LERMITAGE BVHL
WUCB508 RWU187 GFFF0959 VDD181 VIA WUI RJB842 00187 ROMA
MARTIN SCORSESE
HOTEL ERMITAGE
BEVERLY HILLS CA
BT

DEAR MARTIN IWILL GIVE YOU ONE OF MINE CONGRATULATIONS
TO ROBERT AND THELMA
INGRID

NNN
1253 EST

LERMITAGE BVHL

June 13, 1980

Michael Franklin
Directors Guild of America
7950 Sunset Blvd.
Hollywood, Ca. 90046

Dear Mr. Franklin:

I am writing to you regarding my screen credit in the main titles on my latest film RAGING BULL. At this time I would like to request a waiver from the Directors Guild, in order to use the words, DIRECTOR: MARTIN SCORSESE, rather than the usual form of DIRECTED BY. This matter is important to me and hopefully you will see fit to grant me the requested permission.

I will expect to hear from you shortly regarding this issue.

Thank you.

Best regards,

Martin Scorsese

MS/dg

Hi Inman 6/11/80

RAGINGBULL------

Scenes from 1941-- DEVELOPEMENTS: *characters, situations etc.* "*flaws*"
CONFLICT: GOALS: X The Title
VICKIE
VS.
Jake's OWN SELF-DESTRUCTION. !
and PRIDE.

to 1943 MONTAGE to 1947: MONTAGE SHOWS CAREER BUILD and
FAMILY SITUATION:
a) New House, etc.
b) Children
c) State of goals--
Not near TITLE yet.
Got VICKIE but Self-
destructiveness is more
EVIDENT. (Jealousy--
Mistreatment of Vickie--
Attempt thru Physicality
to make up. Vickie ob-
viously not entirely happy)

1947: KEY YEAR --1. BREAKFAST (as discussed above)......-
2. DOPA: #1: Jealousy--to further extent --
Questioning her based on
evidence of what he thinks
he sees.
FORCING CIRCUMSTANCES: He goesto

Copa Knowing who'll be
bek there.....then....(PRIDE)
his demeanor at table
with Como etc.........im-

plied threats...distrust...
of not only those he should
distrust: Como etc. BUT
also those closest to him
Joey and Vickie.

3. VIckie: Bedroom: STRONGER SENSE OF DESTRUCT-
IVENESS--THREAT: VICKIE AND
JANIRO.
4. JANIRO FIGHT: DEMONSTRATION OF POWER (PHY-
SICAL) AND DESTRUCTIVENESS.
(Damage done to Janiro also
done to Vickie and Como etc)
5. STEAMROOM--WORK, ALONE, CUTTING OFF. OF OTHERS.
AFTER DISPLAY OF POWER.
6. COPA #2.: JOEY AND VICKIE ARGUE.
JOEY AND OTHERS FIGHT.
IN THE COURSE, OF THE ARGUMENT
BETWEEN JOEY AND VICKIE WE SHOULD
UNDERSTAND THAT THESE CIRCUMSTANCES
ARE FORCED BY JAKE--his ATTITUDES
Thru towards Vickie and Joey and others.
Pride & self --shown in earlier scenes which
destruction should grown in intensity re: JAKE'S
FORCING CIRCUMSTANCES--RESULTING
IN DISASTROUS CONSEQUENCES--
XXXXX Vickies' alienation and
Actions, Joey--caught in the mid-
dle, between Jake and Vickie
and Como. If he lets Vickie do

LEFT: REVEALING SCRIPT NOTES BY SCORSESE ON THE
INTERACTION BETWEEN <u>RAGING BULL</u>'S MAJOR
CHARACTERS.

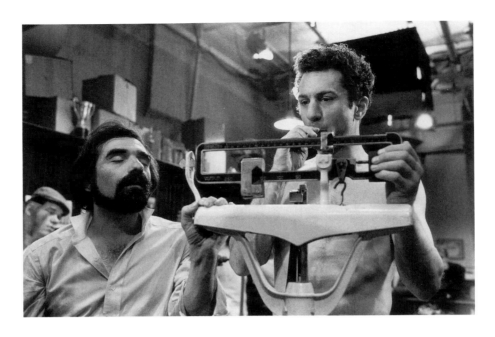

THE TWO JAKES: THIN (ABOVE) AND FAT (BELOW).

THE MANNIX CLINIC
2021 PONTIUS AVENUE
LOS ANGELES, CALIFORNIA 90025
TELEPHONE (213) 477-6511

February 2, 1979

Mr. Hal Polaire
Chartoff-Winkler
110 West 57th Street
New York, N.Y. 10019

Dear Mr. Polaire:

It has been brought to my attention that an actor
in your production of "Raging Bull", Mr. Robert
DeNiro, will be gaining a significant ammount of
weight for his role.

The Mannix Clinic is an exclusive treatment center
working with the problems of addictive behavior and
specializing in weight control using the techniques
of behavior modification. Although weight loss is
the primary goal for most of our programs in weight
control, Mr. Mannix is extremely interested in the
antithetical problems of the anorexic patient and
individuals who need to gain weight effectively and
safely.

We would be very interested in assisting Mr. DeNiro
and his physician in designing and monitoring a
program of weight gain. The research opportunity
would be invaluable to us, and we would like to
offer our services free of charge.

We will look forward to your reply.

Sincerely,

Arana Greenburg,
Director of Program
Development

Chartoff-Winkler Productions, Inc.

MEMORANDUM

TO: JUNE/SHAWN/TERI/HELENE/HAL/DONNA

FROM: KYLE

DATE: March 22, 1979

SUBJECT: BOBBY'S LUNCH

Please be advised that as of Friday, March 23rd,
Bobby or anyone on his behalf will be able to order
ROOM SERVICE directly from the Conservatory Restaurant
at the Mayflower Hotel at any hour.

If there is any problem with his special menu, please
let me know and I will see that they accomodate him.
They have already been informed of the liver and
roast chicken routine.

Thank you.

RAGING BULL: THE SECRET WORLD OF MEN.

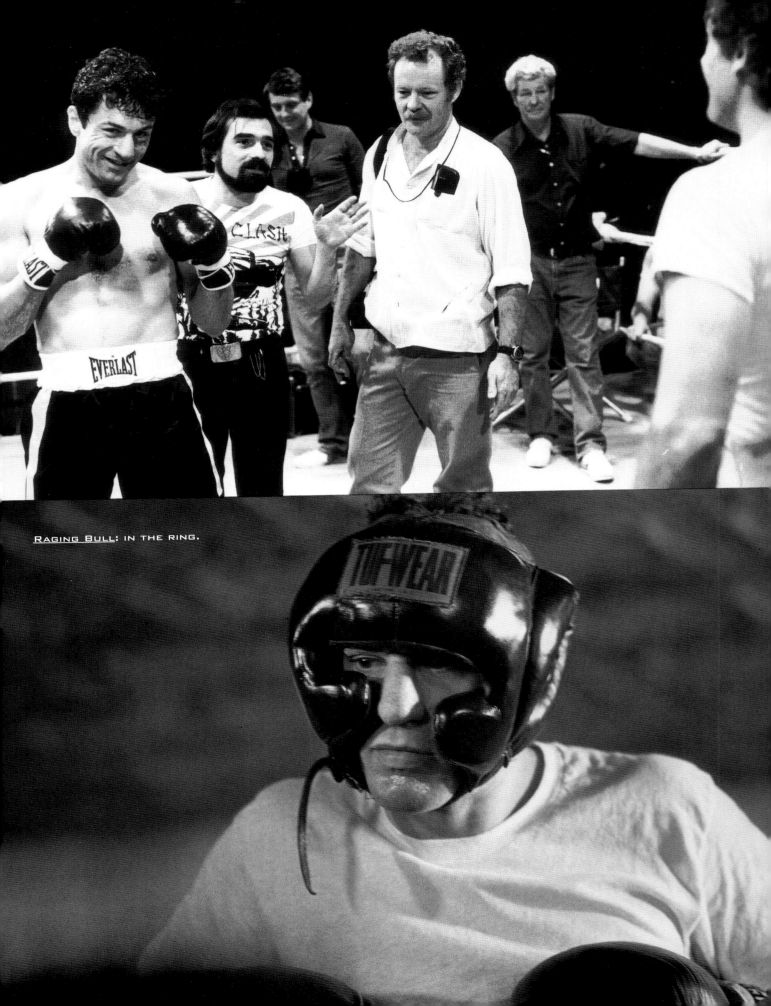

RAGING BULL: IN THE RING.

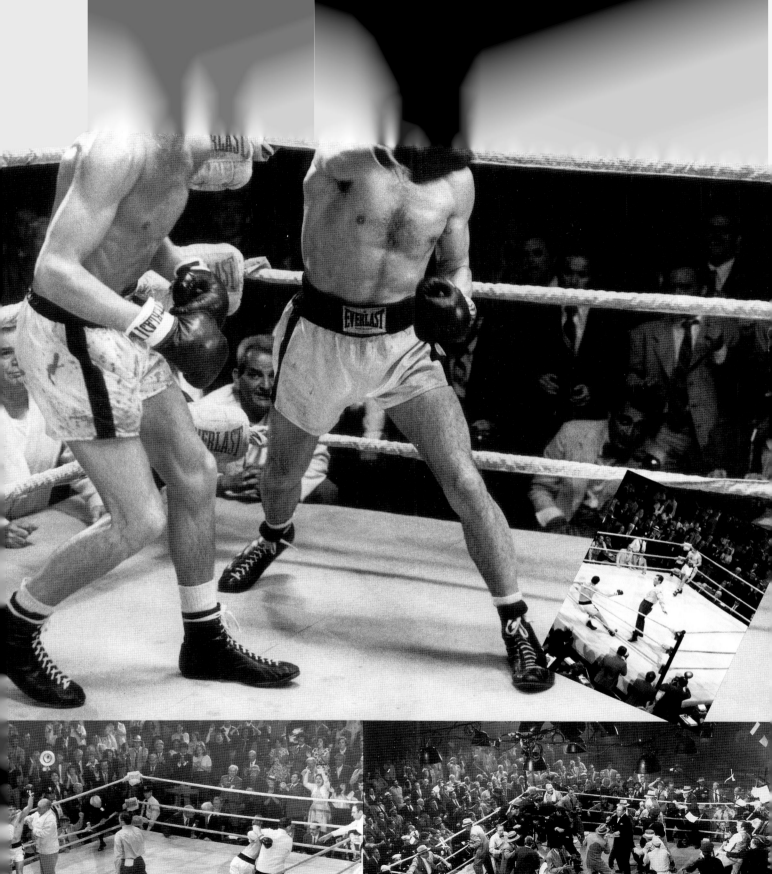

IN <u>THE PATSY</u> (1964), UPPER RIGHT, DIRECTOR AND CO-WRITER JERRY LEWIS PLAYED A SHOW BIZ OUTSIDER WHO, BY CHANCE, BECAME AN INSIDER, A STARTLING CONTRAST WITH THE PREDATORY OUTSIDER ROBERT DE NIRO PLAYS ALONGSIDE LEWIS'S SHOW BIZ INSIDER IN <u>THE KING OF COMEDY</u>.

DAY#	DATE	DESCRIPTION	SC #s	PG CT	D/ N	INT/ EXT	LOCATION
MON	9/14	TIMES SQUARE PHONE BOOTH Pupkin calling Langford	32, 33, 34	7/8	D	EXT	TIMES SQUARE
		LANGFORD'S OFFICE Wirtz throws Pupkin out	50	5/8	D	EXT	PARAMOUNT PLAZA 51st Street & Broadway New York City
TUES	9/15	POSSIBLE TRAIN OR CAB On way to Langford's home	51	1-5/8	D	EXT	T.B.D.
WEDS THURS FRI	9/16 9/17 9/18	CHET'S APARTMENT Attempted seduction of Rita by Chet	16, 18, 20, 22, 24, 26	5	N	INT	110 HUDSON STREET Apartment #8A New York City
		END OF SIXTEENTH WEEK					
MON TUES	9/21 9/22	BAR - CLUB 478 Pupkin enters bar; turns on tv as monologue starts	117 pt	1-4/8	N	INT	CLUB 478 478 9th Avenue Between 36th & 37th Stre New York City
WEDS	9/23	STREET - CLUB 478 Pupkin arrives at Rita's bar, looks in window	8	2/8	N	EXT	
THURS	9/24	N.D. CAR (CLUB 478) Pupkin taken to Rita's	114	1-2/8	N	INT	CLUB 478
FRI	9/25	BAR - CLUB 478 Pupkin goes into bar	116	2/8	N	EXT	CLUB 478
		BAR - CLUB 478 Pupkin being taken away	118	4/8	N	EXT	
		END OF SEVENTEENTH WEEK					

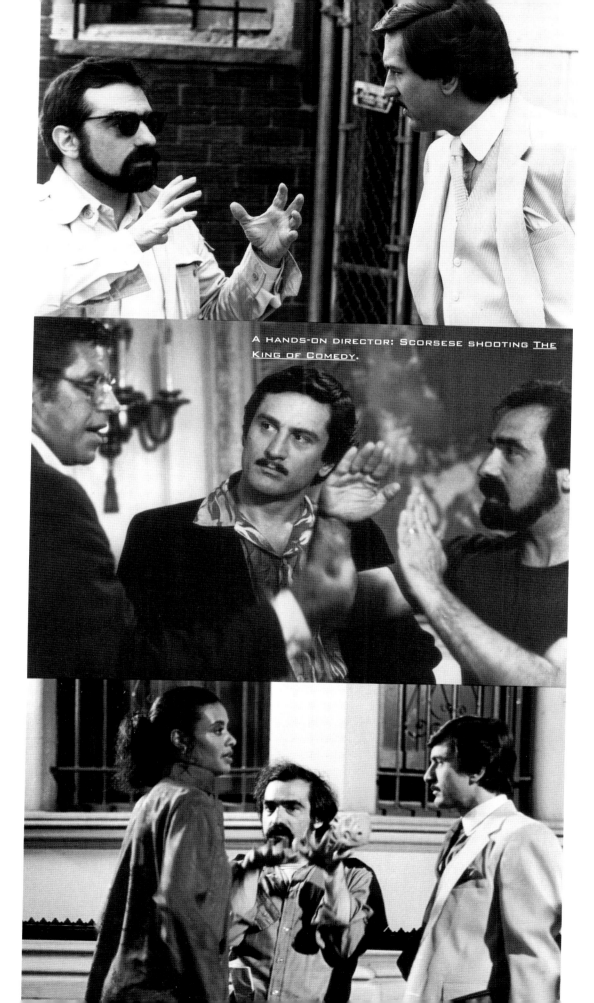

A HANDS-ON DIRECTOR: SCORSESE SHOOTING The King of Comedy.

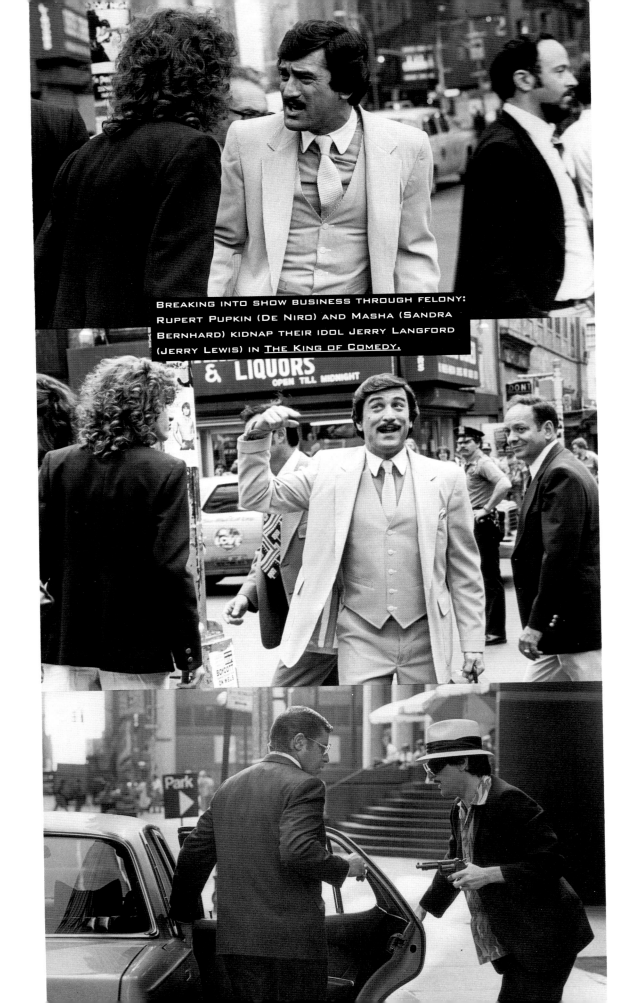

Breaking into show business through felony: Rupert Pupkin (De Niro) and Masha (Sandra Bernhard) kidnap their idol Jerry Langford (Jerry Lewis) in <u>The King of Comedy.</u>

RUPERT FINALLY HAS JERRY WHERE HE WANTS HIM.

"I'M GONNA LOVE YOU LIKE NOBODY'S LOVED YOU,
COME RAIN OR COME SHINE."

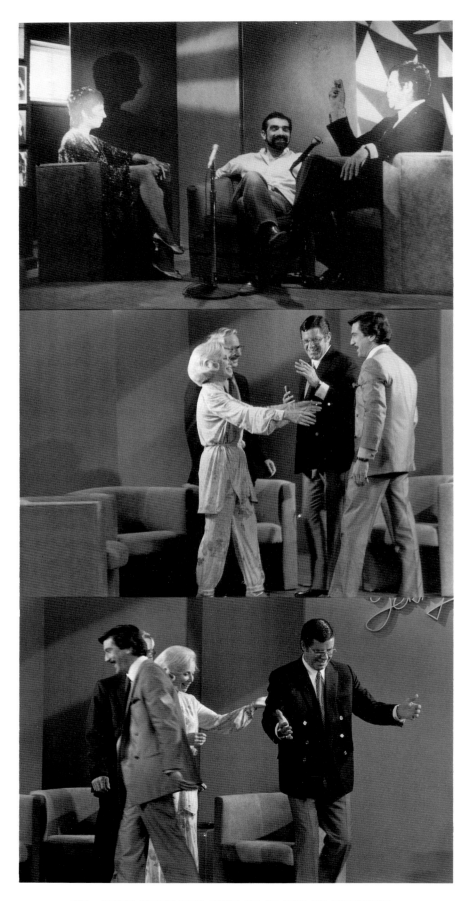

DR. JOYCE BROTHERS POPS UP IN ONE OF RUPERT'S
FANTASIES OF SHOW BUSINESS SUCCESS.

LIZA MINNELLI, WITH DE NIRO AND LEWIS IN A
FANTASY SCENE THAT WAS CUT FROM THE FINAL
VERSION OF <u>THE KING OF COMEDY</u>.

THE KING OF COMEDY

TO: ARNON MILCHAN

FROM: BARBARA DE FINA

RE: MAIN TITLE CHANGE

DATE: Oct. 15, 1982

Martin would like to change his production credit from
"A MARTIN SCORSESE FILM" to "A MARTIN SCORSESE PICTURE."
I understand from Frank Reel, that in order to make this
change, Martin's contract must be amended. If you would
like to proceed with this change, please let me know so that
Frank can prepare the proper amendment for your signatures.

cc: Martin Scorsese
    Frank Reel
    Donald Baraf
    Thelma Schoonmaker
    Bill Goldberg
    Debbie Schindler

GURENA A.G.
120 Duane Street, New York, N.Y., 10007, 212-962-2882

THREE: "SOMETHING YOU BELIEVE IN"

SCORSESE: I don't think anyone sets out to make a courageous film. I think you start out by trying to make a film about something you believe in. I knew what Kazantzakis was trying to do, and I believe in the teachings of Jesus. So I figured you couldn't go wrong making a film of *The Last Temptation of Christ*. Look, I'm not a cleric, I'm not in the Church — I'm a movie director. I wanted to use Kazantzakis's concepts to tear away at all those old Hollywood films — even though I love them — and create a Jesus you could maybe talk about, question, get to know. I wanted to try to get people to see something of *themselves* in Him. I never imagined the reaction against doing something like this would be so vociferous. It may be hard to understand now, but at the time I first decided to do it, I really thought a film of this nature would be quite acceptable.

On August 11, 1988, a crowd estimated at 25,000 marched in front of Universal Pictures in Los Angeles demanding that the studio halt its release, scheduled for the next day, of *The Last Temptation of Christ*. One of the largest public demonstrations the city had ever seen, the march was the climax of five years of carefully orchestrated harassment and intimidation by a network of right-wing religious groups of a production that Morality in Media's Joseph Reilly described as "an intentional attack on Christianity." Most of the protestors probably never realized that the ideas they found objectionable had first been raised when Nikos Kazantzakis's novel was published in 1951.

The Last Temptation of Christ was both the most personal and the most controversial work of Kazantzakis's, a novelist, poet, and religious philosopher best known for *Zorba the Greek*. A student of French philospher Henri Bergson, Kazantzakis's career choices ranged from monk to Greek Minister of National Education. A philosophical gadfly, Kazantzakis allied himself at one time or another with movements ranging from Buddhism to Marxism. However, Christianity, was the most important force in his life.

Kazantzakis was a deeply religious man; his most important writings deal with the meaning and impact of faith. But his often unorthodox views on spiritual matters, based on a philosopical bent similar to the existentialism of Jean-Paul Sartre, led him to frequent clashes with the hierarchy of the Greek Orthodox Church. The publication of his book *The Greek Passion* nearly caused his excommunication, and on his death in 1957, the archbishop of Athens refused to grant him an official church burial.

Described by Kazantzakis scholar P. A. Bien as "the summation of the thought and experience of a man whose entire life was spent in the battle between spirit and flesh," *The Last Temptation of Christ* stands at the heart of the writer's conflicts with the church establishment. Using Christ's life as the arena for his between spirit and flesh battle, Kazantzakis investigates the means by which Jesus could be both man and God, by granting him a psychological dimension, much in the manner of the hero of a novel by Tolstoy or Dostoyevski, two of his favorite writers. While psychological depth may be a prerequisite for fiction, when Christ is the central character, such examination is bound to be strongly resisted by many of the faithful. The Scriptures indicate the importance of Jesus' human dimension, but the entire thrust of standard religious practice has been toward his absolute divinity. To evoke his humanity is therefore to risk charges of blasphemy. Secure in both his faith and his literary methods, Kazantzakis took the risk.

Kazanzakis's Jesus is a tormented young man whose talents as a carpenter are used by the Romans to make the crosses on which rebellious Jews are executed. Jesus is subject to visions, voices, and blinding headaches, but fearful that their origin may be demonic rather than divine. Confused and terrified by sexuality, he spurns marriage to Mary Magdalene — a decision she claims is responsible for driving her into prostitution. His best friend, Judas Iscariot, encourages him to forgo his personal crisis and join the Jews in rebellion against their Roman rulers. But after a retreat in the desert, in which the Devil tests him by questioning his spirituality, Jesus assembles his disciples and begins to preach.

From this point, the novel's account of the events in Christ's life generally match the Scriptures, although the psychological superstructure Kazantzakis created around Jesus enables the novelist to treat the frequent divergences and contradictions in the Gospels in a new way. The Christ who declares peacemakers to be "blessed" in one sermon only to assert he brings "not peace, but the sword" in another, is seen as a single, gradually evolving personality, struggling to comprehend his own divinity. The final stage is the "last temptation," in which the crucified Christ has a vision of what it would have been like for him to have lived as an ordinary man with a wife and children. Jesus realizes at the last moment that the author of this vision is the Devil, and rejects it. His death, therefore, becomes the moment of his full transformation from man to God.

Before Scorsese, Hollywood was loathe to consider the dramatic possibilites inherent in Christ's dual nature. Moviemakers felt more comfortable presenting a God whose human dimension is never explored. In both the 1927 and 1961 versions of *King of Kings* Jesus appears as a benign, smiling white male with a mellifluous voice, a carefully trimmed beard, and a glowing halation about his body. This image has in turn been reproduced in countless pieces of religious kitsch — aesthetically debased versions of classic Christian icons of the Middle Ages and Renaissance. The most noteworthy of these items are three-dimensional glow-in-the-dark reproductions of Da Vinci's "The Last Supper," and tiny plastic statuettes affixed to automobile dashboards with magnets or rubber suction cups. Through constant repetition, these pop icons have created an image of Christ so culturally overwhelming that even those who reject it on an intellectual level recognize its power over the popular imagination. Still, this "pop Christ" has its limitations, seen most dramatically in George Stevens's film *The Greatest Story Ever Told*.

One of the most expensive and elaborately produced Hollywood films of its era, this 1965 release, highlighted by guest appearances by major box office stars in supporting roles (John Wayne, Charlton Heston, and Sidney Poitier among them), placed the kitsch Jesus against a series of spectacular natural vistas, shot on location in the mountains of Utah. Plainly inspired by salon painting of the nineteenth century, Stevens's film was tasteful and reverent, but completely indifferent to the needs of drama. A solemn pageant compared by numerous critics to a series of greeting cards, *Greatest Story* was a box office disaster that signaled to many in Hollywood the end of the Biblical epic.

Yet a year after this fiasco, Pier Paolo Pasolini's *Gospel According to St. Matthew* was released in the United States to enormous critical acclaim and considerable "art house" box office success. Shot in black and white with a cast of nonprofessionals in a quasidocumentary style, Pasolini's film, though made in 1964 a year before the release of *Greatest Story*, seemed to many to be a deliberate reproach to it. Treating the life of Christ respectfully but straightforwardly, the film was free of the sanctimony of Hollywood epics. Pasolini's Christ (played by Enrique Irazoqui, a Spanish college student) maintained the pleasant features of conventional icons, but was free of their artificial glow. This alone proved precedent shattering, not only were critics and lay audiences pleased with Pasolini's film, religious groups were impressed as well — particularly Protestant denominations.

The Gospel According to St. Matthew was frequently shown by Protestant church groups as a visual aid for religious discussions. After its initial U.S. run, a Protestant organization purchased the film's distribution rights for a time. This enthusiasm can only be interpreted as a testament to the power of Pasolini's imagery. The film's fans couldn't have been paying full attention to Pasolini's dramatic thrust, which frequently underscores the ambiguous nature of Christ's teachings (loving one moment, warriorlike the next), and carefully establishes an image of a Jesus whose behavior could easily be interpreted as paranoid schizophrenic. They also failed to note that the admired film was written and directed by a gay, Marxist atheist.

In the 1970s two efforts were made by Protestant groups to duplicate Pasolini's success. The first came in 1975 when Roberto Rossellini was commissioned to direct *The Messiah*. Since Pasolini's film was directly inspired by the style of many of Rossellini's works (particularly his 1950 *The Flowers of St. Francis*), he was a logical choice. But Rossellini had long ago lost interest in conventional drama, and *The Messiah,* like Pasolini's *Gospel* shot with a nonprofessional cast, was nearly as dramatically moot as Stevens's *Greatest Story*. It was little seen in the United States.

In 1978, a group called the Genesis Project set about making its own Christ movie à la Pasolini. Simply called *Jesus*, it was shot on location in Israel by Peter Sykes and John Krish with a professional cast of unknowns. Released by Warner Bros. to poor reviews and little audience interest, it indicated that the life of Christ was a "greatest story" told once too often. Only the 1978 film version of the Broadway musical hit *Jesus Christ Superstar* dealt, however obliquely, with the Gospels. When in 1977 director Franco Zeffirelli decided to make his Pasolini-inspired *Jesus of Nazareth*, few were surprised that he chose television as the medium.

It was against this background of financial risk, rather than religious controversy, that Scorsese mounted his initial campaign to make *The Last Temptation of Christ*. His greatest asset, he felt, was the very point that eventually caused so much controversy — the Kazantzakis portrayal of Christ. Instead of the bland deity of Hollywood epics, or the more vital, yet emotionally remote Christ of Pasolini, Kazantzakis's version of Jesus gave Scorsese the chance to create a Christ with whom audiences could empathize personally.

In 1983, Scorsese began preproduction on *The Last Temptation of Christ* for Paramount Pictures. Immediately, angry letters demanded that production cease on a film that the letter writers claimed would portray Christ as homosexual. Though homosexuality figured in neither Kazantzakis's book nor Scorsese's film, the charge continued to be leveled right up until the film's release in 1988. Spurious as they were, in 1983 these charges were deeply frightening to Paramount executives.

"It's obviously an organized campaign," Michael Eisner, then Paramount production chief, remarked in a *Los Angeles Times* interview, "but we've never been able to figure out what group is behind it." As the angry deluge continued, the studio realized that identifying the campaign's leaders was less important than managing the crisis. Paramount decided to convene a group of eminent theologians to discuss the merits of making *Last Temptation*.

"They [Paramount] knew that the book had been controversial," said symposium participant John B. Cobb of Claremont College School of Theology. "They knew they were going to have to take a lot of flak. They asked us to look at the script and give them feedback." Cobb, along with Catholic feminist Rosemary Reuther, Jesuit Reverend John L. McKenzie, and Methodist Reverend Jack Elliot, informed Paramount that, while there were obvious risks, *The Last Temptation of Christ* deserved to be made. However, Paramount disagreed and canceled the project weeks before shooting was scheduled to begin.

The studio had given up, but Scorsese had not. He announced his intention of perservering with *Last Temptation*. The motion picture trade papers soon carried stories of offers for Scorsese to produce the film under other auspices. For example, French cultural minister Jack Lang, in association with producer Humbert Balsam, tried to set up a coproduction deal. But French Catholic prelates protested, and plans were quickly scotched. Also the growing independent company Cannon Pictures expressed an interest in the project. This offer didn't get much beyond the first press release. Scorsese threw himself into other movie work, directing the low-budget black comedy *After Hours* in 1985 and *The Color of Money,* released by Disney the following year.

Coming off *Money*, one of his greatest popular successes, Scorsese felt in a good position to propose *Last Temptation* again. In 1987, Universal Pictures agreed to back the film. The studio was encouraged to do so partly on the advice of Michael Ovitz, head of the all-powerful Creative Artists Agency, who was courting Scorsese as a client. But a far more important factor in the studio's decision was Martin Scorsese himself.

In the years after the Paramount fiasco he had reshaped *Last Temptation* into a far different project from the one he'd first attempted. Budgeted at $15 million at Paramount, Scorsese scaled down the film to a lean $6.5. million for Universal. Learning from the mistakes of his more expensive box office failures, Scorsese knew that the film he wanted to make wouldn't be a "blockbuster." However, a low-budget "art" film could return its investment and make a profit. With actors working for scale and limiting himself to three takes of any scene, Scorsese undertook a carefully planned sixty-five-day shoot on locations in Morocco.

Universal learned from Paramount's mistakes in dealing with expected attacks from religious groups. The studio hired Tim Penland, a marketing consultant for Christian organizations, to help with public relations. The move backfired, however, when Penland suddenly quit, claiming Universal had failed to show him the finished film in advance. Since *Last Temptation* was still in the editing process at the time of his departure, a screening would have been impossible. However whether Penland would have cared to look at *Last Temptation* in any state is open to question. Soon after leaving Paramount he joined Bill Bright of Campus Crusade for Christ, Larry Poland of MasterMedia, the Reverend Jack Gayford of Church of the Way, and the Reverend Lloyd Ogilvie of Hollywood Presbyterian Church at a press conference at Los Angeles's Registry Hotel, to demand that Universal destroy all copies of the film.

A new series of protests, far more vociferous than when the project was at Paramount, was launched. This time the offended parties revealed their affiliations. A group calling itself Concerned Women for America circulated an early draft of Paul Schrader's screenplay, taking particular exception to the line addressed by Jesus to Mary Magdalene (not used in the finished film). "Satan is between your legs." The "last temptation" sequence, in which Jesus is seen marrying and raising children, was described by these detractors as a "sex scene," and the Jesus declared "a wimp." "I am appalled," said television evangelist and one-time presidential candidate Pat Robertson, "that anyone would ever consider producing a film which portrays the Son of God as a sex-crazed mental defective."

At that time, Robertson had not seen *The Last Temptation of Christ.* Neither had Mother Angelica of the Eternal World Network, of Birmingham, Alabama, when she declared viewing it would be "a deliberate act of blasphemy" and that its release would bring the entire country under "a heavenly chastisement." Neither had James Dobson, president of Focus on Family, when he said, "God is not mocked. I do not know how long it will take him to speak, but he will speak." Neither had Archbishop Roger Mahoney of Los Angeles, Archbishop John J. O'Connor of New York, California Republican congressmen William Dannemeyer and Robert Dornan, singer Pat Boone, Donald Wildmon of the American Family Association, or any of the scores of other individuals and organizations raising an uproar.

Soon, anti-Semitism began to creep into the protest. MasterMedia's Larry Poland claimed that Universal's Tom Pollack had told him "the Christians aren't going to stop us from releasing this film." When Pollack denied making such a remark, Poland retracted his statement. The Moral Majority's Reverend Jerry Falwell threatened that the film's release would spark "a wave of anti-Semitism." Reverend H. L. Hymers of Los Angeles staged a noisy protest in front of the home of Universal Chairman Lew Wasserman, claiming that "Jewish money" was behind *Last Temptation*'s attack on the Christian faith. A protester made up to resemble Wasserman posed for the news media with his foot on the back of another protester, who was dressed as Christ carrying a cross. Franco Zeffirelli declared on Italian television that the film was "a product of that Jewish cultural scum of Los Angeles, which is always spoiling for an attack on the Christian world." When the American press reported the statements, Zeffirelli denied making them, but nevertheless, he threatened to withdraw his *Young Toscanini* from the Venice Film Festival when *Last Temptation,* a film he described as "truly horrible and completely deranged," was screened there. Like the film's other detractors, Zeffirelli had not seen it.

The protesters' real agenda soon became clear. The radical religious right, rocked by scandals involving two of its most important figures, the Reverends Jimmy Swaggart and Jim Bakker, saw in *Last Temptation* a golden opportunity to rally their flagging forces. The more enterprising among them, like Donald Wildmon, used the protest as a blatant fund-raising device. For other protesters the film became an excuse for decrying their favorite demons — homosexuals and Jews. They weren't about to be confused by the facts: The book was written by a member of the Greek Orthodox faith, adapted for the screen by a Calvinist, and directed by a Roman Catholic, all heterosexuals.

The atmosphere surrounding *Last Temptation* was now thoroughly poisoned. Universal decided that its only recourse was to release the film the moment it was completed so audiences could judge it for themselves. Universal abandoned plans for a world premiere at the New York Film Festival in September, followed by a careful nationwide release, and rushed it into theaters on August 12.

In the face of the protests, many theater owners balked at showing the film. Some newspapers refused advertisements for it. Picket lines were formed in front of several theaters during the opening days of the run, and scattered incidents of vandalism were reported. In a theater in Paris, firebombs injured several patrons, and several countries — including Israel — refused to show the film altogether. When Universal released *Last Temptation* on home video, there was no advertising of any kind. Blockbuster Video, the largest rental and sales chain in the United States, declared it would not stock *Last Temptation*, a refusal that brought the company a special award from the Catholic Church in America.

Despite the adverse publicity, moviegoers came to see *Last Temptation*, video viewers rented and purchased copies of it, critics praised it, and the Academy of Motion Picture Arts and Sciences expressed its support by nominating Scorsese for Best Director of 1988. Still, it is difficult to gauge whether spectators were able to disregard the circuslike atmosphere surrounding *Last Temptation*'s release, and deal with the film on its own terms.

At nearly three hours, and without major stars or product tie-ins, the film violates nearly every rule of major studio filmmaking. While conventional biblical films boast acres of exposed flesh and crass carnality, *Last Temptation*'s alleged "sex scene" is comparatively chaste. Scorsese's Jesus is free of the piety of the old epics. He walks and talks like a normal man, speaking not the English of the King James Bible that is Hollywood rule, but in an almost contemporary vernacular. On a psychological level he's far more complex than Pasolini's crabby Christ, for as played by Willem Dafoe, Jesus' problems unfold before us in a logical and entirely sympathetic manner.

We see a Jesus who is painfully shy and unsure of himself. When he begins to preach, he does so uncertainly. There is a dramatic excitement in seeing him find his strength. His conflicting views about peacemaking and warfare are seen within the context of the political struggles of the Jews against the Romans. Most important, the logic of his martyrdom is made palpable by Scorsese's sense of intimacy with his every thought. As a result, the entire film is a kind of extended interior monologue of the man coming to terms with himself. In this way, Scorsese suggests that Christ's Passion — his self-realization — can be experienced by us, in our own way.

SCORSESE: In my film Jesus is wracked by doubt and fear. Some of the people who were protesting have called him a "weakling" because of that. But he's not weak at all. He just has the doubts we all have. He struggles all the time because it's part of his human nature. And in the Last Temptation what he sees is part of that nature as well. It's everything he's going to give up in order to complete his mission.

It's going to take a few years to deal with the film. People have had a really difficult time talking about it by itself. All the reviews were forced to deal with the controversy. I don't think the film has had a chance to make a difference yet. Still, we've gotten letters from people who said the film brought them back to their faith, and I'm very happy about that.

It's funny, but even though *Last Temptation* looked to be the opposite of the sort of Hollywood biblical epic I grew up with, I wouldn't mind making an epic in that style. I love the story. In fact, I'd like to do another sort of film about the life of Christ a few years from now. I've thought about doing the story in all sorts of different ways over the years, way before *Last Temptation*. For example, there was a script I wrote that was never filmed called *Jerusalem, Jerusalem*. It dealt with an earlier period in the life of J.R., the hero of *Who's That Knocking at My Door?*, when he went with a group of students on religious retreat. There was a scene in which he imagined the passion of Christ being enacted on the streets of New York, with people in contemporary costumes. I also thought about shooting a film about Christ in a cinema verité style, like a documentary. Then I saw Pasolini's film, and that was *it*.

Maybe I could try to do it another way. Perhaps something extremely traditional — like just dealing with the imagery of Renaissance paintings. But you have to say something fresh about it. I've always been interested in the first hundred years of Christianity — the switchover from the Romans to what came just after — the edict of Milan, and the Emperor Constantine. I'd like to do a historical film on it, but it would be the story of a family. They would be people who were well entrenched in the society, well respected. You could cover the same family over a hundred years — several different generations. At the beginning of the film they would be completely pagan, and into that sort of ritual. And then a hundred years later, their great-grandchildren would be doing the same sorts of ceremonies, only it would all be different because it would be Christian. For example, instead of worshiping pagan gods, they would be worshiping the saints.

That Scorsese would consider doing another film about the life of Christ may seem remarkable. But making *The Last Temptation of Christ* wasn't quite so difficult as it seems. The personal and professional stand he had to take in order to make *Last Temptation* was in essence made years before, during the production of the film that changed the course of his career, *Taxi Driver.*

SCORSESE: *Taxi Driver* was a very personal film for me because of the way Paul Schrader wrote it and what he felt about the character of Travis. It was a labor of love. Yet it was primarily an interpretation of what Schrader wrote. It's not an original work of mine. But he felt so strongly about the character, and so did De Niro. That's why I fought everybody and everything that came down the line in getting it made. I was ready to destroy the picture rather than have it compromised.

No, take that back — that's too smooth, too easy a word for what they wanted to do with it. They would have cut the violence out completely, and emphasized anything that, in their view, would have made it more — "appealing." They would have turned it into a

love story! But what's the point of making a film like that if it's not going to be done in the way it was . . . inspired? Schrader was inspired when he wrote it. What was I going to do? Sell him out? I couldn't. First of all, there was hardly any money to make the picture. $1.3 million. I was going to compromise over that? What would be the point? I might as well just go off and do another genre picture for Roger Corman. So I became obsessed with the film, and was really quite unpleasant to be around when I was making it, because I had to fight. Every day was a battle to get what I wanted.

The big trouble came in the scene in the coffee shop when I put Cybill and Bob against the window, and you can see all of Columbus Circle — the buses, the lights of the city. It doesn't sound like much, but it's very important, because the city is a character in the film, and the scene really establishes that. It's basically a two-shot profile with a number of panning movements where the camera goes back and forth between the actors. Well, what happened was I was to take a shot of Cybill alone, and one of Bob alone. Half the frame would have been the window and what was just outside it, and the other half would have shown each of them. It was very hot and rainy that summer, with a lot of thunderstorms, and when I went back to get those shots I couldn't get them to match the ones we'd already taken. I had to wait for the weather to change. That took time, and time is money.

The studio said, "Well, can't you cheat it? Can't you pan the camera over to the right and have her against a white wall?" Now to go and just throw the actors against a wall would just kill *everything* we were trying to create. I needed that shot, and the studio didn't want me to wait to get it. They said, "Tell him to shoot against the white wall." I said, "I can't do that." I remember saying that to Michael Phillips, who coproduced the film with his wife Julia. I don't think the studio knew what I'd said, because their response would have been, "To hell with this guy, fire him." After all, it was only the second week of shooting, and they could have gotten somebody else. I told him I would stop shooting unless this was settled and they got off our backs. In that moment I came to realize the kind of film director I had become, and I was willing to take responsibility for it. I told Michael, "I *will* get this, and I'll work faster and compress other things to make up for it." Michael came back an hour later and said, "It's okay, shoot it the way you want it." I don't know what he did, but it worked.

Then, after all the shooting was over, there was the Motion Picture Association of America to deal with about the rating. We couldn't afford to get an X. I remember we had a meeting and I was going to take notes, but I didn't. I blanked out. I knew we weren't going to get what we wanted. It wasn't a meeting where people were going to be reasonable. It was a meeting where people were saying, in effect, "You do it or else." I guess I had the old Sicilian thing of "How *dare* you speak to me like that!" All I said to them was "I know what has to be done." I guess what I meant was I knew I had to fight them too. I hated that, because the fight was going to have be done in a very showy sort of way: "I'm an artist." And the response to that, of course, is "So what?" They don't want to see you, they don't want to know you, they don't really want this movie, and thank you very much.

Julia and Michael Phillips were very good in what they did, helping me deal with both the studio and the ratings board. In her book, *You'll*

Never Eat Lunch in This Town Again — which is very accurate about what went on when we made *Taxi Driver,* by the way — Julia says when she saw the rough cut for *Mean Streets* that by reel three she wanted to make a deal with me to make the film, but it also hinged on De Niro playing Travis. Well, I can certainly understand that now, but when I heard it then, all I could think of was how was I gonna trust her and Michael too, you know? But there was something about Julia Phillips that was tenacious. I knew she loved the picture, and I liked her a lot personally. I knew she would fight like I was gonna fight. That was the most important thing. But in my street-paranoid way I said to myself, "I can't trust *anybody!*"

Still, Julia Phillips finally put it together. I don't know how she did it. The only compromise was in the big shoot-out scene at the end where I ended up saying, "Yes, I will pull some frames of fingers being shot off, the blood coming through the fingers, and the knife through the hand." Those changes didn't really matter because the power of the scene was still there. On top of that, to really stop Columbia from redoing things, I suggested the idea of draining the color out of that scene. I had wanted to do that originally, because I wanted to do an experiment in draining colors out of the shots like John Huston did with *Moby Dick.* But it was also a way of making it appear that I was doing something to tone things down in the scene itself. So I toned down the color, and we got the R rating, but I didn't tone down the scene. When I finally saw the scene with Julia, we started laughing — the toning down of the color made it look even *worse!*

Anyway, there was one important thing I came to realize from that whole horrible experience. All that anger, all the rage that was in the character that you hoped to work out for yourself in making the film *stays with you!* Making the film helps, but it's not enough.

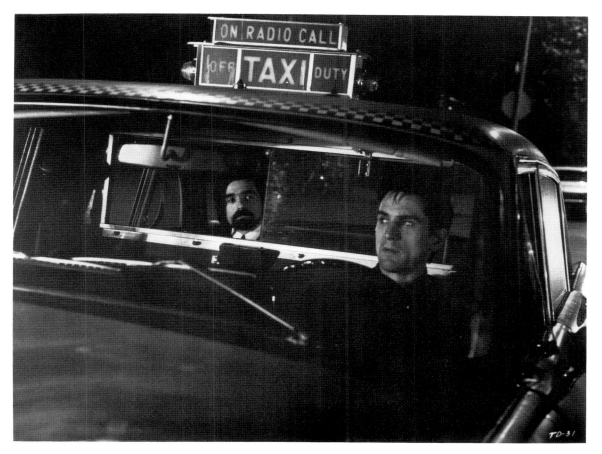

"PUT THE METER BACK." SCORSESE AND DE NIRO IN TAXI DRIVER.

THE CRUCIFIXION IN <u>THE GREATEST STORY EVER</u>
<u>TOLD</u> (1965), A LEGENDARY BOX OFFICE DISASTER
THAT SCORSESE ADMIRES FOR ITS VISUAL STYLE.

MOSES ADDRESSES THE THRONG — CHARLTON HESTON IN CECIL B. DEMILLE'S <u>THE TEN COMMANDMENTS</u> (1956).

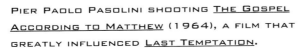

PIER PAOLO PASOLINI SHOOTING <u>THE GOSPEL ACCORDING TO MATTHEW</u> (1964), A FILM THAT GREATLY INFLUENCED <u>LAST TEMPTATION</u>.

THE HOLY FAMILY (MYRIEM ROUSSEL AND THIERRY RODE) IN JEAN-LUC GODARD'S <u>HAIL MARY</u> (1985), THE FILM THAT, PRIOR TO <u>LAST TEMPTATION</u>, CREATED THE GREATEST RUCKUS IN THE ORGANIZED RELIGIOUS COMMUNITY.

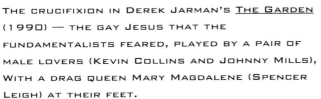

THE CRUCIFIXION IN DEREK JARMAN'S <u>THE GARDEN</u> (1990) — THE GAY JESUS THAT THE FUNDAMENTALISTS FEARED, PLAYED BY A PAIR OF MALE LOVERS (KEVIN COLLINS AND JOHNNY MILLS), WITH A DRAG QUEEN MARY MAGDALENE (SPENCER LEIGH) AT THEIR FEET.

RICHARD BURTON AND JEAN SIMMONS IN <u>THE ROBE</u> (1953), A FAVORITE RELIGIOUS EPIC OF SCORSESE'S YOUTH.

JESUS WITH HIS FAMILY — WILLEM DAFOE
IN <u>THE LAST TEMPTATION OF CHRIST</u>.

JESUS ADDRESSES THE THRONG.

The Passion

Photos by [illegible]

DAVID BOWIE AS PONTIUS PILATE.

SCORSESE DIRECTS BOWIE.

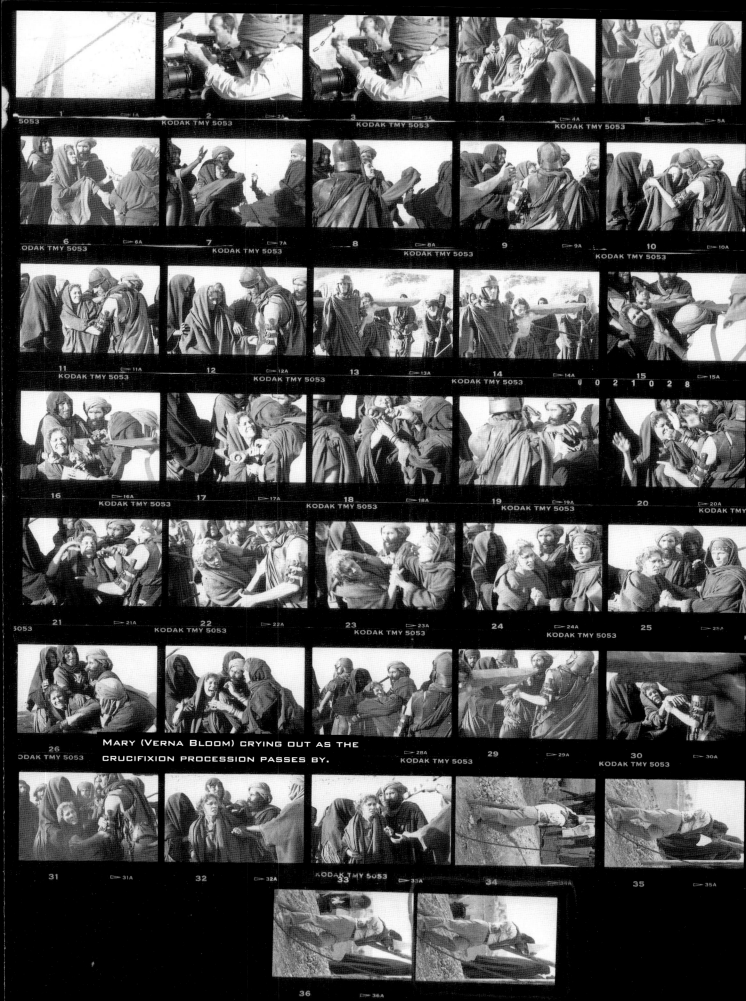

MARY (VERNA BLOOM) CRYING OUT AS THE
CRUCIFIXION PROCESSION PASSES BY.

18 ▷18A   19 ▷19A   20 ▷20A

23 ▷23A   24 ▷24A   25 ▷25A

28 ▷28A   29 ▷29A   30 ▷30A

▷33A   34 ▷34A   35 ▷35A

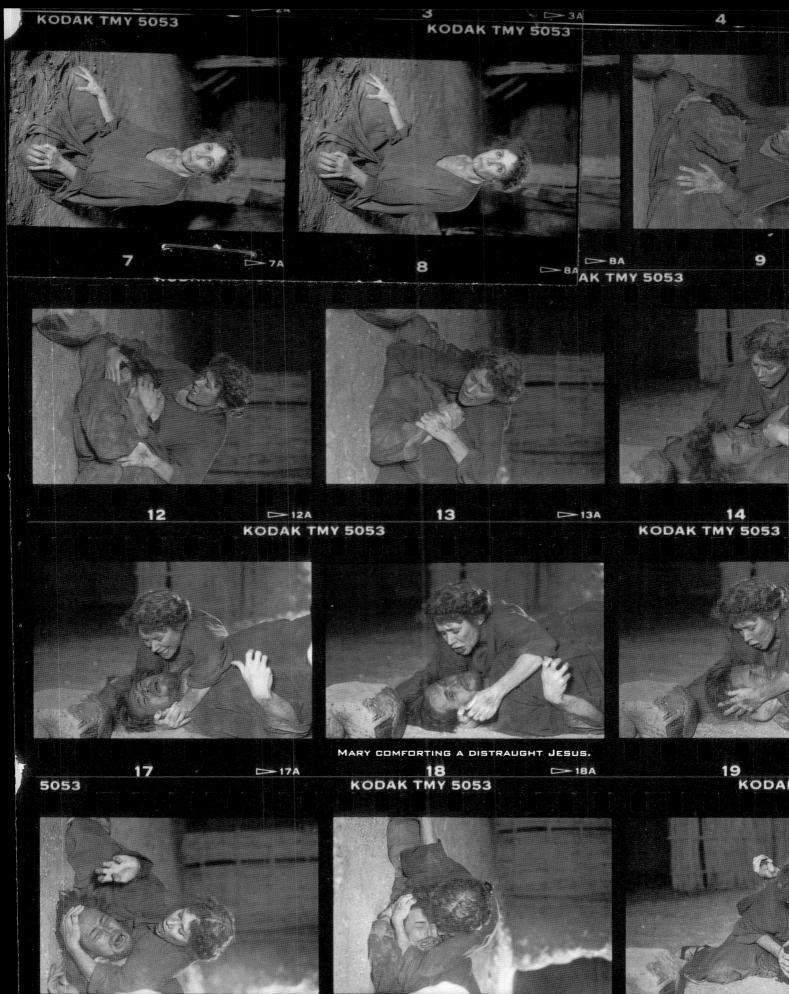

MARY COMFORTING A DISTRAUGHT JESUS.

8 ▷ 8A 9

28 ▷ 28A
KODAK TMY 5

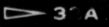

KODAK TMY 5053
33 ▷ 33A

is no rea~   should buy
prod~   ~nally and
~   Christ.

Stop Universal Studios

Donald E. Wildmon
Executive Director

home to help us

tcard to
~
Studios.

is phone
k with Mr.
's not in,
~al's plans
" and ask
ay for
ith Mr.

Dear Christian Friend,

Please tear the enclosed "movie ticket" in half.

Write "NO THANKS" on one half. Tape it in the space
marked on the enclosed postcard and mail it. Here's why.

On Friday, August 12, Universal Studios
released a movie titled "THE LAST TEMPTATION OF
CHRIST". Here's what young people in your
community will learn about Jesus from this movie:

++ He is a fornicator;
++ He is a weak, unstable traitor to the Jews;
++ He is one who curses the poor and sick; "I
   marries Mary Magdalene and tells her: "I
   worship you. God sleeps between your legs."
++ He believes He is the devil: "I haven't been
   in my right mind. I am Lucifer."

Your enclosed SCRIPT SHEET (found on back of your
PETITION TO LOCAL THEATER OWNERS) gives you more details.
Here's one more example:

"When pressed by a crowd of poor and sick asking
Jesus to heal and cure them, Jesus says, 'Get away. You
sicken me.' You're selfish and full of hate. God won't
help you.'"

This is what young people in your neighborhood will see
and hear about Jesus in Universal's movie "THE LAST
TEMPTATION OF CHRIST".

We must alert all Christians to this movie's
blasphemies and lies.

We couldn't stop Universal from releasing its movie.

But here's what we can -- and must -- do:

(1) Work to convince theater owners -- out of respect
    for Christians in their community -- not to book
    "The Last Temptation of Christ" for their theater.
    (To date we've been successful; read on for details).

(2) Send SCRIPT SHEETS from the movie to as many
    Christians as possible as a warning about what the
    movie contains.

(3) Organize a nationwide boycott of MCA Incorporated
    -- the company that owns Universal Studios. There

U
a~

non~
to u
Stud~

~
millio~

Bu~
of prote
Christia~
protest c

~
m~

So we m~

And just   ~ is again
leading the fi~

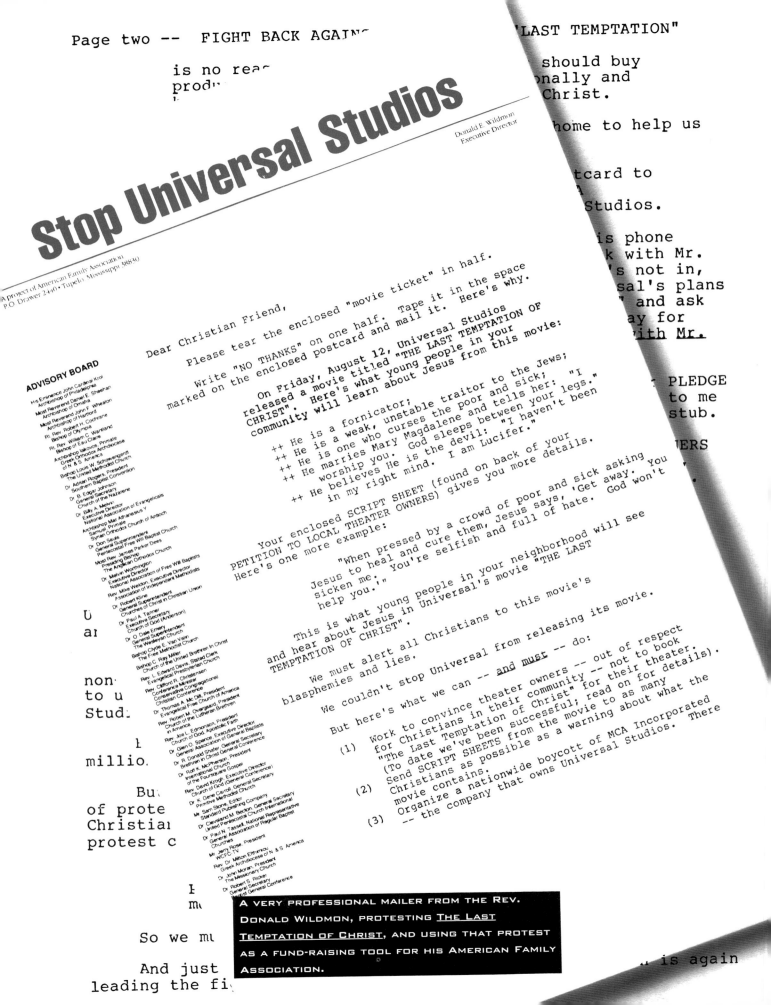

A VERY PROFESSIONAL MAILER FROM THE REV.
DONALD WILDMON, PROTESTING THE LAST
TEMPTATION OF CHRIST, AND USING THAT PROTEST
AS A FUND-RAISING TOOL FOR HIS AMERICAN FAMILY
ASSOCIATION.

TO: DAVID EHRENSTEIN (HERALD EXAMINER STAFF WRITER)
RE: "TEMPTATION" FILM
_____

I am a Catholic -- not a very orthodox type, but a good one -- and I resent your
DISRESPECT towards my religion.

Freedom does not license a person to: say what he wants, do what he wants, etc --
cross the limits and the law is behind you. The "Enquirer" has been sued a few times
for misrepresentation of facts. Try and say something derogatory about me, and I'll
take you to the cleaners.

Surely, you as a Jew and very much the bigot, would come to Wasserman's & Kazantsakis'
defense to knock down and ridicule Catholicism and the rest of the Christian world --
just for a few "shekels". When Wasserman produced this film, he knew he would irritate
the Christian spirit...and, afraid he would have to shelve it, he went along and did it.
You people are so used to fighting the Palestinians, grabbing what you can, that you
don't know where to draw the line of decency. If we are zealots, as you call us in
your article, you are very much the BIGOT (look the word up in the dictionary).

I don't need to see this junky film -- I know what the story of Jesus Christ is --
I don't need the Jewish version. I am a civilized person and do not cherish seeing
Jesus Christ crowned with thorns, flogged, and drag his heavy cross all the way to
Golgotha, where he was mercilessly crucified by Jews. No, I don't need to see this
again -- it's brutality and terorism. But, you seem to gloat over his ordeals.
Surely, there are a lot of mentally-deficient derelicts who indulge in senationalism,
brutality, killing, bloodbaths, pornography, and the likes of it -- these will be your
customers. What are the Jews trying to do? Cause more hatred and widen the rift that
exists between them and the Gentiles? I have heard that bombs will be placed in some
of the theatres showing this film. If this happens...you only have yourselves to answer.

Jerry Rubins said on TV -- think of all the free advertising they are getting, and
all that money. How vulgar! but I'm sure he said the truth, while Wasserman drools
with his satanic-look-alike-face behind his eight-ball. I promise you, that every
recipient of "Temptation" monies will be accursed.

As for me, and legions of others, it has maximized my Faith in Jesus Christ and gained
DISRESPECT for you and your sick ilk.

By the way, what has happened to your Shechinah? Maybe he is busy helping your version
of Jesus Christ with his leftover prostitutes!!

YOU ASKED FOR THIS!

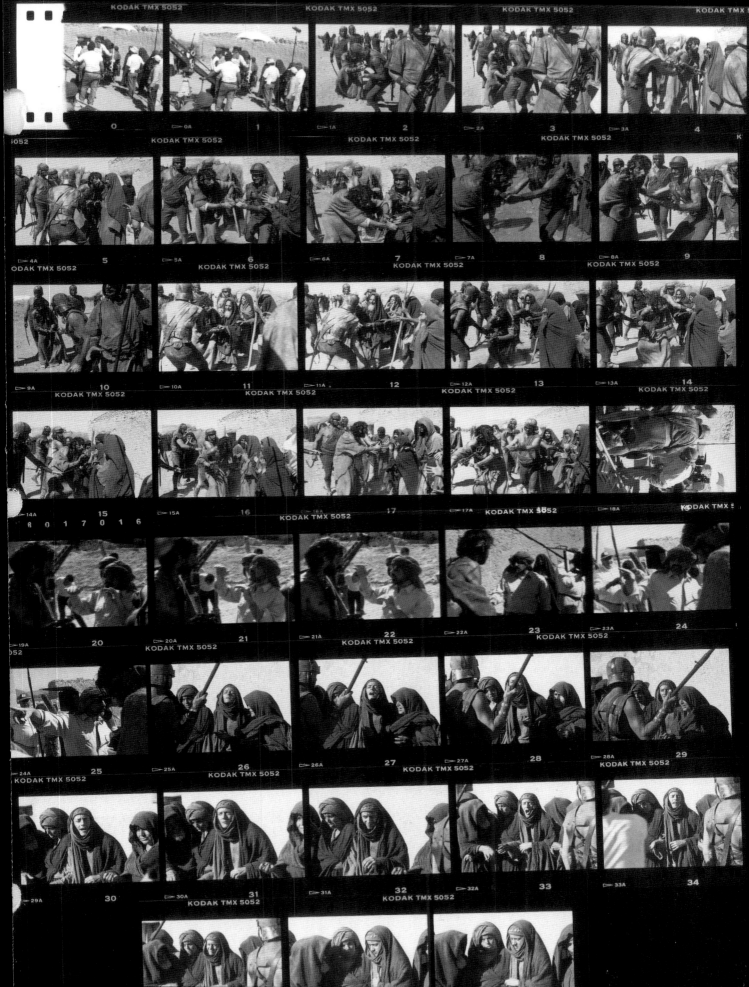

JESUS IN THE DESERT.

21 ▷ 21A 22 ▷ 22A 23

TMY 5053 KODAK TMY 5053 KODA

26 ▷ 26A 27 ▷ 27A 28

KODAK TMY 5053 KODAK TMY 5053

31 ▷ 31A 32 ▷ 32A 33

5053 KODAK TMY 5053

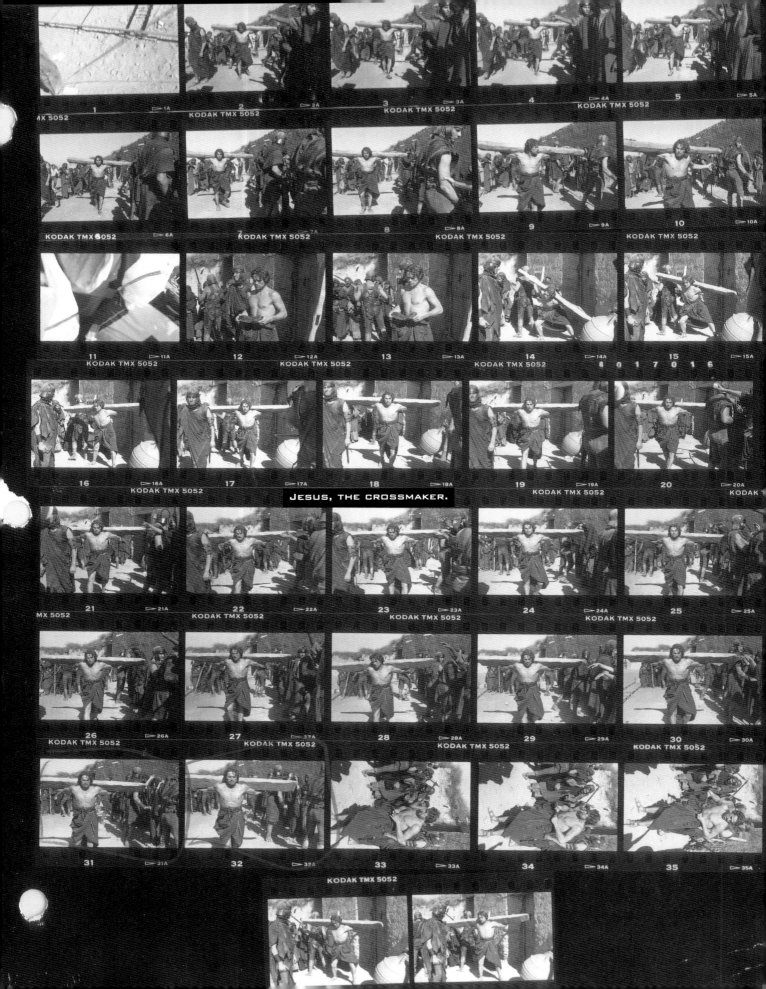

JESUS, THE CROSSMAKER.

"GOD'S LONELY MAN." DE NIRO AS TRAVIS BICKLE AT
THE BEGINNING AND END OF <u>TAXI DRIVER.</u>

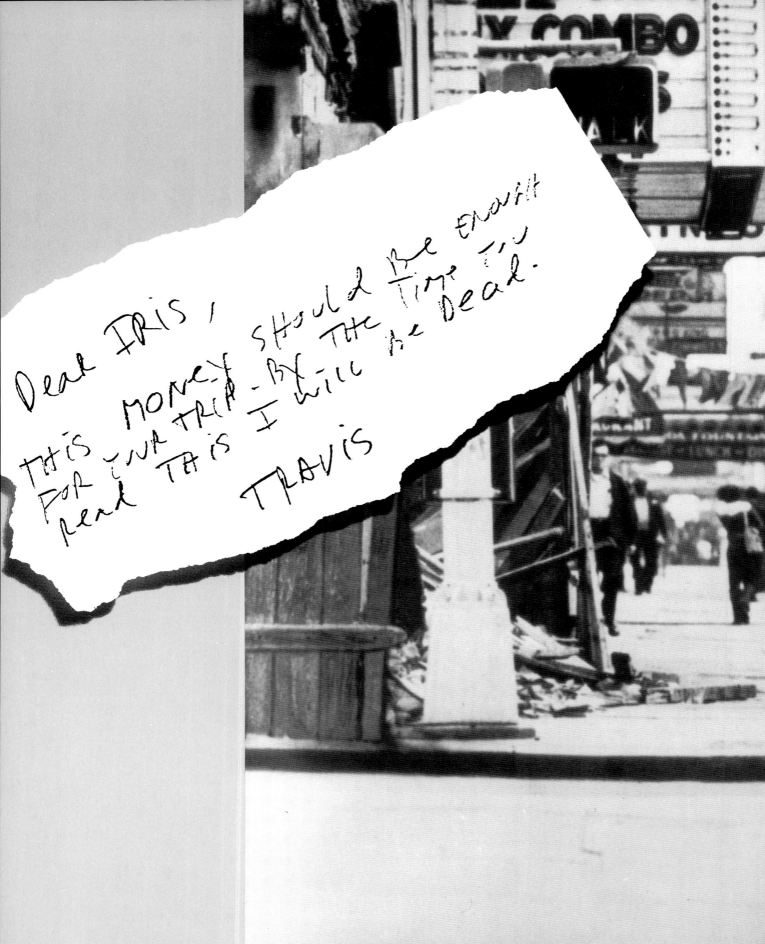

A HOLY FRAGMENT FROM <u>TAXI DRIVER</u> — TRAVIS'S
LETTER TO IRIS, WRITTEN IN SCORSESE'S HAND.

A TEENAGE PROSTITUTE AND HER PIMP: JODIE FOSTER
AND HARVEY KEITEL IN A SCENE FROM <u>TAXI DRIVER</u>
THAT SCORSESE AND SCREENWRITER PAUL SCHRADER
SAY WAS INSPIRED BY JOHN FORD'S WESTERN CLASSIC,
<u>THE SEARCHERS.</u>

LOSING CONTACT: TOM (ALBERT BROOKS) STOPS
TRAVIS (ROBERT DE NIRO) FROM SEEING BETSY
(CYBILL SHEPHERD).

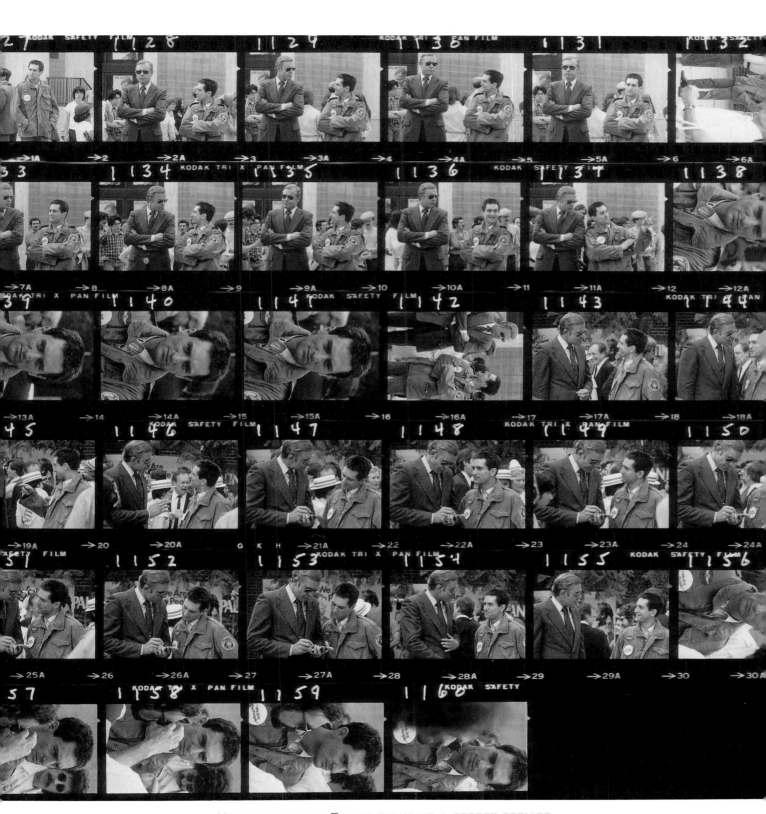

MAKING CONTACT: TRAVIS TALKS UP A SECRET SERVICE
AGENT (RICHARD HIGGS).

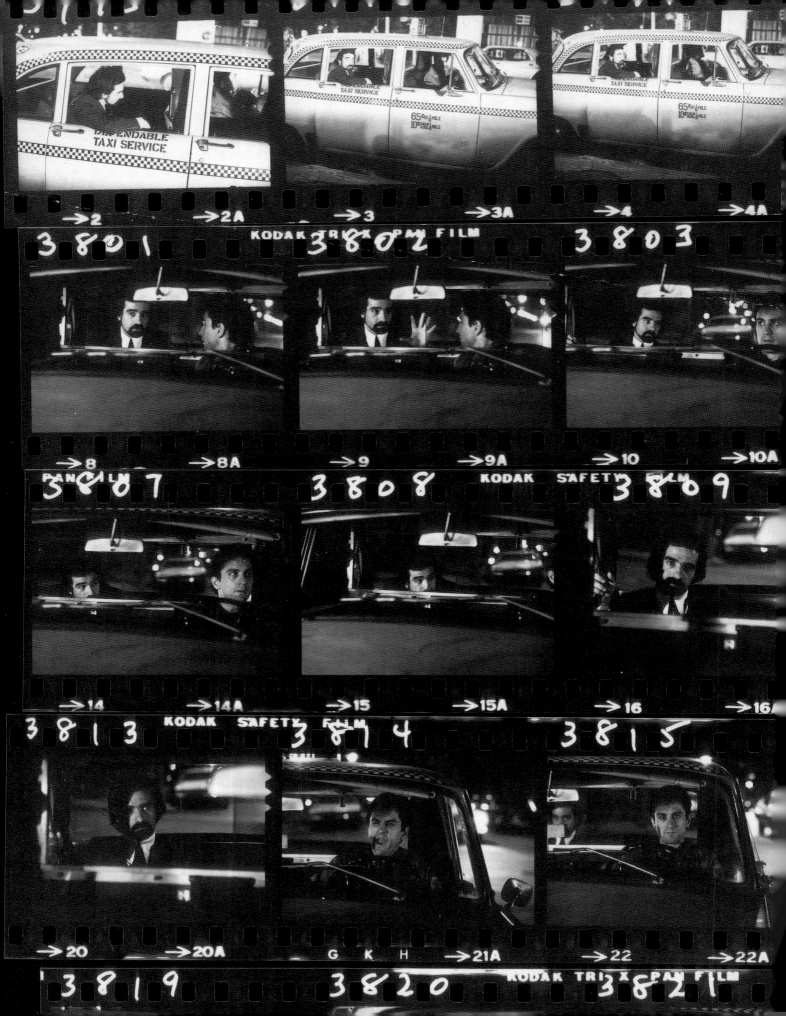

"Did you ever see what a .44 Magnum could do to a woman's face?"

CLICK TEMPO ______
WARNING CLICKS ______
SCORING ST. MARK ______

TITLE OF PRODUCTION "TAXI DRIVER"

PRODUCTION # 132327 TOTAL TIMING 1:34

TITLE OF CUE ______

SEQUENCE R2P2 STARTS AT 318 FEET 2 FRAMES DATE 11-20-75

PREV. SEQ.

IN PALATINO CAMPAIGN HEADQUARTERS, BETSY IS ANNOYED BY THE STARE OF TRAVIS WHO SITS IN HIS CAB, HER FELLOW CAMPAIGN WORKER CHASES HIM AWAY AND HE DRIVES OFF IN A RAINY NIGHT.

:00	CUT	CU OF RED TRAFFIC LIGHT.
:02	CUT	MS OF TRAVIS WAITING, STARING UP AT O.S. LIGHT.
:06		THE LIGHT CHANGES TO GREEN, REFLECTED ON THE WINDSHIELD.
:08	•	HE STARTS TO DRIVE OFF. (MELODY IN HEAD)
:11	CUT	CU OF TRAVIS' POV OF A STREET LIGHT PASSES BY, SEEN TRHOUGH THE WINDSHIELD AS THE CAB DRIVES ON IN THE RAINY NIGHT.
:12	CUT	ANOTHER CU OF TRAVIS' POV OF A STREET LIGHT PASSES BY.
:13	CUT	CU OF TRAVIS DRIVING.
:14	CUT	CU OF THE METER WHICH IS OFF.
:17	CUT	MCU OF TRAVIS DRIVING, SHOT THROGH THE WINDSHIED.
:19	CUT	LS OF TRAVIS' POV OF PEOPLE ON A BUSY SIDEWALK.
:21	CUT	MCU OF TRAVIS STARING AT OS. SIDEWALK.
:22		HE COCKS HIS HEAD AND STARES AHEAD, DRIVING. A BUSY TRAFFIC.
:26	CUT	LS OF TRAVIS' POV OF A CAR AHEAD OF HIM. THE CAR STARTS TO SPEED UP AND DISAPPEARS AS TRAVIS' ATTENTION CHANGES TO PEOPLE ON SIDEWALK.
:30	CUT	MCU OF TRAVIS SEARCHING FOR A CUSTOMER.
:34	CUT	LS OF TRAVIS' POV OF A SIDEWALK, WITH FULL OF PEOPLE. HE SEES A GIRL WAVING AT HIM.
:37	CUT	MCU OF TRAVIS STOPS AND LOOKS AT THE GIRL GETS IN. (WE DON'T SEE HER)
:39		HE PICKS UP HIS PASSE

MUSIC TIMING SHEET USED BY COMPOSER BERNARD HERRMANN FOR TAXI DRIVER, HIS LAST MUSICAL SCORE.

(CONTINUED)

91-259   Bobby coming in through window. Fight scene.
         Tracking camera good. Violence blocked. Good exit.
         Very good. <u>Great</u>

260   1st better.

263   Imrovisation.

266   Didn't care for first one. This has some good moments.

267   The one with the shout. Old man looking at them.
      Probably the best one.

271   Other angle. Pretty good. Especially living in Hell.
      Moves away from the cars-very good. Bus blocks them
      out. Nice.

273   Very good. Heavy traffic very nice.

63-277

278   Very good also.

First master and she's laughing. Last part is good. The rest
   is not so good.

Take two of master. "senator's stand on welfare" good. "What
   exactly do you want?" is good w/ Albert in BG. Beginning
   still not too good. Coaxing good at the end. End of 2nd
   take master better w/ Albert.

290   CU of her. 1st line excellent. "Thanks, what do you
      think of Palantine"good. "C Palantine, person you're
      volunteering to help elect president" not too good.
      "Want to canvas" good. Welfare line good. "You're sure
      of that"is good. "Think I'm a lonely person" is no good.
      Tail not too good. Coaxing good. "I'm sure you will"
      is good. Albert cut off at end-don't know if it's
      necessary.

291   "Why volunteer to me?" is better. smile is better.
      What so you think of Palantine-better than other.
      "Charles Palantine, the man you're,..." good.

292   "Why do you feel you want to volunteer to me" is good.
      "Thanks" good. "What do you think of Palanting?" good.
      very good. "Man you volunteered to help elect pres."
      is the best. "Want to canvas?" excellent. "Stand on
      welfare" good, but maybe not as good as other one.
      "Be my friend" is good. She looks down is good.
      Nervousness very good. Arm business very good, his arm.
      So far best of coaxing. "I'm sure you will" out of place.

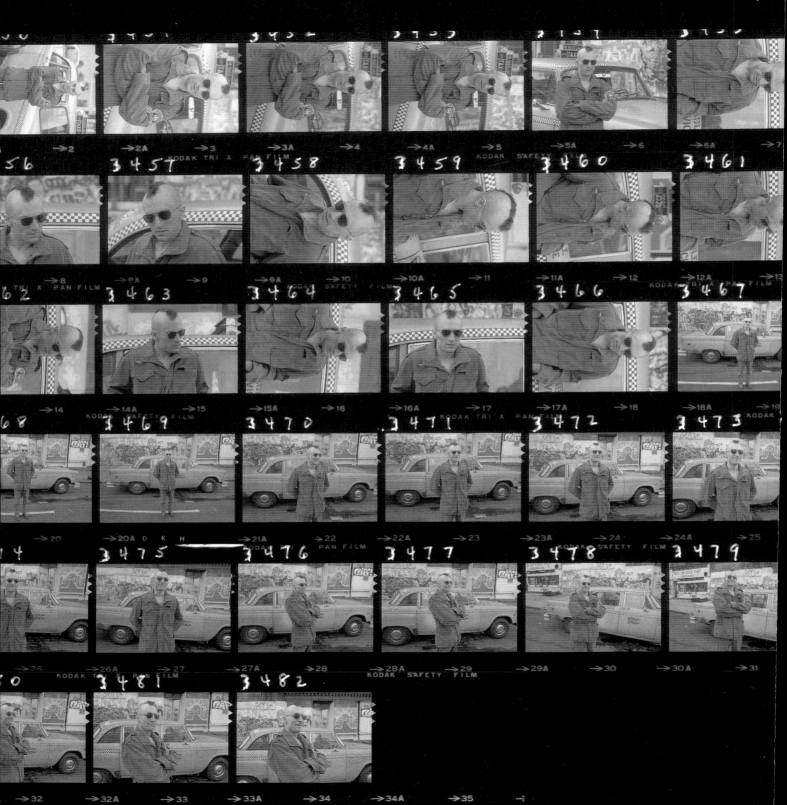

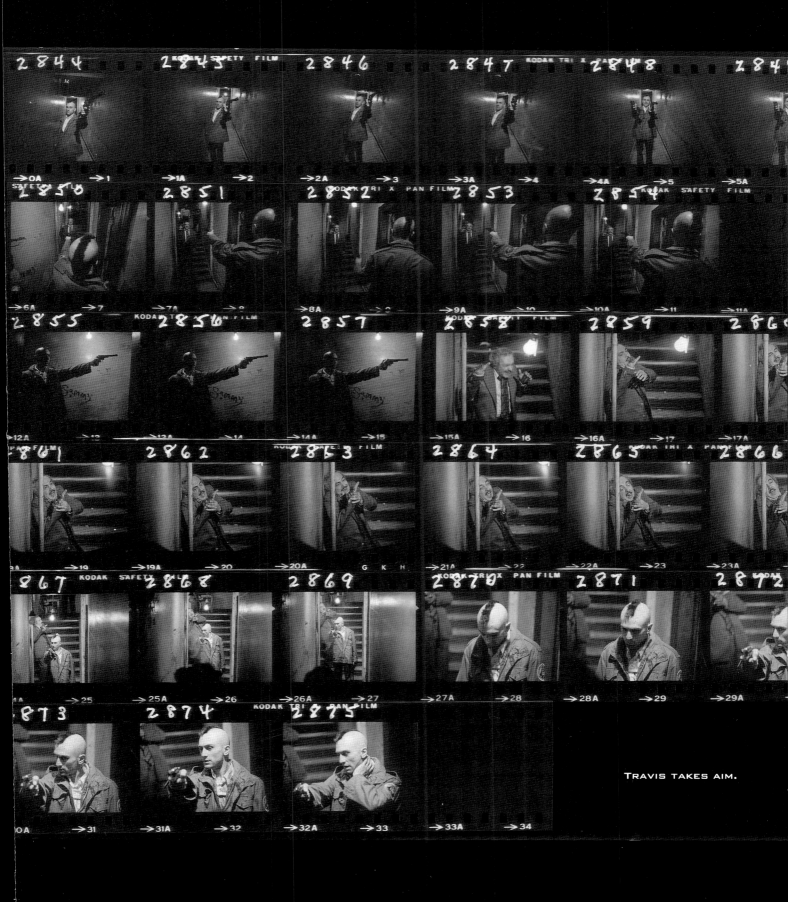

TRAVIS TAKES AIM.

FOUR: "ALL THE ARTS CULMINATE IN FILM"

"Is it a great movie? I don't think so," said critic Pauline Kael about *GoodFellas*. "The filmmaking process becomes the subject of the movie. All you want to talk about is the glorious whizzing camera, the freeze-frames and jumpcuts. That may be why young film enthusiasts are so turned on by Martin Scorsese's work: they don't just respond to his films, they want to be him."

Considering the quality of much current filmmaking — plodding and unimaginative, slapdash and sloppy — it's odd to see a director criticized both for his technical prowess and for inspiring others to follow his example. Still, Kael can't be blamed for being taken aback by Scorsese's intoxication with the visual possibilities of the medium: The boxing sequences of *Raging Bull,* with its subjective shots that pull you into the ring; the camera's slow-motion prowling through nighttime New York streets in *Taxi Driver*; the bravura Steadicam take through the Copacabana night club in *GoodFellas,* one of the longest and most complicated and emotionally exhilarating tracking shots in movie history. To suggest that this technical flash is at the expense of other equally important filmmaking qualities isn't unreasonable. But it is unreasonable to imply, as Kael does, that there's a simple way to separate Scorsese's style from his film's content.

Generations of American critics of all artistic pursuits have found the word technique to be unprintable unless it's preceded by the adjective mere. In Scorsese's case, this prejudice has a special edge, inasmuch as he's never been interested in exploring uplifting themes of the *Gandhi* or *Chariots of Fire* variety. Neither has he been drawn to social themes for their own sake. His films may touch on "hot-button issues," such as feminism (*Alice Doesn't Live Here Anymore*), organized crime (*GoodFellas*), wife-beating (*New York, New York, Raging Bull*), mental illness (*Taxi Driver*), and vigilante justice (*Cape Fear*), but they do so within the context of specific characters and unique circumstances. More important, the creative choices in Scorsese films aren't made to supplement the actors' performances or express a "message" that exists solely on a literary level. Scorsese's messages are inextricably tied to the means by which he conveys them. His methods *are* his message.

SCORSESE: I've always believed all the arts culminate in film. Camera movement is dance, lighting is painting. Camera movement is also a lot like painting — and like music. I feel it's always a combination of lighting, camera movement, the use of music and the impact of the actors on the screen. The way the actors move into the light and relate — or not relate as in *The King of Comedy* — is very important. In

The King of Comedy it's all a series of frozen frames. The characters never penetrate each other's areas. They just can't get in.

The King of Comedy isn't the first work mentioned in discussions of Scorsese's technical mastery. Camera movements in the film are few and simply executed. In the precredit sequence there is a very brief bit of slow motion. But with the camera placed firmly in the middle distance, calmly observing the action, Scorsese would appear to be making a work in polar opposition to the pyrotechnics of *Raging Bull*. Yet because of this very simplicity — more apparent than real — *The King of Comedy* is central to any discussion of the methods and purposes of Scorsese's work.

One of the key scenes takes place in a Chinese restaurant where Rupert Pupkin, autograph hound and would-be stand-up comic, takes his date Rita, a barmaid. Rupert tries to impress Rita, first by showing her his autograph book, then by telling her that his signature will have greater value than any of the others in his collection, because he's going to make his television debut on the "Jerry Langford Show." With Rupert's overconfidence squared off against Rita's cynical bemusement, a basic comic conflict unfolds. Scorsese's method of filming the scene is equally straightforward. He uses a standard reverse-angle shot setup: a medium shot of Rupert, with part of Rita's head and shoulder on the right of the screen, alternating with a medium shot of Rita with part of Rupert's head and shoulder on the left of the screen. While three additional medium shots of the two of them facing one another in the booth (Rupert on the left, Rita on the right) are integrated into the editing of the sequence, the primary shot alternation is between two talking-head images in isolation.

In his book, *The Filmmaker's Art*, Haig Manoogian notes that, while the reverse angle is a valuable filmmaking tool, it must be used with care: "The technique of reverse angles has always been popular with filmmakers, because crosscuts in which fairly close shots are taken are an expedient method. Once characters are in a reverse-angle setup, there is a tremendous conservation of shots as the camera concentrates first on one, then on the other. But to conserve shots does not appear to be the objective so much as to maneuver the characters into set positions so they can talk, talk, talk. Reverse angles have been used so often in the manner described that they have become a visual cliché. It is often overlooked that staging and dialogue are not half so important as the action and reaction on which the reverse angles should be based."

In the Chinese restaurant scene, Scorsese takes his former teacher's lesson very much to heart. Instead of using the reverse angle setup to simply convey information through dialogue ("talk, talk, talk"), Scorsese draws our attention to the curiously tense atmosphere surrounding their conversation. The contrast between Rupert's self-conscious body language — rocking back and forth like a waterbird toy — and Rita's poised, relaxed demeanor plays a part in this tension. But the most important factor is Scorsese's awareness of the dramatic impact of editing.

A director working in the "talk, talk, talk" mode that Manoogian disdains would concentrate on Rupert speaking, and cut to Rita only when she replies. Scorsese nervously cuts back and forth between the characters at points not cued by anything specifically stated in the dialogue.

Behind Rupert, a man sitting at another table (Chuck Low) mimics the would-be superstar's every gesture. Does this man's appearance mean the scene, like several others in the film, is a fantasy? If it's "really happening," how does it relate to the rest of the story? Scorsese doesn't supply an answer. The man in the other booth is there precisely to *create* such a disturbance. Where *Taxi Driver* and *Raging Bull* brought us into its protagonist's view through subjective camera positions, *The King of Comedy* delineates Rupert's character through a deliberate avoidance of subjectivity. The flat effect of the screen is the mirror image of the flat effect of the face Rupert shows to the world. In underscoring this fact through a reverse-shot sequence, Scorsese uses Rupert's character not only to undermine assumptions about fame, show business, and romance, but the very nature of the way these ideas have been represented through techniques like reverse-angle setups. Scorsese makes *The King of Comedy* more than a simple piece of social criticism; it questions the nature of film narrative itself.

Martin Scorsese is hardly the first director to examine the nature of the medium. But over the past two decades few directors have been disposed to question the filmmaking process. What sets Scorsese apart from the run of the Hollywood movie mill, is best indicated by his preferred credit: "A Martin Scorsese Picture." Not "a film by Martin Scorsese," not a "Martin Scorsese film," or even a "Martin Scorsese Production." "Picture" emphasizes something quite different. For, while Scorsese is dependent on the talents of other artists and technicians to bring his films to life, his controlling vision of the film is the ultimate force that shapes it into a "picture" of a very particular kind.

SCORSESE: With Hollywood in the old days, being a director was like, "So-and-so has a project and you have so many days and you devise the shots and work out the themes in the script." That's being an interpretive artist. Well, I do interpret material to a degree, but it's not the same sort of thing. I can never bring myself to be just "the director." For example, *The King of Comedy* was an assignment, in a way, because it was a film that Bob De Niro wanted to do. I had to find something coming from myself — personally — in the film, in order to do it. I found it during the shooting, which is why the film took as long as it did. But I *had* to find it. It couldn't be any other way.

Though Scorsese has officially taken screenwriting credit only for *GoodFellas* (cowritten with Nicholas Pileggi), he has had a hand, to some degree in

the screenplay of every film he has directed. *Raging Bull,* credited to Paul Schrader and Mardik Martin, was almost entirely rewritten by Scorsese and Robert De Niro before production began to accommodate their evolving vision of the film. Even when he's less involved with the actual writing process, his influence predominates, as in *After Hours,* where his rewrite requests to screenwriter Joseph Minion resulted in the alteration of several important scenes. On *Cape Fear,* Scorsese collaborated with screenwriter Wesley Strick in a way that was new to him.

SCORSESE: Wesley Strick was with me on the shooting of *Cape Fear.* It was the first time I ever had a writer on the set. He just had the right personality. Universal wanted the film made as quickly as possible, so I made a calculated risk of getting the script up to, say, the fifteenth draft, and then working through it scene by scene with the actors as they came aboard. Wesley was so sensitive to what was happening with the whole production that I actually had him standing right by the video monitor on the set to see everything that was going on.

Beyond traditional notions of the *written,* there is a "visual writing" that Scorsese executes on every film, translating words into meticulous storyboards of each and every sequence. Alfred Hitchcock used the same method, making his visual signature unmistakable despite a range of script collaborators. Hitchcock aimed to produce specific effects of suspense. Scorsese's visual signature is applied for a very different purpose. Rather than simply producing emotional responses, his films question the emotions they arouse. The sequence in *Vertigo* in which James Stewart stares at Kim Novak as she slowly walks through a restaurant toward him, establishes a feeling of romantic longing that Hitchcock wants us to share. By contrast, a similar sequence in *Life Lessons,* in which Nick Nolte watches Rosanna Arquette disembark from a plane, places the character's sense of romantic longing under a critical eye. Carefully constructed shots of Nolte's face, of the cigarette in his hand, and Arquette moving in slow motion as Procol Harum's "Whiter Shade of Pale" is heard on the sound track, are offered as material to be carefully analyzed, not simple scenes to be passively consumed.

Life Lessons was written by Richard Price, a well-established novelist (Ladies Man, The Wanderers) when he came to work with Scorsese. Paul Schrader also has enjoyed an independent career as a writer-director (Blue Collar, Mishima, Patty Hearst). Joseph Minion's brilliant screenplay for Robert Bierman's film Vampire's Kiss indicates he's developing a satirical vision of upscale New York life that is only hinted at in After Hours. Despite the independent talents of these writers, King of Comedy screenwriter Paul D. Zimmerman, said that seeing the finished product was "like having a baby that looks like Martin Scorsese."

Over the years, Scorsese has come to depend on a cadre of collaborators: editor Thelma Schoonmaker, cinematographer Michael Ballhaus, musician Robbie Robertson, assistant director Joe Reidy, and, until his death in 1988, production designer Boris Leven, who designed the sets for The Silver Chalice.. But Scorsese's work with Leven had little to do with film-buff nostalgia. Besides Chalice, Leven had executed remarkable designs for such diverse films as The Shanghai Gesture, Anatomy of a Murder, West Side Story, and The Sound of Music. When Scorsese needed to recreate the glamour of the set-bound films of the studio era for New York, New York, Leven was the obvious choice. Scorsese also used Leven on such unusual projects as the music documentary The Last Waltz (Leven created the sets for the concert sequences and the musical numbers shot, like New York, New York, on the sound stages of MGM), and The King of Comedy. Leven designed the sets for Scorsese's 1983 attempt at The Last Temptation of Christ. Because the 1988 version was a scaled-down production, Leven's designs had to be abandoned in favor of those by John Beard.

Scorsese's work with Leven highlights his interest in maintaining a continuity between the cinema's past and present, in forging a moviemaking tradition from which he can draw and learn. It's not surprising that he worked on Cape Fear with cinematographer Freddie Francis (Room at the Top, The Innocents, Sons and Lovers, and The Elephant Man) veteran production designer Henry Bumstead (The Sting, To Kill a Mockingbird, and Vertigo), and composer Elmer Bernstein, who adapted the late Bernard Herrmann's score of the first version of Cape Fear. Herrmann's last score was for Taxi Driver.

The artist who has had the greatest influence on shaping Scorsese's notion of film as a living tradition is Michael Powell. The British director whose most famous work, The Red Shoes, first opened Scorsese's eyes to the medium's possibilities, remains one of the most controversial figures in the history of the cinema. Powell first made a name for himself in the 1930s and 1940s, when he collaborated with screenwriter Emeric Pressburger to create a dazzling series of dramatically rich, visually stunning Technicolor films. In addition to The Red Shoes, these include The Life and Death of Colonel Blimp, Black Narcissus, and A Matter of Life and Death (released in the United States as Stairway to Heaven). Working against the British tradition of well-mannered realism, Powell strove to create a cinema of imagination and emotion. Most of his films met with audience approval, but they won few critical allies at the time they were made.

In 1960, Powell released his most daring film, Peeping Tom. Like Psycho, which debuted the same year, it featured a sympathetic murderer as a protagonist. However, Powell's antihero was also an amateur filmmaker. Using the filmmaking process to underscore the intimate relationship between films and their viewers, Peeping Tom drove Powell's critics into an unprecedented rage. One of them suggested that "the only satisfactory way to deal with it" would be to "shovel it up and flush it swiftly down the nearest sewer. Even then the stench would remain." Labeled a filmmaking pariah, Powell was forced to direct episodes of television series like *Espionage* and *The Defenders*. He emigrated to Australia and resumed filmmaking in the mid-1960s with the charming comedy *Age of Consent*. But by the 1970s Powell's career, by and large, was over.

In 1973 Michael Powell saw *Mean Streets*, and was so impressed by it that he wrote to Scorsese. Several letters were exchanged and, shortly after the completion of *Alice Doesn't Live Here Anymore*, the two met. The result was both a friendship and a unique intellectual partnership of mentor and student that lasted until Powell's death in 1990.

SCORSESE: Michael became such a part of my life over the years it's difficult to talk about him. I remember our becoming especially close right after *Raging Bull*. He gave us some very important advice on that film. For example, originally we were going to end it with Jake reading something from Shakespeare's *Richard III*. It was a speech he actually read in his night club act. Michael said it would be wrong to have a literary reference of that kind come at the end in that way — that we'd really be criticized for it. So we changed it to a quote from *On the Waterfront*, and that worked perfectly. He did the same thing on *After Hours*. We weren't satisfied with the ending we originally had, where the hero, Paul, was just taken away encased in plaster. He kept pushing me to find a solution. It was his idea that Paul should somehow end the film back where he started, and that's how we came up with the ending we finally used.

Scorsese returned Powell's favor. In 1979 he sponsored the American rerelease of the long-unseen *Peeping Tom*, which spurred a revived interest in Powell's work. He helped in any way he could to put Powell back behind the cameras. Scorsese lent his acting talents to *Pavlova*, the Soviet-produced drama about the ballerina, for which Powell was hired to supervise an English-language version. In 1987, Cannon Pictures announced it would back a Powell-directed film of Philip Glass's opera *The Fall of the House of Usher*, but the production never materialized. However, Powell happily continued to serve as Scorsese's most important advisor, virtually marrying into the director's "family" when he wed Thelma Schoonmaker in 1982.

SCORSESE: Michael was a very direct man. He would tell you exactly what he thought about something. That's part of the reason why he found it increasingly difficult to work. He couldn't handle the diplomacy involved. I remember a dinner, right before the shooting of *Raging Bull*, when we'd just met. We all went out to eat with him — Thelma, Bob, and several of our other friends. Halfway through dinner, Michael turns to me and says, "When is Mr. De Niro arriving?" Bob was sitting right next to him. Now you must understand, this didn't have anything to do with any shortcoming of Michael's faculties. It's just that Bob, when he's not on screen, is so reserved that you wouldn't know him! In a social situation he's a completely different person, and that's one of his most endearing qualities.

The Scorsese/De Niro partnership is one of the most productive in film history. It has fascinated critics because of the high quality of their films and the air of mystery surrounding their work habits. Notoriously nonverbal, De Niro has had little to say about how and why he and Scorsese work so well together. Scorsese also finds it difficult to explain their working method, which has developed into an instinctual rapport.

It's become common to speak of De Niro as Scorsese's alter ego, but a closer look at the films doesn't bear this out. In *Who's That Knocking at My Door?* and *Mean Streets*, Harvey Keitel, who resembles Scorsese in physical stature, vocal intonation, and low-key demeanor is far closer to an alter ego. In *Mean Streets*, De Niro's first appearance for Scorsese, the actor is cast as Johhny

Boy, whose emotional volatility is contrasted with the moral uncertainty of Keitel's Charlie. De Niro's subsequent work for Scorsese proceeds directly from this mold — not playing Scorsese's direct reflection, but a nightmare image of the worst side of himself.

Being the prime mover behind the decision to film *Raging Bull* and *The King of Comedy,* as well as the center of both films, De Niro qualifies as a kind of codirector. Scorsese concedes to the idea. At the same time, the differences that separate his goals and De Niro's are equally plain — signaled by the actor's establishment of his own film production facility in New York.

SCORSESE: It's the old story. One has to be very careful about such a strong collaboration, because at a certain point in time, one of the collaborators will begin to get more satisfaction out of it than the other. And that's when it's time to make changes.

The change is apparent in *GoodFellas,* where De Niro does not take the lead role, but plays what Scorsese has described as "a major cameo."

SCORSESE: On *The King of Comedy* Jerry Lewis was all *there* by the sixth take. It was great, because in a way he *was* Jerry Langford. But Bob was playing all these different levels of Rupert — seeing how far he could go with the aggressiveness, how far he could go "over the top." Like when he said to Sandra, "I gave you my spot! I live in a hovel and you live in a town house!" We shot that scene for three days. I saw Bob do that scene once in rehearsal and it was so funny that I had to get it into the film. But we had chosen the worst street in New York to shoot on, and when we finally started doing the scene it was five o'clock and the light was going. The shots had to match so we had to shoot the rest of the scene at five each day. Today I wouldn't do that. I would rehearse more and be ready to shoot a scene like that before lunch. But it was important because I

think that it's one of Bob's greatest performances.

The only thing I have going with actors is to try as best I can to create an atmosphere on the set where they're as free and relaxed as possible. I've gotten to know a lot of them personally, especially over the past few years, and they know that with me they have to do their best work.

Scorsese's attentiveness to actors is the cornerstone of his Hollywood esteem. Ellen Burstyn and Paul Newman have won Oscars with his help. Other performers, including Nick Nolte *(Life Lessons, Cape Fear)*, Rosanna Arquette *(After Hours, Life Lessons)*, Barbara Hershey *(Boxcar Bertha, The Last Temptation of Christ)*, and Sandra Bernhard *(The King of Comedy)*, have turned major corners in their careers through Scorsese films. Despite his apparent ease with the various aspects of the filmmaking process today, Scorsese feels his shaky beginnings didn't suggest the director he would become.

SCORSESE: In some ways I don't particularly like my first feature, *Who's That Knocking at My Door?* because of all the problems we had making it. I know what I wanted to do when I started the film, but I couldn't do it with the amount of money I had. I was trying to learn about 35mm cameras. I should have shot the whole thing in 16mm and blown it up to 35. I made a lot of errors, which came about because of the very process of making a feature in a noncommercial manner. I didn't have access to the equipment on a daily basis. The crew was constantly blowing out the fuses in people's buildings. It was all stopping and starting. You start shooting a scene, then two months later, when you want to reshoot, the actors have cut their hair, or have other jobs and can't work. It's a nightmare.

Bad as this experience was, it prepared Scorsese

for *Boxcar Bertha*, Roger Corman's low-budget variation on *Bonnie and Clyde*. Believing cost cutting to be the key to creativity, Corman gave Scorsese on-the-job training, but little else. It took the more professional production contexts of *Mean Streets* and *Alice Doesn't Live Here Anymore* to give Scorsese the sense of control he needed, and the freedom to let go in certain areas of his work.

SCORSESE: On *Taxi Driver* we had two or three editors, but basically it was supervised by Marcia Lucas. Tom Rolfe was one of them, and he was the person responsible for the "Are you talking to me?" scene. We had tons of footage of Bob playing around in front of the mirror, but I liked those "Are you talking to me?" takes and asked Tom to try to edit it. It was the first time I ever worked the old way with an editor — just leave the room and let him cut it himself. I wouldn't touch it. It was beautiful. But in another part of that sequence I added a little jump cut at the end where Travis says, "Listen, you screwheads," and seems to pop suddenly into the frame. Tom disowned that cut. He said, "I had nothing to do with it." But he is a great professional editor.

Scorsese enjoys the editing room more than the set, except on *New York, New York*. The most improvisational piece of filmmaking Scorsese has ever attempted, this musical drama of the unhappy marriage of a band singer and a jazz musician was shot on some of the most elaborate studio sets ever devised. It was a madly inspired attempt at wedding the irreconcilable extremes of a Vincente Minnelli-style fantasy with a Cassavetes drama. Unfortunately, the result was a mass of interesting footage, almost impossible to edit into a unified whole.

In the end, Scorsese's troubles come down to whether he should keep "Happy Endings," in the film. An elaborate production number designed to be placed at *New York, New York*'s climax, "Happy Endings" was, on a narrative level, a means of underscoring the show business success of the film's heroine, Francine Evans (Liza Minnelli). It wasn't crucial to the story, but on a thematic level "Happy Endings" was very important. Both a parody and a homage to the production numbers from the golden era of Hollywood musicals, it symbolized everything connected to Scorsese's desire to make *New York, New York* in the first place.

SCORSESE: "Happy Endings" was the first thing we shot. It was beautiful — a little movie all to itself. Shooting it was the happiest time I had on the picture. But by the time we were into the rest of the film, everything changed. When it was all over, we had a very difficult time editing. It seemed that every week we had a different cut of the thing. It was a long film and, in some places, slow. We wanted to speed it up somehow. So sometimes "Happy Endings" was in, and sometimes it was out.

Toward the end of the shoot I was having personal problems, and a bout with drugs. One of my friends said, "Marty, you're thinking about this thing too personally." I said, "No, no, no. Next version, we'll cut it!" So we did, and the film moved faster. But was it better? No. "Happy Endings" *made* the film. It gave the audience the happy ending that it otherwise didn't get. "Happy Endings" made one side of the film complete and whole — the part connected to all the old Hollywood musicals that I adored. The real ending made complete the other side of the film — the Cassavetes-like story about creative people in romantic relationships. It was a bad experience, but thank God it happened, because after *New York, New York* I knew what *not* to do.

Scorsese felt he had failed with *New York, New York* because he'd let his imgination run riot. He also blames his own lack of discipline for the problems that plagued much of the shooting of *The King of Comedy*.

His return to low-budget filmmaking with *After Hours* was a deliberate attempt to regain control. This lesson in cost-conscious filmmaking paid off on *The Last Temptation of Christ* when he was forced to film only three takes of any shot. In addition, the film's remote location forced him to shoot *Last Temptation* "blind." He couldn't see the daily rushes and had to rely on one telephone call per day to Thelma Schoonmaker in New York to find out if the shots were usable.

SCORSESE: I can't make every picture the way I made *After Hours* and *Last Temptation*, where it's all planned down to the smallest detail. But sometimes you're forced into those kinds of situations. Planning is always the hardest part of the writing of a film — figuring out what shots you're going to use. Sometimes it's so frustrating to try to figure shots out. I sit here with my dog, Zoe, and I end up turning to her and saying, "Come on, contribute!" The truth is, I'm lazy.

It's doubtful that Scorsese really is lazy. There are enough films now in the planning stages to keep him busy past the turn of the century; he appears to work at a feverish pace. The question is, "Why?" The answer can be found in one of Scorsese's most graceful films, *Life Lessons.*

Paulette, a frustrated young artist who has become the unwilling mistress of famous painter Lionel Dobie, asks him whether she has talent, or should give up painting entirely. Dobie is madly in love with her and fearful of driving her away, so he hedges his reply. Telling Paulette that she's the only one who can decide whether or not she's an artist, he adds that art is something "you do because you *have* to."

Nobody needs as much to make films as Martin Scorsese does. The carefully composed individual shots of *The Last Temptation of Christ*, the complex texture of sound effects in *Raging Bull*, the unusual camera angles of *Life Lessons*, the dynamic editing of *The King of Comedy*— none of it is needed by an industry that demands that directors produce simple, commercial, product. Martin Scorsese can't do that. He does what he does *because he has to.*

INANIMATE OBJECTS: PAUL (GRIFFIN DUNNE) WITH SCREAMING-MAN SCULPTURE . . .

. . . AND WITH THE SCULPTURE'S NEAR-COMATOSE
CREATOR (LINDA FIORENTINO), IN <u>AFTER HOURS</u>.

MARTIN SCORSESE AND MICHAEL POWELL.

ANNA MASSEY AND CARL BOEHM IN <u>PEEPING TOM</u>,
A KEY POWELL FILM OF 1960, REVIVED BY
SCORSESE IN 1980.

JACK PALANCE AND VIRGINIA MAYO IN <u>THE SILVER</u>
<u>CHALICE</u> (1954); PRODUCTION DESIGNED BY BORIS
LEVEN. SCORSESE HIRED LEVEN TO DESIGN
SEVERAL OF HIS PICTURES, INCLUDING <u>NEW YORK,</u>
<u>NEW YORK</u> AND <u>THE LAST WALTZ</u>.

HAIG MANOOGIAN, SCORSESE'S FILM TEACHER AND
MENTOR. <u>RAGING BULL</u> WAS DEDICATED TO HIM
"WITH LOVE AND RESOLUTION."

The war was over
and the world was falling in love again.

A love story is like a song. It's beautiful while it lasts.

LIZA MINNELLI   ROBERT DE NIRO
"NEW YORK, NEW YORK"

A ROBERT CHARTOFF - IRWIN WINKLER Production   A MARTIN SCORSESE Film
LIZA MINNELLI · ROBERT DE NIRO in
"NEW YORK, NEW YORK"
Screenplay by EARL MAC RAUCH and MARDIK MARTIN · Story by EARL MAC RAUCH
Directed by MARTIN SCORSESE · Produced by IRWIN WINKLER and ROBERT CHARTOFF
Original Songs by JOHN KANDER and FRED EBB · Musical Supervisor and Conductor—RALPH BURNS
Production Designed by Boris Leven · Director of Photography Laszlo Kovacs, A.S.C.

PG | **PARENTAL GUIDANCE SUGGESTED**
SOME MATERIAL MAY NOT BE SUITABLE FOR PRE-TEENAGERS

ORIGINAL MOTION PICTURE SOUNDTRACK ALBUM AND TAPE AVAILABLE ON UNITED ARTISTS **UA** RECORDS

United Artists
A Transamerica Company

T H E A T R E

Liza Minnelli, Robert De Niro Star In Romantic 'New York, New York'

(Advance Production Feature)

Producers Irwin Winkler and Robert Chartoff, fresh from their triumph with an Academy Award Best Picture win for "Rocky," are looking to new laurels with their latest film, "New York, New York," starring former Oscar winners Liza Minnelli and Robert De Niro and directed by Martin Scorsese. It is a romantic musical drama about the struggling careers of a young danceband vocalist and the saxophone player who falls in love with her, played by Minnelli and De Niro. Also starred are Lionel Stander and Barry Primus.

A Robert Chartoff/Irwin Winkler Production of a Martin Scorsese Film, "New York, New York" is released by United Artists, a Transamerica Company, and will open . . . . at the . . . . Theatre.

The screenplay was written by Earl Mac Rauch and Mardik Martin from a story by Mac Rauch. Original songs are by John Kander and Fred Ebb; Ralph Burns is Musical Supervisor and Conductor. Production design is by Boris Leven and Laszlo Kovacs is director of photography.

This lavishly mounted production opens at the close of World War II when the big bands were at their peak, and pays nostalgic tribute to that era by showcasing twenty-four timeless songs made famous by Glenn Miller, Tommy and Jimmy Dorsey, Benny Goodman and other bandstand stars of 1940's. The story moves on into the changing tempo of the 1950's, with four new songs written by Kander and Ebb of "Cabaret" fame providing a musical bridge.

This blend of music forms a fitting accompaniment to the story line, which has the girl singer, played by Miss Minnelli, sky-rocketing to the top while the sax player, De Niro, must wait for public taste to catch up to his new "bebop" style.

"In 1945 the mellow, joyous Dorsey sounds underlined the mood of the country," comments Producer Irwin Winkler. "From 'Opus One,' the first music you hear in our film, you find this feeling continually expressed in song."

"Then we are in the Fifties and Liza sings the title-song. The lyrics reflect a different attitude in America. Times have changed. Euphoria has given way to the reality of the Cold War. The mood of the country now is to struggle forward."

Still NY-7   **Mat 24**
Liza Minnelli, playing a popular singing star of the 1940's, performs at a solo appearance in "New York, New York." The United Artists release will open .... at the .... Theatre.

Still NY-15   **Mat 34**
Liza Minnelli as a big band vocalist who has become a Hollywood star, appears in a big musical production number, "New York, New York," a United Artists release, will open .... at the .... Theatre.

who met producers Robert Chartoff and Irwin Winkler through a mutual friend and the producers commissioned him to write "New York, New York." Rauch later adapted the screenplay into a novel just published in a paperback edition by Pocket Books. The picture, a United Artists release, is currently playing at the . . . . Theatre.

Martin Scorsese Tries New Dimension With 'New York, New York'

Several years ago, on the release of his penetrating "Mean Streets," virtually all the critics singled out Martin Scorsese as a "young director to watch." He hasn't let them down. In 1976 his gripping drama—one of the year's big hits—"Taxi Driver" won the prestigious Cannes Film Festival top prize, the Palme D'Or. He has now explored a whole new area by directing Liza Minnelli and Robert De Niro in the Robert Chartoff-Irwin Winkler production "New York, New York," a United Artists release about the romance and music of the Big Band era of the '40s. Written by Earl Mac Rauch and Mardik Martin from Mac Rauch's story, it opens . . . . . at the . . . . Theatre.

Scorsese's obvious sensitivity and deft direction of film, amply demonstrated in "Mean Streets," became even more evident with the release of "Alice Doesn't Live Here Anymore."

It took twelve years for Scorsese to fully make the jump from Little Italy to Hollywood. Born in New York in 1942, he originally planned to enter the Roman Catholic priesthood. He was always a film buff, and, while attending New York University as an English major he decided on a film-making career when he found himself totally involved in the film arts department.

While at New York University, Scorsese produced two short films, "What's a Girl Like You Doing in a Place Like This?" and "It's Not Just You, Murray." Both won awards from film foundations.

Film editing next became his bread and butter with the documentary films "Woodstock," "Medicine Ball Caravan" and "Elvis on Tour." Realizing that all film directing roads must lead to Hollywood, Scorsese left New York in 1970 and moved to the West Coast. As Francis Ford Coppola and Peter Bogdanovich before him, he was given a feature—"Boxcar Bertha" —to direct by exploitation filmmaker Roger Corman. This was followed by the realization of his dream picture, "Mean Streets." While editing "Alice Doesn't Live Here Anymore," Scorsese made a short documentary about his parents and Italian heritage called "Italianamerican," which became the hit of the 1974 New York Film Festival.

Scorsese is married to writer Julia Cameron; they recently became parents of their first child, Domenica Elizabeth, who was born on Labor Day, 1976.

Robert De Niro, Hot-Tempered Jazz Musician in New Role

Robert De Niro, who achieved an Academy Award as Best Supporting Actor for his striking performance in "The Godfather, Part II," adds still another new dimension to his acting talents as the hot-tempered and talented jazz saxophonist in the romantic musical-drama of the Big Band era of the '40s, "New York, New York." The actor stars with Liza Minnelli in the Robert Chartoff-Irwin Winkler production directed by Martin Scorsese for United Artists release. The picture will open . . . . . . at the . . . . Theatre. Earl Mac Rauch wrote the screenplay from his own story, with Mardik Martin.

Robert De Niro has won plaudits for a succession of roles in Chartoff-Winkler's "The Gang That Couldn't Shoot Straight," the unforgettable "Bang the Drum Slowly," the hard-hitting "Mean Streets," the Oscar-winning "The Godfather, Part II," Martin Scorsese's "Taxi Driver,"

tours in the classics and in motion pictures.

He has played a wide spectrum of roles. The ball-player in "Bang the Drum Slowly" was vastly different from the ruthless young mafia leader in "The Godfather, Part II" and still further removed from the role of the lonely stalking figure he portrayed in "Taxi Driver," or of the movie studio boss in "The Last Tycoon."

He'll next be seen on the screen in Bernardo Bertolucci's controversial "1900."

Robert De Niro was born in New York City's tough lower East Side on August 17. His first professional pay check was earned on a tour of the high schools in the New York and New England area in Chekhov's "The Bear." Later he did the almost mandatory "dinner theatre circuit" in New York's suburbia in such standard fare as "Cyrano de Bergerac," "Captain..."

directed by Brian De Palma, who also guided him in two other films, "Greetings" and "Hi, Mom." He co-starred with Shelley Winters in "Bloody Mama" under the direction of Roger Corman and, in 1972, the film public singled him out as star material in "The Gang That Couldn't Shoot Straight."

It was in 1973, however, that he won special recognition. De Niro's heartbreaking performance as the dying ball-player in "Bang the Drum Slowly" brought out all the accolades of the critics and audiences. Also released that same year was Martin Scorsese's "Mean Streets," a powerful film that won him the Best Supporting Actor Award by the New York Film Critics Circle. This triumph was topped in 1974 by winning the Academy Award in "The Godfather, Part II." De Niro is married to Diahann Abbott.

Mac Rauch and Martin Write 'New York, New York'

"New York, New York" was filmed

BERNICE (MARY KAY PLACE) SINGS IN THE "UP CLUB" SEQUENCE; PRODUCTION DESIGNED BY BORIS LEVEN.

LIZA MINNELLI AS FRANCINE EVANS IN <u>NEW YORK,</u>
<u>NEW YORK</u>.

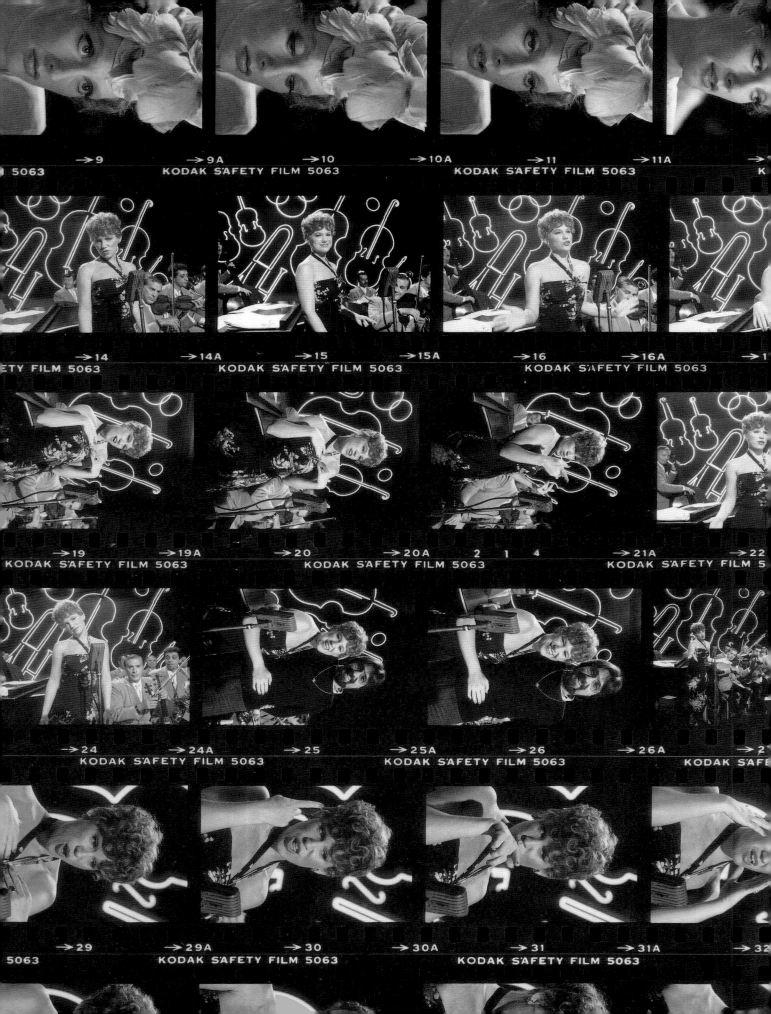

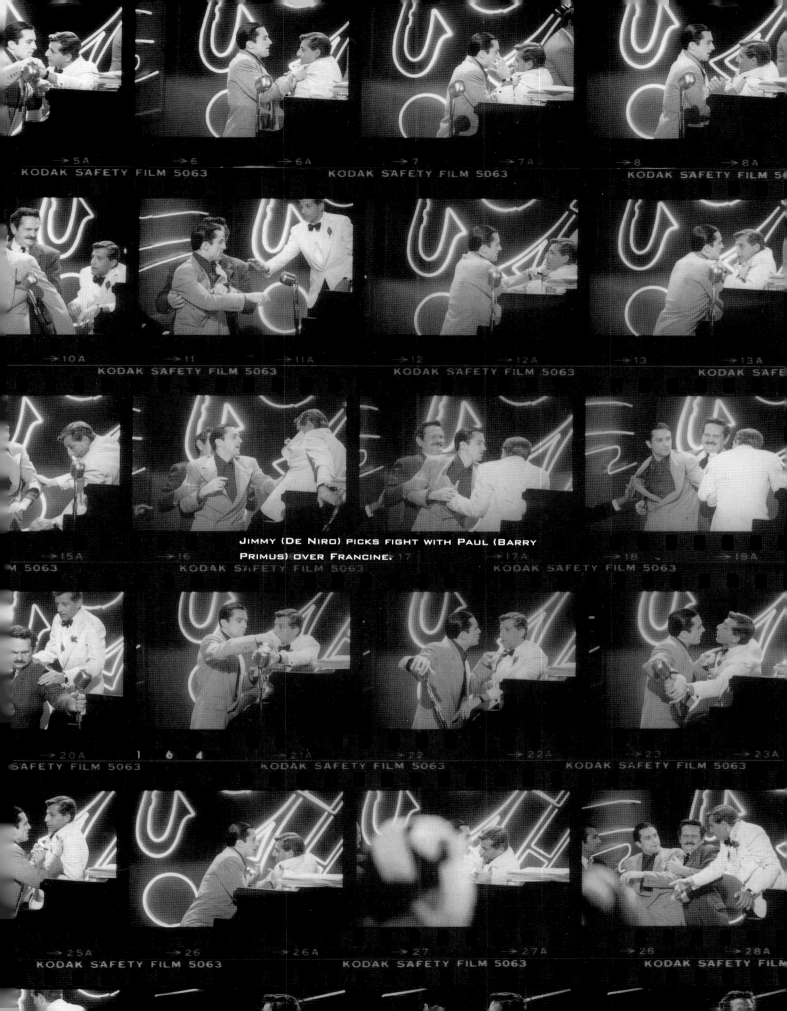

Jimmy (De Niro) picks fight with Paul (Barry Primus) over Francine.

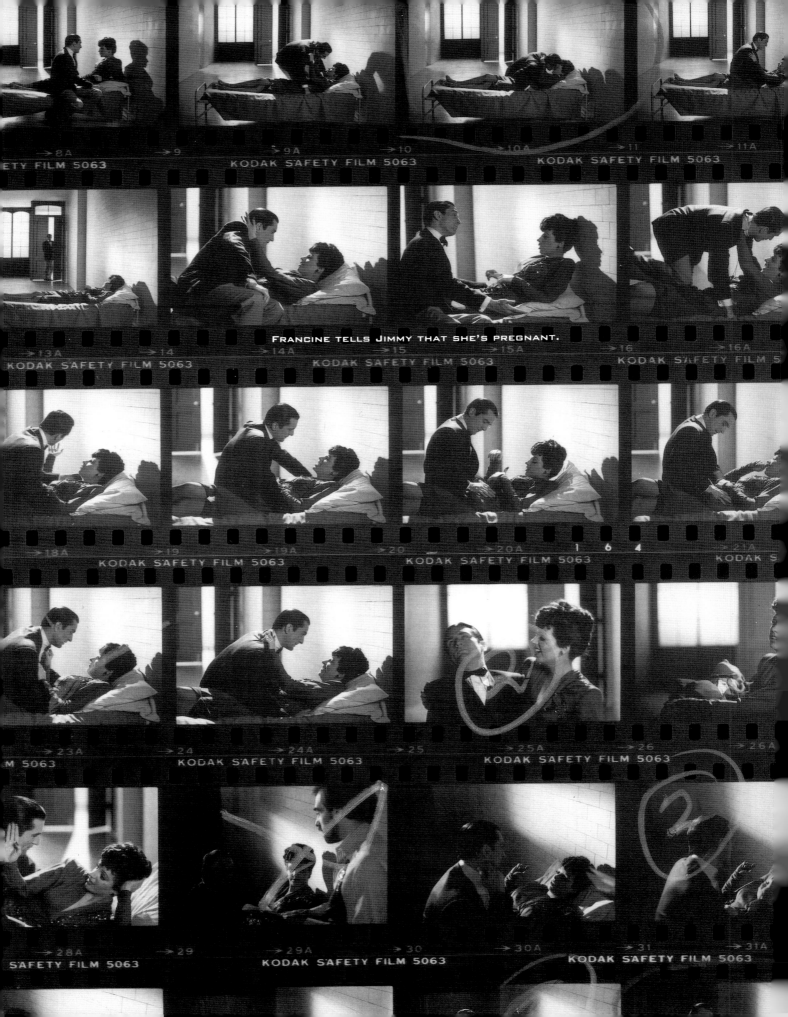

FRANCINE TELLS JIMMY THAT SHE'S PREGNANT.

PAUL (BARRY PRIMUS) ON THE ROAD WITH THE BAND.
THESE IMAGES ARE USED IN A <u>NEW YORK, NEW YORK</u>
SEQUENCE IN WHICH LIZA MINNELLI PASTES PICTURES
INTO A PHOTOGRAPH ALBUM AS A DJANGO REINHART
TUNE PLAYS ON HER PHONOGRAPH.

(TOP) SCORSESE SHOOTING IN THE HALLWAY OF "UP CLUB" SET. (CENTER) PAUL COMFORTS FRANCINE. (BOTTOM) REHEARSING THE PICTURE HANGING SCENE: SCORSESE IS REFLECTED IN A MIRROR HELD UP BY KATHY MCGINNIS AS LIZA MINNELLI LOOKS ON.

3   → 21A

KODAK SAFETY FILM

THE "HAPPY ENDINGS" NUMBER. LIZA MINNELLI,
LARRY KERT.

EPILOGUE: "IT'S 3:28, THELMA!"

May 6, 1991. 2:00 P.M.. Martin Scorsese's editing room at the Brill Building in midtown Manhattan. Film editor Thelma Schoonmaker and director Martin Scorsese, accompanied by his faithful dog, Zoe, are editing the climactic sequence of *Cape Fear*. At this point, the two have already made a preliminary rough assembly of sequences. On the wall above the editing table is a chart of 149 separate segments with descriptive titles (e.g. "Family Leaves House"). Most of these numbered segments represent specific scenes; some refer to pivotal shots linking scenes together.

The sequence being edited today takes place on a small boat adrift in a river. Robert De Niro, as the vengeful ex-convict Max Cady, has handcuffed his adversary, lawyer Sam Bowden (Nick Nolte), to the boat. His face horribly scarred by fire from an earlier scene, Max is conducting a mock trial of Sam while holding Sam's wife, Leigh (Jessica Lange), and daughter, Danny (Juliette Lewis), at bay with a handgun. Outside there is a storm that in the course of the scene tears the boat apart.

Schoonmaker and Scorsese normally approach editing a film from scene one to the end, but with *Cape Fear* they are working out of sequence because shots of exteriors of the boat, made with miniatures, still have to be executed. They are looking for the most effective place to insert reaction shots of Jessica Lange and Juliette Lewis as De Niro beats — and browbeats — Nolte.

Thelma Schoonmaker edited Martin Scorsese's first feature, *Who's That Knocking at My Door?* and worked with him on *Woodstock*. In 1980 she was reunited with Scorsese on *Raging Bull*, for which she won an Academy Award for Best Editing. She has edited nearly every subsequent Scorsese picture. Holding a marking pencil in her right hand, her left in a white glove, Schoonmaker's attention is divided between the editing flatbed and the reels of picture and sound track that she regulates by hand. Scorsese observes from an easy chair just behind her. When she stops to make adjustments, Scorsese takes the opportunity to make notes on his next film, *The Age of Innocence*, browse through the latest issue of *Video Watchdog*, and consult film catalogs for titles he wants to add to his burgeoning personal collection. He also talks to Zoe, who is occasionally disturbed by the sound of the actors' screaming voices on the sound system. The rhythm of the afternoon's work is one of constant stopping and starting, talk when decisions are being made, and silence (save for the whir of the film reels) while they're executed.

NICK NOLTE'S VOICE: *It said that she was*

promiscuous, and had three different lovers in one month.

ROBERT DE NIRO'S VOICE: *At least three! At least three!*

MARTIN SCORSESE: Could we tighten that?

THELMA SCHOONMAKER: The second "at least three" is from another take.

Schoonmaker makes the appropriate cut.

MS: On to the next one.

TS: On to the next one.

DAVID EHRENSTEIN: I gather that the shooting isn't your favorite part of movie-making.

MS: I'm always irritable during the shooting. I complain to my assistant director, Joe Reidy. On *Cape Fear* one day, he came into my camper in the morning, wearing rain gear and all wet, with a big "Good Morning!" I said, "What's so good about it?" I couldn't *imagine* stepping out of that trailer. I say to him, "Look at you — you're a mess! How can you be smiling at six A.M.? Don't push me today. I won't be forced to go any faster!" He doesn't say a word. I start in, and by the time I'm on the set with the actors it's a whole different thing.

TS: I have to find this other "*Talk to me*" On "*Talk to me!*" I have another really nice loud one of Bob.

MS: Can we look at that one?

TS: I'm trying to find it now, real quick, and then we'll look at the shots of the women and then we've *got* to move on.

RD: *Talk to me!*

MS (TO DE): It took us six weeks to shoot this sequence, with water shooting out of hoses hitting every part of our bodies.

TS: Zoe, aren't you being a good girl! She's very slow to warm up to people. She has to do it on her own time.

MS: It's torture for her to hear all this yelling, especially later on, when we pull the window shade down to keep out the lights. She doesn't understand it.

RD: *Talk to Me!*

TS: That was a good one.

DE: I can't help but notice that one of the scenes on the chart is titled "Nietzsche is discussed." What's that about?

TS (TO DE): Marty always has fits about this. I give all the scenes names, because I hate learning numbers. The one he really hated was on *Raging Bull*. It was the bedroom scene with Vickie where Jake pours ice on himself to keep from getting aroused. Because we had other scenes I'd marked as love scenes, I didn't call it that.

MS: So she called it "Sink/Ice"! My big love scene!

RD: *Talk to me! I'm standin' here!*

TS: It's so fast I think we're going to have to go back to the beginning to see if we can put a clip of the ladies in there.

RD: *Would you care to tell the jury why? Would you care to tell the court why?*

MS: You could put it after he says, "*Would you care to tell the jury why?*" and Nick doesn't answer. Then you could cut to the ladies. Is he going to answer or not? How long is this going to go on? Because the "judge" is supposed to be up there. (**TO DE**) Bob's obviously talking to nobody, you know.

TS: Do you want to see the whole scene first? You might have to loop his voice on this. These are the "selects." They're a very complicated set of Marty's favorite takes — sometimes just only one line — in order of preference. We run it on this second monitor. He can pull things out that way, judge sections instead of wholes. So that's what we're running through now, alternate takes of the women.

Jessica Lange appears on the second flatbed monitor. She is holding on to Juliette Lewis who is out of camera range. Lange flinches as a gun goes off.

MS: A gun doesn't really go off at that point. I was firing guns to make them jump. They're supposed to be reacting to punches being thrown at Nick, and things like that.

Zoe barks, then strikes a pose when attention is paid to her.

DE: What breed of dog is she?

MS: She's a bichon frise.

TS: Isn't it amazing how they pose? It's bred into them.

MS: That's what it is. When they survived the French Revolution they became show dogs. They were the favorite lapdogs of the French aristocracy, and during the Reign of Terror they were executed right along with the aristocrats. A couple of centuries earlier they were raised by pirates who had them on their ships. Right, Zoe? Oh, those damned boats! They were raised to sit on people's laps. Oh, the lazy afternoons, Zoe! Her eyes are closing. I got her for Barbara but . . . I never had a dog! I was always allergic to animals. I've learned a lot from her. She has a real sense of humor.

TS: This is too long.

RD: *Was her prior sexual history prepared in connection to my defense?*

MS: Let's go down to the head of the reel, and then get the other stuff out, give up on the damned thing and get on to the last scene. Let's *drown* the guy! I'm sick of him. How long have we been at this sequence?

TS (*in mock exasperation*): Oh, Marty, it's only been thirty minutes. It's a very complicated sequence.

MS (*sheepishly*): Yeah, yeah, I know.

Other takes of Jessica Lange reacting are run on the monitor.

MS: Look. Here, with the waves hitting in the background. She opened her mouth a little bit too. There, like that, see? There where the kid moves and she opens her mouth. Hey, you know what? You know where it zooms in? Cut before the zoom settles.

TS: For when Bob hits Nick?

MS: No, not even for the hit. Cut here and give it an extra frame. Just then he'll yell, and it'll overlap half of his first word.

Schoonmaker follows Scorsese's directions and they review the results.

MS: Oh, well, that's a mess. So much for that idea!

TS: I think it would be nice if we made the hit with the camera on Nick.

MS: Oh, yeah, you're right. Let's try it!

TS: Yeah, terrorize `em!

Schoonmaker edits the sequence, and she and Scorsese are pleased with the result.

RD: *Was her prior history ever prepared in connection to my defense?*

MS: Bob wants to get his point across. He's been waiting around for nearly two hours on this picture, trying to get his point made, and he's a little — no pun intended — *burnt up* about it!

TS: I like that bit there, where he turns to the invisible jury.

MS: You see that shot? It's the old Mario Bava zoom! I got a new 16mm print of *Black Sunday*, by the way. What a movie! The whole thing is like one long dream. You see that rocking, there? I'm telling you, once we got on that boat, it was like an amusement park ride. It was pretty nauseating, especially for the camera crew, who wore wet suits.

DE: Hot, wet, and cold all at the same time.

MS. Exactly. I got Freddie Francis to shoot this film, mainly because of what he's directed and photographed over the years. Films like *The Innocents*. I wanted that edge. You know, the classic horror-film image of a woman walking down the hall with the candle at night.

TS: It's gonna work!

MS: You think it's gonna work, Thelma? Gee, I should be in the editing room more often.

Schoonmaker runs the sequence through the monitor again.

MS: One more frame off the zoom shot, I think. One more frame off then you put a couple of frames on the tail.

TS: And then we look at another reel.

MS: Yeah. Another reel coming up, you bet. You want shots? We got! Right, Zoe? We got 'em. "Uh oh," she's thinking. "What's he gonna do now?" Yes, Zoe, we got the shots!

A different reaction shot of Jessica Lange runs on the second monitor.

MS: I like that she put up the hands a little bit. I storyboarded the whole thing. But how do you use them with a boat that's rocking in a storm? It's like, "What happened? Where was the image? Was that it?" It really humbles you because the film takes on a life of its own.

RD: *You betrayed your country. You derogated your oath. Guilty of judging me and selling me out!*

MS: It's three twenty-eight, Thelma!

TS (*in mock despair*): Oh, God!

MS: I'm telling you I'm getting one of those big digital clocks and putting it right in front of your eyes. Let's make the picture, right, Zoe?

TS: She gets upset when she thinks we're arguing.

MS: She wants to calm us down. That's what they do, you know, that's what their job is. They lick you to calm you down.

RD: *This is between you and me, captain. Leave them out of it. This is my night, captain.*

Don't you step on —

De Niro begins to rhythmically pound Nolte with his foot as he delivers the last line.

JESSICA LANGE: *Stop! Stop! Stop!*

De Niro stops, his foot suspended in midair.

MS: Let's see it again from a different vantage point. Closer. Put a different cry over it. Every time it starts coming in on that frozen foot there it just . . . Ultimately I don't think we'll need a cut in there, but I like the idea of the kid panicking because her father's being kicked in the head.

TS: There's another possibility — putting the cry in *after* the shot of Bob's foot stomping Nick.

MS: Where?

TS: After "Leave them out of it" and just before he turns around.

These alterations are made, and the scene is reviewed.

MS: I don't know, Thelma. I think it'll have to go back to where it was before.

TS: Maybe it could be earlier?

MS: Before the close-up? Right between those two cuts? Or before the leg stops moving? Would that be too much? Yes, before the leg stops! Go, Thelma, Go!

She does, and they observe the results.

MS: That's better. Let's go with that for a little while. Come on, get this damned thing off! Let's make another movie! Right Zoe?

The scene runs on the moviola without sound at an accelerated speed. A wave hits the boat; it starts to turn over and break apart. The camera turns upside down as the actors are thrown about by the force of the wave. In the tumult, Nolte is freed from his handcuffs. He immediately cuffs the now semiconscious De Niro to what's left of the boat. Scorsese narrates as the scene runs by.

MS: There we are. The gun slips in his hand. Noise. Music. Now they get out. Crash, bang, crash. (TO DE) Where it says Scene Missing is to indicate a shot of the boat breaking up. That's one of the miniatures we're going to shoot. Crash, bang, crash. It's going to work! It's just a matter of getting the right miniature in there.

DE: I gather one of the problems you're having now has to do with making sure that the viewer sees everything that's going on in each shot.

MS: Even though this is all storyboarded, sometimes basic narrative information just doesn't come across. This was why I forced myself to make this film. I mean with me — narrative — forget it! It's all just character. Here we need shots like "Man being dragged away by the current." The problem is to get a shot that makes it clear that that's happening. We've got all these angles on the scene. Like here — we need a shot of Bob's head coming out and just missing the rock that Nick's about to drop on him.

TS: We could put in the shot with one of the stuntmen.

MS: Where he goes out? You're right. Bob doesn't seem to be going out with the tide here. We're shooting in a torrential storm and water's covering his face. If it were still water there would be no problem in seeing this.

The telephone rings.

MS: This is for me. When I'm taking private calls Thelma can go out and I can buzz her back in, but if I'm too lazy I can go over there into the "Booth of Silence" and take the call.

DE: It looks just like the isolation booth they used to have on the $64,000 Question TV show.

MS: That's what it is! In fact when we put it in the room, the editing assistants rigged it so it played the show's theme music.

Schoonmaker edits as Scorsese takes the call.

MS (*off the telephone and looking at the scene again*): Bob goes out of the shot too slowly there. Use a shot where he goes out faster.

As she looks for the take, Scorsese glances out the editing room window.

MS: There's a place across the street that sells T-shirts between the Circus Cinema and the video store. It's called "The Eye-Catcher." There's always a fight there. They're always chasing out guys dressed in caftans, running across the street with garbage pails, and the police always come by on horseback to stop it.

DE: They've got to be selling more than T-shirts.

MS (*chuckles*): It looks like it.

DE: I noticed from the window in your office, the sign for Liza Minnelli's show at Radio City is staring straight at you.

MS: Yes, I know. I wanted to go to Liza's show, but I don't know if I'll have time. You know, I haven't had a vacation since 1987. It's hard to find time for anything anymore. Tomorrow night I'm taking my father out to dinner — it's his birthday. Next week I have to go to Washington, D.C., for a day and a half for a tribute to Michael Powell. The rest of the time I'm here in this room.

They look at the reedited scene.

MS: You slowed it down. Skip-frame this bit here and you've got it. And trim the tail end of the shot of the rock. See, where his hands are almost coming off? Lose that. Right there. No, lose one more frame. That's it. Now you're talking! The images are really all here, it's just a matter of placement.

They review the sequence.

MS: If we didn't get the idea that Bob's slipping out of the frame, and floating away after that, let's go home!

TS: I like that cut from the rock to the sand.

MS: Yeah, it gives us more indication of movement.

TS: We've never had a shot of Bob inside this wave, did we?

They look at the shot.

MS: Hmm. Much better.

TS: Wait, wait, let's see if it works.

MS: Is it necessary to know that he's moving? Two cameras on him and the lens distortion, and it still doesn't seem like he's moving out.

DE: This is your first widescreen film.

MS: Yeah. I was thrown by Panavision at first. It doesn't have the variety of lenses you have normally. But I really like it now. Thelma and I are going to recut *Cape Fear* for TV, using different shots and making another version so you won't have that awful pan-and-scan thing when they show widescreen movies, cutting half the image off the screen. How about that for driving you crazy, Thelma? You know how much I want to come back in the middle of *Age of Innocence* and say, 'Yeah, let's use a close-up here.' Maybe we could edit *Cape Fear* on the set.

TS: Well, you *do* have to wait a long time for the lighting.

MS: You're right! We could start cutting a little bit of *Age of Innocence* right there too, if we can. Lord knows there won't be any improvisation. The dialogue is . . . the dialogue. I've been working at choosing all the paintings that the families in *Age of Innocence* would have had in their houses. You wouldn't believe some of the stuff these people liked. Genre paintings of cows and sheep, faces of street urchins and nudes. Imitation Pre-Raphaelite stuff. Some of the taste these people had is amazing. The Hudson Valley painters were considered modern then. Only certain kinds of people dealt with them. The older families had Gainsborough. In a way I'm finding the characters through the paintings. Everybody will be very formal in the film. I looked at William Wyler's *Heiress* again last week. I just adore it.

They look at the sequence of Nolte attempting to strike De Niro with a rock, and De Niro floating away from him on a piece of wreckage.

MS: Keep going, keep going. He's actually moving now.

TS: We're almost there.

MS: I had a thought. Take the shot of the wave and fill the screen with water and rock and roll it back and forth, then superimpose him in the center of the shot and zoom out. I know — "But it'll cost a fortune!" What about skip-framing it? You know those skip-frame shots that are so obviously skip-frame that they work? Like Hitchcock — the scene in *North by Northwest* where Cary Grant's car goes out of control and then comes to a stop really quickly. Come on Thelma, be daring, be bold!

TS: I think that, no matter what, we'd better have the shot of Nick's shoe with *something* next to it.

MS: I agree.

TS: It's got to be the shoe and the wreckage.

MS: Yes, with the camera tight on the water somehow.

TS: Of course, maybe the music could convince us we're seeing something.

MS: Convince us we're sinking.

TS: Not sinking, so much. Remember, the wave is washing away slowly. I was surprised not to see the wreckage move.

MS: I have an idea — skip-frame the first part of the shot.

TS: And then cut back later?

MS: Cut back to the piece we're taking off of

the shot of Nick.

TS: Well, that might work with the B cameras, because there's movement with the A cameras. But it's too slow.

MS: I still think we should skip-frame the first part of the shot, cut back to Nick, dolly further out, then cut to Bob.

TS: Cut close here with the wave over it, and then we cut to Nick and it's normal.

MS: Yes.

DE: It's a bit like Chabrol here with the rock — *This Man Must Die*.

MS: Oh, yeah — all the blood.

DE: And the final fight in *Blade Runner*, too.

MS: Yeah, that was really nice, the way Rutger Hauer didn't want to die. When I first saw that film, I didn't quite get it.

They look at a shot of De Niro handcuffed to the wreckage, slowly sinking into the water and drowning. As he does, he begins to babble, "speak in tongues."

MS: There'll be noise and music here as he's going under singing. What do you think, Thelma? It seems to be okay. Let's do the rest of the scene, and then check the whole thing against the storyboards 'cause it's going to be coming up on six o'clock exactly.

They look at the scene again.

TS: Should we go that far?

MS: I think so. Henry Bumstead was our art director on this. He's in his early seventies, and he's just incredible. He worked on so many of Hitchcock's films.

TS: Here?

MS: Yeah, this close-up of Sam, then we trim the head of the shot a bit and you're fine. Six eighteen Thelma!

TS (*mock horror*): Oh, God!

MS: I'm getting a damned digital clock so you can see. Red numbers. I'm going to get the one

from Hammacher Schlemmer that projects the numbers on the wall. Time is ticking away. We have to make another picture! (*to DE*) Better not sit too close to her now — she's mad. (He *points at the chart*) What you're looking at is from number 144 to the end. We've only put together a rough assembly of up to number 22. Tomorrow we'll cut up to number 22.

As Nolte, Lange, and Lewis huddle together on shore, we hear Lewis's off-screen monologue, the last moment of the film.

JULIETTE LEWIS'S VOICE: *After all that happened folks treated us differently, and I guess we are different than before. But that's okay, because I think if you hang on to the past you die a little every day. As for myself, I know I'd rather live.* (in a fierce whisper) *The End.*

MS: Not bad. It's a little bit as if the whole picture is in her eyes.

TS: Well, what time is it now, Marty?

MS: It's six forty-two.

TS: Well, we've done enough for today.

MS (*looking out the window at the Holiday Inn across the street*): Look at that, all those neon lights. You should have seen what was going on when they were building the place.

TS: It's ridiculous. It's part of the "Times Square Revival." Everything has to be neon. It's Las Vegas. It's all pink and it makes it vibrate in here.

MS: When we were cutting *Life Lessons* and *GoodFellas*, the flickering was theatening to throw off our judgment of the cuts.

TS: Remember when Bill Murray dropped by, and was doing his eye-rolling routine? He was trying to convince them he couldn't work with the sign on because it was affecting his eyesight. They said "We're sorry you didn't come down to the Planning Commission." That was five years ago.

187

MS: At first it was very beautiful. Before the building came along you could see down five blocks. But everyday they were laying concrete.

TS: And the noise!

MS: She said, "Marty, they're putting up lights." I said, "Don't be silly."

TS: And then it started!

MS: The lights went on at four-thirty that day!

TS: All over the Brill Building filmmakers were going crazy — all those pink lights.

MS: They were running around like that scene out of *The Fountainhead* where Gary Cooper's yelling, "You compromising fools!" Everybody wanted to blow the place up.

TS: It's just not Times Square anymore.

MS: Thelma, you grew up in Aruba! Get out of here!

TS: Have you seen the front?

MS: I haven't ventured past. Well, I'm gonna go now.

TS: We've really got to hunker down.

May 8, 1991. Same place, same cast. As the editing begins, Kristi Zea, production designer on *GoodFellas* and *Life Lessons*, visits the editing room with her newborn daughter, Norma. Scorsese is on the telephone as she enters.

MS (*into the telephone*): Kristi Zea dropped by to show us her new baby, and it's petting my dog. So I'm having to hold onto the dog, and David Ehrenstein is here writing a book on me at the same time. So, aside from that, the film's coming along just fine!

KRISTI ZEA: Boy, I have to tell you, Thelma, I have so much respect for you guys. I'm editing my little thing upstairs for the HBO Women and Men series. Its based on a Carson McCullers story and it's supposed to be twenty-six minutes long. I've got it down to twenty-eight, and I

don't know *what* I'm going to do.

TS: It takes years of experience. We're learning every day. We've never done a thriller before. Ordinarily what we'd do when we're coming to the end of a film is to start to punch it up and make it go faster and faster. Here we have to slow things down and draw them out.

MS (*now off the telephone*): Zoe's never seen a baby before.

TS (*holding the baby in her lap*): She's sitting up so well.

MS: And she's in the movie business too!

TS: Kristi's been in editing agony upstairs.

KZ: I was just telling Thelma we had eight days to shoot and I did it in eight and a half.

MS: Just starting out, and already she's becoming decadent!

KZ: So how are you?

MS: A little tired, because I've had no break. Well, when we were shooting in Florida — you know me — I was in the sun all the time, I was in the pool! I'm kidding — it was me and Zoe in the shade. I rented a house with a pool in the back. When my daughter Domenica came down she went in it, but I wouldn't. Zoe just stared at it. She loved Florida but had to be dipped once a week because of the fleas. Actually, it was like an animal movie because eveyone brought their dogs with them. All of them would park themselves right by the entranceway to the set, where the grips would be going in and out, and they got into this proprietary thing about it — guarding the place. One night we did this scene where Jessica and Nick come home to their house and discover that Bob has killed this private detective that was involved in the case. There's a pool of blood on the floor and they keep slipping in it and falling over the detective's body. Nick is really upset and he grabs a gun and runs out into the yard at night firing the gun and yelling, "I'll kill him!" He climbs this pillar and Jessica is pulling him back. Later I said to everyone, "Finally I got these WASPS to act like Italians!" But when we were at the climax of the scene, the dogs went crazy and started running all over the set. We had to stop the take — it was pandemonium.

The telephone rings.

MS: *This* one I know I'll have to take in the Booth of Silence.

KZ: I was reading that on the first film you did with Marty that none of the cuts matched, and I'm thinking, "Thank God!"

TS: Well, you know when John Ford started out as a director and he was making two-reelers, it had to be explained to him that he couldn't just do "master" shots [medium-to-long shots taking in an entire scene] and expect to be able to cut them together. So at one point they had to make a shot by blowing up a tiny detail of the corner of the frame of a "master" where there was a parrot. Every time they went from one "master" to another they inserted the shot of the parrot to make the cut work.

KZ: It's been an incredible experience for me, making this first film.

TS: You know, Marty always wanted to do an article about filmmaking by wearing a tape recorder so he could pick up all the questions that are asked on the first day of shooting. Everything from, "Do you take milk in your coffee?" to "Where do you want the camera?" and "Who do you want miked?" People just don't understand him when he talks about the need for quiet and concentration. When we were scouting locations, he would say, "Everybody be quiet, I gotta think," and everybody thought he was just being crazy.

KZ: Well, if I didn't know how complicated it is before, I know now.

TS: Marty's getting interested in shooting in a studio for the first time. That's one of the things he and Michael [Powell] used to argue about. He could never understand why Marty wanted to shoot on location.

KZ: There are good things about both ways. You get a certain leverage with sets, but locations add credence to things.

TS: Actors like Bob De Niro like the ambiance of a location.

Having finished the call, Scorsese leaves the booth.

KZ: So how far along are you?

MS: We've had to start cutting the end of the picture because we still have to shoot miniatures. People like Michael used to do films with miniatures all the time.

They run a scene from early in the film where the principal characters are in a movie theater watching the film Problem Child. *Norma giggles.*

MS: See, you like Max, don't you, Norma? He's a funny guy. Movies are fun, huh, Norma?

Kristi Zea makes her goodbyes, and she and Norma leave.

MS: Where's the tissue supply?

TS: There should be an extra box there.

Zoe begins to rummage around the room, looking for something.

MS: Zoe's upset because the couch has been taken out. Don't worry, Zoe, you're getting a new couch tomorrow.

TS: It isn't coming tomorrow.

MS: It isn't? I signed the check. (*to* **DE**) I sign everything they give me. You can't do this to Zoe — look at her!

TS: Okay. Here we go.

They are now looking at scene number 10 "Ice Cream Parlor." Nolte is about to pay for ice cream that he has bought for Lange and

Lewis, only to be told that it has been paid for by someone else. He looks across the street and sees De Niro sitting in a car. De Niro is revealed slowly; the camera moves closer and closer through a series of jump cuts ending on a close-up of his extended tattooed arm.

MS: Is it nervy enough?

TS: We'll see.

MS: Cut right there after the car passes.

TS: That's not your preferred shot?

MS: No, the car seemed to be moving too slowly. Pick it up a little later, I guess. It's only two frames.

They briefly review a scene in which Nolte and Illeana Douglas, who plays his secretary, play racquetball. They move on to a nighttime scene where Nolte, looking in a bathroom mirror, sees Lange, just behind him, massaging her shoulder.

NN: *Honey, do that again.*

JL: *Oh, come on!*

MS: I like her *"Oh, come on!"* The colored lights in the background are from the fireworks display outside the house.

DE: It looks a bit like the opening of *Contempt.*

MS: Oh yes, always *Contempt!* Why not? Somebody's got to do it. Everybody's trying to get new prints made of that film. Just tighten the shot of her head a bit.

They look at a scene of Lange getting out of bed in the middle of the night.

MS: Here it's negative and then back into color when she opens her eyes. I'm going to use images in negative at certain points in the film. They're such a nice couple — tall Aryan, very good features.

DE: The perfect victims.

MS: Right!

TS: Should I trim the tail of this a bit?

MS: I think it's too long to hold on negative,

don't you? After that mark, go to black-and-white positive. It'll be green, and they'll look like lizards!

Scorsese takes a telephone call from legendary B movie director Joseph H. Lewis.

MS: They're showing some of his films at the Public Theater. Jay Cocks and I just wrote an article for the *New York Times* about him, and he really liked it. He's eighty-one now, and he looks fine. You know, his films are great, but at first I found them very intellectual. I reacted more to someone like Phil Karlson. It took me awhile to understand what was happening in Lewis. Of course, *Gun Crazy* was no problem. I got that immediately.

TS: Okay, now?

MS: Yes. Now it goes to green, then red — like *Black Narcissus*, where Kathleen Byron faints. That cut worries me a bit, because it looks like the beginning of an action.

TS: We could put a tail on it here, but it doesn't look like we need it.

Lange is shown looking out a window blind. The next shot shows De Niro sitting on a wall. In the background, pieces of the set are visible.

MS: These shots of Bob are going to be bluescreened so you'll see fireworks behind him. I've never done bluescreen before.

TS: I'm going to try and remove more of this shot and then jump the shot of her in.

MS: Maybe we're resting on her a little too long. Pick it up right . . . there.

Lange is shown waking Nolte, who is in bed.

JL: *Sam, Sam, somebody's out there. (pause), No leave the light on.*

MS: With the right sound effects it would be nice.

TS: We're going to end on her.

Lange and Nolte are looking out of the window.

JL: *He's gone.*

MS: Maybe there's a little bit too much on the head of "He's gone." If we don't start trimming we'll end up with a three-hour rough cut, and I can't take that.

TS: He's ranting again!

MS: It's going to be a five-hour movie!

TS: Oh, come on!

MS: You see? I *want* to get nervous. I *want* to get sick to my stomach.

TS: Yeah, right.

MS: Sixteen reels. No, wait, that scene called 'Reveal Cady,' that's three reels from number 142.

TS: No, we started at 'Cape Fear sign.' Number 143 is the beginning of the last three reels.

MS: Two-thirds of a card is three reels.

TS: Marty, that's insane. The charts are not done that way!

MS (*sheepishly*): I know, I know.

TS: You can't go by the charts.

Lange, alone on screen, is wiping lipstick from her mouth. There is a brief close-up of her lips as she wipes them.

MS: Here it's too long. Begin with her hands, then punch right in before the audience realizes it. God forbid an image should stay on the screen too long these days!

DE: There seems to be a kind of Hitchcock feel here; the way you do the closeup of her lips especially.

MS: I love that sort of thing. To me, the best movie kiss is in *Marnie* — the branches breaking through the window and the extreme close-up of Sean Connery kissing Tippi Hedren during the storm. If you speak to "Bummy" — Henry Bumstead, the production designer — he'll tell you that, from the fifties on Hitchcock didn't

want to go on location. He'd say, "Build me this." It's funny, but the more films you do, the more you want the total control of the studio. Can we jump cut to Nick from the image of Jessica's lips?

TS: No, because we're cutting to her next.

MS: Oh, really? Another one of my bright ideas! Well, we'll just end the scene on her lips.

DE: The way she wipes off the lipstick is a bit like *The Naked Kiss.*

MS: Oh, yeah, we were talking about that the other day. But here you can see her tongue. Thelma, no tongue!

TS: Come on!

MS: You see, it gets to be that time of the day. No respect. That's why they don't want directors in editing rooms. What about cutting here, before the tongue?

TS: Then you're not going to see her exit the shot. I could jump cut it.

MS: We're making so many jump cuts!

DE: It's *Breathless* all over again.

MS: Cut the outgoing shot, right before the tongue between the lips. One hand goes out, then punch the other hand in. What's it look like?

TS: I have no idea.

MS: That's what it comes down to.

JL: *He's gone.*

MS: Good.

They look at scene number 22 "Leigh Grills Sam." Nolte and Lange are conversing over breakfast.

JL: *What was he in prison for?*

NN: *I think it was battery.*

JL: *You think it was battery? What do you mean "battery"? Did he batter a man? Did he batter a woman?*

TS: Does this line have to be with camera on him or her?

MS: I think I like it on Nick more. You can see

him try to hide his face in the cup. Stay on him. Lose the shot on her. These are very hard shots to get. It's like the scene in *GoodFellas* where Bob and Ray Liotta are at the diner. The camera is literally in front of the actors. They're talking to the lens, and they're supposed to be having a conversation with another person.

DE: He throws a little sidelong glance there, [as if to say] "Is she buying this?"

MS: He doesn't want to worry her.

TS: I don't think we should stay on this shot too long.

Schoonmaker trims the shots and they review the scene again.

MS: About Friday, when do you want me to come in?

TS: If you just want to come in to look at scenes you can come at anytime. If you want to look at what I've been working on, I don't know. It doesn't matter because it's going to take awhile to cut those scenes. "Sam offers money to the police" is a big scene. Why don't we decide tomorrow?

MS: You know it's going to be a pretty-looking picture.

DE: Your salute to family values?

MS: Yes! That's the way I've always looked at it. Nick plays a guy who's trying to keep everything together in life, trying to keep the lid on.

Scorsese prepares to leave.

MS: You know I must show you this review of *Raging Bull* that was in a laserdisc newsletter. I read it to the whole crew on *Cape Fear*. It tries to be very respectful, but the guy obviously doesn't like the film. It's all sort of "I don't know why anyone would want this in their house, but it's a great movie and can be used for reference." He said about the commentary Thelma and I did for the second track of the

disc, "Listening to these comments it would seem the film was put together through blind artistic luck." So later in the day on the *Cape Fear* shoot we were having some problems and the camera operator Gordon Hayman said, "Well, we'll just have to rely on blind artistic luck!" So that's it. It's all just blind artistic luck! Well, good night, Thelma. I shall *try* to return.

SCORSESE OBSERVES THE EDITING AS ZOE SLEEPS.

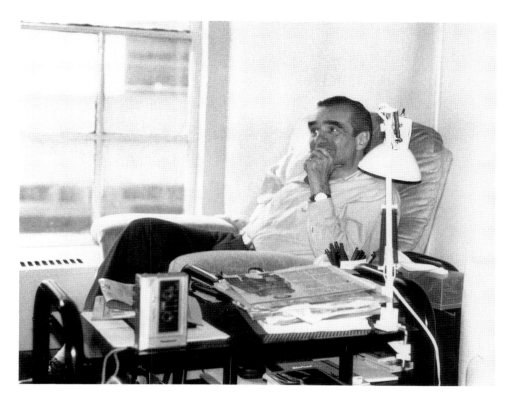

SCORSESE WATCHES THE EDITING: "GO, THELMA, GO!"

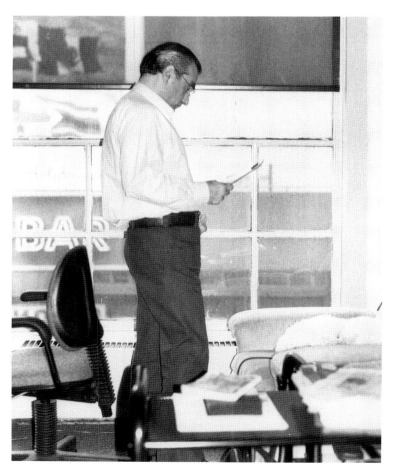

SCORSESE IN THE EDITING ROOM.

DESCRIPTION	SCENE		DESCRIPTION	SCENE
			LEIGH GRILLS SAM	44
			LEIGH ASKS FOR GUN	45
			SAM CONFIDES IN BROADBENT	46
	5		OMIT	47
			STUDIO/SLASHER	48

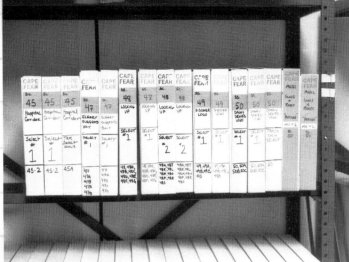

SAM ARRANGES POSTPONEMENT	30
MOVIE THEATER	31
ICE CREAM PARLOR	32

THELMA SCHOONMAKER EDITING _CAPE FEAR_.

	STRIP SEARCH	55
	PARADE	56
	LORI PICKED UP	57
	LORI RAPED	58
		59

Zoe lends moral support.

Three of the many films on Scorsese's mind while editing <u>Cape Fear</u>.

Constance Towers and Michael Dante in Samuel Fuller's <u>The Naked Kiss</u> (1964).

Tippi Hedren and Sean Connery in Alfred Hitchcock's <u>Marnie</u> (1964).

James Stewart in Alfred Hitchcock's <u>Vertigo</u> (1958).

[TOP] PSYCHOLOGICAL VIOLENCE — NICK NOLTE AND
JESSICA LANGE IN <u>CAPE FEAR</u>. [BELOW] PHYSICAL
VIOLENCE: ROBERT MITCHUM AND POLLY BERGEN IN
THE ORIGINAL VERSION OF <u>CAPE FEAR</u> (1962).

NOLTE AND DE NIRO IN <u>CAPE FEAR</u>;
JULIETTE LEWIS AND
JESSICA LANGE IN <u>CAPE FEAR</u>.

THE RETURN OF THE REPRESSED — DE NIRO AND
NOLTE IN <u>CAPE FEAR</u>.

SCORSESE DIRECTING THE LAST SCENE OF <u>CAPE FEAR</u>.

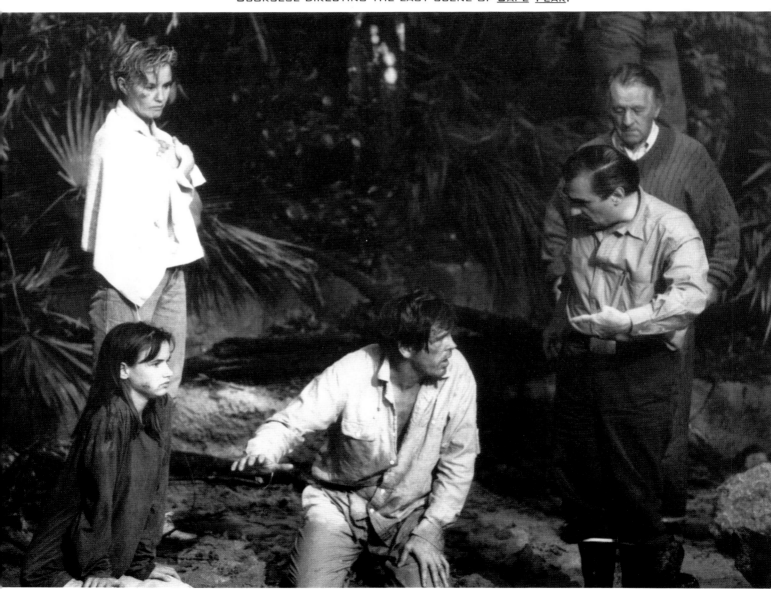

CADY (DE NIRO) AND BOWMAN (NOLTE) BATTLE TO THE DEATH.

JULIETTE LEWIS, JESSICA LANGE, AND NICK NOLTE.   "I COME FROM THE BLACK FOREST!"

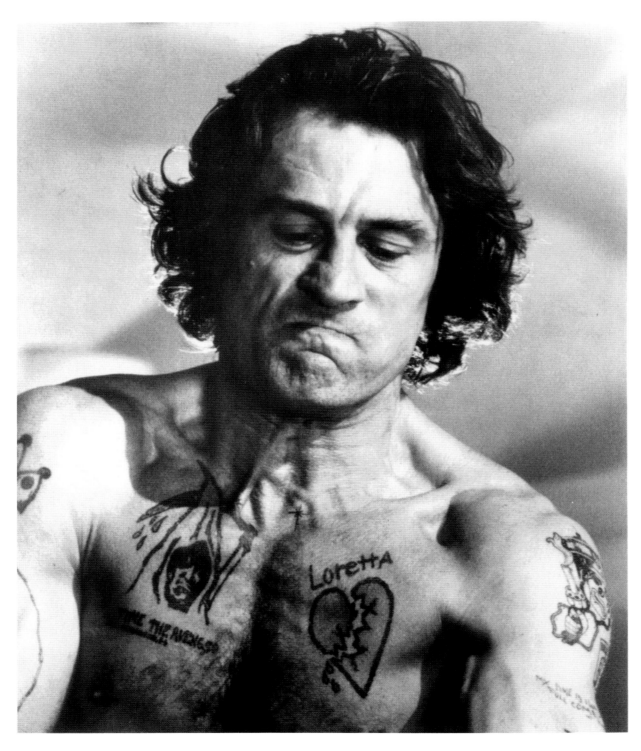

Cady on top: Robert De Niro in the rape scene
in <u>Cape Fear</u>.

CADY GOING DOWN FOR THE LAST TIME.

<u>Taxi Driver</u> (left),
<u>Raging Bull</u> (below)

A unique filmmaking partnership: Robert De Niro
and Martin Scorsese.

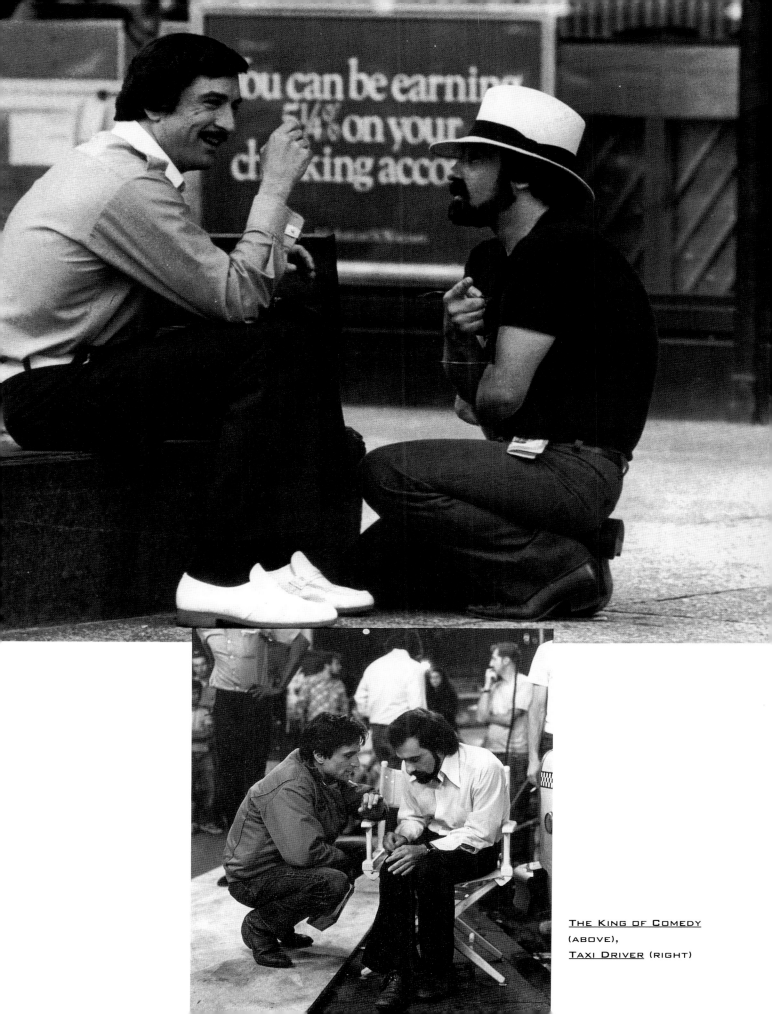

THE KING OF COMEDY
(ABOVE),
TAXI DRIVER (RIGHT)

On the set of <u>GoodFellas</u>.

TWO OF MARTIN SCORSESE'S FAVORITE PERFORMERS.

FILMOGRAPHY

This filmography represents all of Martin Scorsese's screen work to date, not only the films he directed (indicated in all capital letters) but also those he edited, produced, and appeared in as a performer. Also included are all the commercials and music videos he has directed.

The cast and production credits are full listings for all of Scorsese's works.

1963

WHAT'S A NICE GIRL LIKE YOU DOING IN A PLACE LIKE THIS?

A New York University Department of Television, Motion Picture and Radio Presentation, Summer Motion Picture Workshop. Faculty Advisors: Haig P. Manoogian, John Mahon.

Director/Screenplay: Martin Scorsese.

Cast: Zeph Michaelis (Harry), Mimi Stark (Wife), Sarah Braveman (Analyst), Fred Sica (Friend), Robert Uricola (Singer), Martin Scorsese (Man in the photograph). *Music Score Composed and Conducted* by Richard H. Coll. *Song*: "Swivel Hips Sal;" *Music by* Richard H. Coll, *Lyrics by* Sandor Reich. *Assistant Director*: Louise Stephanic. *Still Photography*: Frank Truglio. *Sound*: Sandor Reich. *Sound Editor*: Maria Stoller.
Running Time: 9 minutes.

Synopsis: A young writer is obsessed with a photograph of a man standing in a boat. Desperate to take his mind off the picture that is "really nothing to look at," he throws a party, where he meets and falls in love with a girl. They marry, and the photo of the man in the boat no longer haunts him. But he becomes obsessed with another photo, one of an empty seashore. His analyst advises him to confront his fears. In doing so, he is absorbed into the photo — swimming off into its ocean waves shouting, "Life is fraught with peril."

> *Commentary:* Scorsese has said *What's a Nice Girl* was inspired by the Mel Brooks/Ernest Pintoff short *The Critic*. The narration has much of the flavor of Brooks's offhand absurdist humor. Visually, the film is influenced by the work of early 1950s television gagman Ernie Kovacs. The hero merging with the photo that obsesses him is typical of the Kovacs neosurrealist comedy style.

> The rapid editing style, New York bohemian atmosphere, and tone of comic paranoia foreshadow *After Hours*. The resemblance between the photograph of the seashore and the strikingly similar photograph in Michael Snow's *Wavelength* (1967) is perhaps coincidental.

1964

IT'S NOT JUST YOU, MURRAY!

New York University Department of Television, Motion Picture and Radio Presentations. Faculty Advisors: John Mahon, Haig P. Manoogian.

Director: Martin Scorsese. *Screenplay*: Martin Scorsese and Mardik Martin.

Cast: Ira Rubin (Murray), Sam DeFazio (Joe), Andrea Martin (Wife), Catherine Scorsese (Mother), and Robert Uricola, Bernard Weisberger, Victor Magnotta, Richard Sweeton, John Bivona.

Cinematography: Richard H. Coll. *Editor*: Eli F. Bleich. *Music Composed and Arranged by*: Richard H. Coll.. *Music Performed by*: John W. Dodd Junior High School Band, Freeport, Long Island. *Musical Director*: Leo Ursini. *Production Assistants*: Edwin Grant, Larraine Brennan. *Costumes*: Lancelot Braithwaite. *Still Photography*: Edwin Grant. *Graphics*: Marjorie Rosen. *"Love Is a Gazelle" Cast*: Robert Uricola, Susan Miller, Sydney Anne Seide, Vivian Thompson, Cynthia Koenig, Larraine Brennan. *Sets*: Lancelot Braithwaite. *Costumes*: Victor Magnotta. *Make-Up*: Teresa Brun.

Running Time: 15 minutes.

Prize: Edward L. Kingsley Filmmaker Award, 1964.

Synopsis: Murray, a small-time hood (bootlegging, extortion, gambling, gun-running) who becomes a Broadway impressario, recounts his life story, in which he credits his best friend Joe with his success. As the film progresses, the gap between Murray's upbeat version and the downbeat images we see of his life widens to the point where he asks that the sound track be shut off. What is about to be revealed is that Joe, who has been having an affair with Murray's wife, is the actual father of Murray's children.

Commentary: Coming on the heels of *What's a Nice Girl*, *Murray* suggests that Scorsese was looking to a career in comedy. Seen from the perspective of the films to follow, however, *Murray* is a satirical precursor of *Mean Streets* and *GoodFellas*. Likewise the musical number "Love Is a Gazelle" looks forward to the "Happy Endings" spectacular in *New York, New York*, as does the montage of titles of Murray's other shows: "Tomatos Are Too Cheap" and "Hello, Harriet! Goodbye, Sam!"

While the film's finale is a parody/homage to the end of Fellini's *8 1/2*, the echo of certain Lenny Bruce monologues can be heard in much of Murray's narration. There is also a pointed reference to the newsreel sequence of *Citizen Kane* in the scene in which Murray testifies at a legal hearing.

1967

THE BIG SHAVE

A Scorsese Films Inc. Release.

Director/Screenplay: Martin Scorsese. *Cinematography*: Ares Demertzis. *Blood*: Eli Bleich. *Bathroom*: Ken Gaulin. *Whiteness*: Herman Melville. *Dedication*: Viet '67. *Music*: "I Can't Get Started with You" (1939) performed by Bunny Berrigan.

Cast: Peter Bernuth (Young Man)

Running Time: 6 minutes.

Award: Prix L'Age D'Or at Knokke-le-Zoute Film Festival.

Home Video: Voyager laserdisc; "Three by Scorsese" (including *Italianamerican* and *American Boy: A Profile of Steven Prince*.)

Synoposis: In a bright white bathroom, a young man lathers his face and shaves. Once finished, he shaves himself again. And again. Each time he nicks his face, drawing blood. He gradually shaves himself to death.

Commentary: Made for the "Angry Arts," a protest effort by a group of artists opposed to the Vietnam War, Scorsese's film is intended to be read as a metaphorical antiwar statement (hence "Viet '67"). However, the spectacle of bloody human sacrifice suggests other levels when seen in the context of Scorsese's later films: *Taxi Driver* (the shootout), *Raging Bull* (the final La Motta-Robinson fight), and *The Last Temptation of Christ* (the Crucifixion).

OBSESSIONS

While he was in Amsterdam shooting the erotic fantasy sequence for *Who's That Knocking at My Door?*, Scorsese worked on the screenplay for this parody/homage to American thrillers directed by Pim De La Parra. He is credited as coscripter for this low-budget English-language production (along with De La Parra and Wim Verstappen), which concerns a young doctor (Dieter Geissler) who spies through a keyhole at the beautiful woman (Alexandra Stewart) who lives in the apartment next door. The score is a pastiche of Bernard Herrmann music written for other purposes (chiefly radio shows). *Obsessions* (which was released very briefly in a few American theaters) is not to be confused with Brian De Palma's 1977 thriller *Obsession*, which features an original Bernard Herrmann score.

WHO'S THAT KNOCKING AT MY DOOR?
A Joseph Brenner Associates, Inc. Release of a Trimod Films Production.

Director/ Screenplay: Martin Scorsese. *Producers*: Joseph Weill, Betzi and Haig Manoogian. *Cinematography*: Michael Wadleigh, Richard H. Coll. *Editor*: Thelma Schoonmaker. *Art Director*: Victor Magnotta.

Cast: Zina Bethune (The Girl), Harvey Keitel (J.R.), Lennard Kuras (Joey), Michael Scala (Sally Gaga), Ann Colette (Girl in Dream Sequence), Harry Northup (Harry, the rapist), Bill Minkin (Iggy/Radio Announcer), Phil Carlson (Mountain Guide), Wendy Russell (Sally Gaga's Girlfriend), Robert Uricola (Young Man at Party with Gun), Susan Wood (Susan), Marrisa Joffrey (Rosie), Catherine Scorsese (J.R.'s Mother), Tsuai Yu-Lan, Saskia Holleman, Anne Marieka (Dream Girls), Victor Magnotta; Paul De Bionde (Boys in Street Fight), Martin Scorsese (Gangster).

Music: "Jenny Take a Ride," performed by Mitch Ryder and the Detroit Wheels; "The Closer You Are," performed by the Channels; "I've Had It," performed by the Bellnotes; "El Watusi," performed by Ray Baretto; "Don't Ask Me," performed by the Dubs; "Shotgun," performed by Jr. Walker and the All Stars; "The End," performed by the Doors; "Ain't That Just Like Me," performed by the Searchers; "Who's That Knocking At My Door?," performed by the Genies; "The Plea," performed by the Chantells.
Running Time : 90 minutes.
Home Video: Warner Bros. cassette.

Synopsis: J.R., a young drifter from New York's Little Italy, falls in love with a woman outside of that milieu — identified in the credits only as The Girl. Their budding romance is cut short when The Girl tells him of a date-rape incident in her past. In J.R.'s view, women are either objects of quasireligious respect or "broads," casual sexual outlets. Unable to deal with her story, he ends the relationship, retreating into his old life of aimless male camaraderie. After a raucous all-night party he attempts a reconciliation — by "forgiving" The Girl. But she refuses to continue their love affair on these terms.

Commentary: A rough sketch of certain themes that would be explored more fully in *Mean Streets*, Scorsese's first feature went through many changes before reaching its final form. It began in 1965 as *Bring on the Dancing Girls*; a free-form set of sketches of Little Italy street life. In 1967 Scorsese began to create a new film out of his original, focusing on the love story between J.R. and The Girl. Shown at the Chicago Film Festival as *I Call First*, it was highly praised by film critic Roger Ebert. Finally in 1969 the film was released in slightly reedited form, with an additional sequence, as *Who's That Knocking at My Door?* (in some areas of the United States, the film was released under the title *J.R.*) The new material, included at the insistence of the film's distributor, was a fantasy sequence (featuring casual nudity) intended to elaborate on the hero's Madonna/whore complex. Shot in Amsterdam, the sequence features Anne Colette, the female lead of two of Jean-Luc Godard's early shorts, *Tous les garcons s'appellent Patrick* and *Charlotte et son Jules*.

THE HONEYMOON KILLERS

Scorsese directed only five days' worth of shooting on this low-budget melodrama (which began production several years prior to its 1970 release) before writer-producer Leonard Kastle took over the reins. An examination of the life and crimes of "Lonelyhearts" murderers Martha Beck (Shirley Stoler) and Raymond Fernandez (Tony Lo Bianco), *The Honeymoon Killers* recounts the couple's marrying and slaughtering a string of naive middle-aged women for their money. Shot in the style of *True Detective* magazine illustrations, the film was a particular favorite of director François Truffaut.

STREET SCENES 1970
A Project of the New York Cinetracts Collective.

Production Supervisor and Post Production Director : Martin Scorsese. *Post Production Management*: Raini Kaplan. *Post Production Consultants*: Diana Krumins, Maggie Koven, Peter Rea. *Post Production Coordinator*: Nick Tanis. *Editors*: Peter Rea, Maggie Koven, Angela Kirby, Gerry Pallor, Larry Tisdall, Thelma Schoonmaker. *Director/Cameramen #1*: Don Lenzer, Harry Bolles, Danny Schneider, Peter Rea, The Big B (Bob Pitts), Bill Etra, Tiger Graham, Fred Hadley, Ed Summer, Nat Tripp. *Director/Cameramen #2*: Nancy Bennett, John Butman, Dick Catron, Frederick Elmes, Tom Famighetti, Peter Flynn, Robert Foresta, David Freeberg, Tony Janetti, Arnold Klein, Ron Levitas, Didier Loiseau, David Ludwig, Laura Primakoff, Gordon Stein, Oliver Stone, Bruce Tabor, Stan Weiser, Bob Zahn. *Recordist/Interviewers #1*: Jay Freund, Josh Stein, Michael Eppy, Harry Bolles, Danny Schneider, Marty Andrews, Bruce Tabor, David Ludwig. *Recordist/Interviewers #2*: Jim Brown, Burgert, Dick Catron, Dallas Garard, Ron Levitas, Marty Rattigan, Peter Rea, Stan

Weiser, Bob Zahn. *Still Photography*: Ron Levitas, Harvey Keitel, Carole Zeitlin, Bonnie Freer, Charles Baum, Christie Emanuel, Jeff Feiner, Andrew Goldberg, Ira Resnick.

On Camera Appearances by William Kunstler, Dave Dellinger, Alan W. Carter, David Z. Robinson, Harvey Keitel, Verna Bloom, Jay Cocks, Martin Scorsese.

Running Time: 75 minutes.

Description: Scorsese supervised the post production on this collaborative documentary on anti-Vietnam War demonstrations held on Wall Street and in Washington, D.C., in spring 1970. The film premiered at the New York Film Festival the following September. After its festival press screening, the filmmakers held an impromptu discussion of the film, and the antiwar movement in general, in a park in front of Lincoln Center. That discusssion was filmed and incorporated into *Street Scenes* in time for its first public showing to festival audiences.

Commentary: While not a film for which Scorsese can take directorial credit, *Street Scenes* does reflect his abiding interest in the documentary form. Its shooting style, while indebted to such European films as *Far From Vietnam* and *Chronicle of a Summer*, also anticipates *Italianamerican* and *American Boy*. Scorsese collaborators, Harvey Keitel, Jay Cocks, Verna Bloom, and Thelma Schoonmaker were involved in the production, as were several film students from Scorsese's NYU class, including future filmmaker Oliver Stone.

WOODSTOCK

Scorsese served as assistant director on Michael Wadleigh's film of the 1969 event, originally billed as the "Woodstock Music and Art Fair." Applying the split-screen editing techniques used in the experimental "underground" films of Andy Warhol, Stan Vanderbeeck, and Jud Yalkut, Scorsese and his editors, including Thelma Schoonmaker, turned what might have been a prosaic slice of cinéma vérité into a lively display of sight and sound. Scorsese's efforts brought him further "rockumentary" work on Medicine Ball Caravan and Elvis on Tour.

1971

MEDICINE BALL CARAVAN

Scorsese was Associate Producer on this ill-fated Warner Bros. attempt to contrive another *Woodstock*. Directed by veteran cinéma vérité filmmaker François Reichenbach, *Caravan* attempted to create a traveling rock concert in which various acts (The Youngbloods, Delaney and Bonnie, B.B. King, Alice Cooper) were accompanied by specially selected members of the so-called "alternate culture." The musicians traveled through middle America, supposedly spreading the message of "Peace and Love." According to writer John Grissom, Jr., in his book about the making of the film, *We Have Come for Your Daughters,* Warner executives hoped some violent confrontation might be provoked to give the film a dramatic climax. This did not happen. The film played for one week in New York and was withdrawn from release.

MINNIE AND MOSKOWITZ

Scorsese worked as an Assistant Sound Effects Editor on this John Cassavetes comedy-drama about the sometimes-stormy romance of a middle-class divorcée (Gena Rowlands) and a bohemian parking attendant (Seymour Cassel). See Chapter One.

ELVIS ON TOUR

Scorsese served as Montage Supervisor for this documentary of Elvis Presley concert performances directed by Pierre Adige and Robert Abel. It features many of the spilt-screen techniques Scorsese utilized in *Woodstock*.

THE UNHOLY ROLLERS

Scorsese edited this drama about the world of roller derby directed by Vernon Zimmerman for producer Roger Corman. While "Whit." of *Daily Variety* (11/15/72) claimed "Technical credits are expertly handled," Glen Lovell in *The Hollywood Reporter* (same date), declared "Martin Scorsese's editing is amateurish."

BOXCAR BERTHA

An American-International Picture. A Roger Corman Production presented by James H. Nicholson and Samuel Z. Arkoff.

Director: Martin Scorsese. *Producer*: Roger Corman. *Associate Producer*: Julie Corman. *Screenplay*: Joyce H. Corrington and John William Corrington, *based on* "Sister of the Road" *by* Bertha Thompson *as told to* Ben L. Reitman. *Cinematography*: John Stephens and Gayne Rescher. *Editors*: Buzz Feitshans and Martin Scorsese. *Music*: Gib Guilbeau and Thad Maxwell. *Music Production*: Herb Cohen. *Production Designer*: David Nichols. *Visual Consultant*: David Nichols. *Costumes*: Bob Modes. *Sound Mixer*: Don F. Johnson. *Sound*: Ryder Sound Services. *In Charge of Production*: Paul Rapp.

Cast: Barbara Hershey (Bertha), David Carradine (Bill Shelley), Barry Primus (Rake Brown), Bernie Casey (Von Morton), John Carradine (H. Buckram Sartoris), David R. Osterhout and Victor Argo (the McIvers), Grahame Pratt (Emeric Pressburger), "Chicken" Holleman (Michael Powell), Marianne Dole (Mrs. Mailer), Harry Northup (Harvey Saunders), Doyle Hall (Dice Player), Joe Reynolds (Joe Dreft), Martin Scorsese and Gayne Rescher (Brothel Clients).
M.P.A.A. Rating: R.
Running Time: 88 minutes.
Home Video: Vestron Video cassette and Image laserdisc.

Synopsis: Set in the Depression Era south, the film recounts the adventures of Bertha Thompson, a young woman who takes to the road with her lover, union organizer Bill Shelley. Attacked by hired union-busters, the couple is forced into a life of crime. They are joined by two unfortunates: Von Morton, a black farm worker, and Rake Brown, a gambler.

They manage to outwit their pursuers for a time, but eventually fall into a trap set by the authorities. Bertha and Morton escape, but Brown is gunned down, and Shelley is captured. Though he's unable to prevent Shelley's virtual crucifixion at the hands of the authorities, who have nailed him to the side of a railway boxcar, Morton does manage to kill Shelley's executioners.

Commentary: This tale of a union organizer and his girl who become bandits was intended by Corman to be a followup to his *Bloody Mama* — itself a variation on *Bonnie and Clyde*. Corman continued to traffic in this makeshift subgenre in later years when he formed New World Pictures, and produced such outlaws-on-the-run films as *The Lady in Red*, *Crazy Mama*, and *Big Bad Mama*. For Scorsese, *Boxcar Bertha* was simply an assignment, a chance to direct. Despite restrictions of script and budget, he managed to work in a number of personal touches, including a homage to Godard's *Vivre sa vie* in a bordello sequence, and naming two minor characters Michael Powell and Emeric Pressburger. A sequence shot in an abandoned church also has obvious personal meaning for Scorsese; the interior is dominated by a cyclorama of the life of Christ. The film's crucifixion scene, in which Bertha bids goodbye to Shelley as the boxcar to which he has been nailed moves down the track, was not a Scorsese inspiration. It was in the original script. (During the shooting of *Boxcar Bertha* Barbara Hershey gave Scorsese a copy of a novel she thought he might adapt into a movie. It was *The Last Temptation of Christ*.)

MEAN STREETS

Warner Bros. A Warner Communications Company presents a Taplin-Perry-Scorsese Production.

Director: Martin Scorsese. *Screenplay*: Martin Scorsese, Mardik Martin. *Producer*: Jonathan T. Taplin. *Executive Producer*: E. Lee Perry. *Cinematography*: Kent Wakeford. *Editor*: Sidney Levin.

Cast: Harvey Keitel (Charlie), Robert De Niro (Johnny Boy), David Proval (Tony), Amy Robinson (Teresa), Richard Romanus (Michael), Cesare Danova (Uncle Giovanni), George Memmoli (Joey Catucci), Victor Argo (Mario), Lenny Scaletta (Jimmy), Murray Moston (Oscar), David Carradine (Drunk), Robert Carradine (Boy with gun), Jeannie Bell (Diane), Lois Walden (Girl at Bar), D'Mitch Davis (Cop), Dino Seragusa (Old Man), Julie Andelman (Girl at Party), Peter Fain (George), Harry Northup (Soldier), Robert Wilder (Benton), Jaime Alba (First Young Boy), Ken Konstantin (Second Young Boy), Nicki "Ack" Aquilino (Man on Docks), Catherine Scorsese (Woman in Apartment Hallway), Ken Sinclair (Sammy), B. Mitchell Reed (Disc Jockey), Martin Scorsese (Shorty, the Hitman), Barbara Weintraub (Heather Weintraub), Ron Satloff (Carl), Anna Uricola (Neighbor at Window).

Production Manager: Paul Rapp. *Wardrobe*: Norman Salling. *First Assistant Director*: Russell Vreeland. *Second Assistant Director*: Ron Satloff. *Prop Master*: Bill Bates. *Script Supervisor*: Bobby Sierks. *Visual Consultant*: David Nichols. *Re-recording Mixers*: John K. Wilkinson, Bud Grenzbach, Walter Goss. *Pre-production and Post-production Coordinator*: Sandra Weintraub. *Production Coordinator*: Peter Fain.

Songs: "Jumping Jack Flash" and "Tell Me," performed by the Rolling Stones; "I Love You So," performed by the Chantells; "Addio Sogni Di Gloria," "Canta Per' Me," and "Monastero Di Santa Chiara," performed by Giuseppe de Stefano;

"Marruzella" and "Scapricciatiello," performed by Renato Carosone; "Please Mr. Postman," performed by the Marvelettes; "Hideaway" and "I Looked Away," performed by Eric Clapton; "Desiree," performed by the Charts; "Rubber Biscuit," performed by the Chips; "Pledging My Love," performed by Johnny Ace; "Ritmo Sabroso," performed by Ray Baretto; "You," performed by the Aquatones; "Ship of Love," performed by the Nutmegs; "Florence," performed by the Paragons; "Malafemina," performed by Jimmy Roselli; "Those Oldies But Goodies," performed by Little Caesar and the Romans; "I Met Him On Sunday," performed by the Shirelles; "Be My Baby," performed by the Ronettes; "Mickey's Monkey," performed by the Miracles.

M.P.A.A. Rating: R.

Running Time: 110 minutes.

Home Video: Warner Bros. cassette and laserdisc.

Synopsis: Charlie, a young drifter in New York's Little Italy, is marking time until his Uncle Giovanni, a protection racketeer, gives him a chance to enter the restaurant business. Charlie's ambitions are complicated by his devotion to his best friend, Johnny Boy, and his love affair with his cousin Teresa, alliances opposed by Uncle Giovanni. When Johnny Boy gets into serious debt with Michael, a local loan shark, Charlie tries to help. But Johnny Boy's taunting defiance of Michael goads the petty mobster into hiring a hitman to settle the score. As Charlie, Johnny Boy, and Teresa attempt to leave town, the gunman shoots, causing the car to crash. Johnny Boy is hit with a bullet in the neck. Charlie and Teresa are seriously injured. All three are still alive at fadeout.

Commentary: See Chapter One.

SCORSESE: I play the hit man in the car. I did the scene on the night of my thirtieth birthday. I shot my own alter egos! And it doesn't work! You think you can exorcise those parts of yourself, and you *can't*!

ALICE DOESN'T LIVE HERE ANYMORE

Warner Bros. A Warner Communications Company presents a David Susskind Production.

Director: Martin Scorsese. *Screenplay*: Robert Getchell. *Producers*: David Susskind and Audrey Maas. *Associate Producer*: Sandra Weintraub. *Cinematography*: Kent L. Wakeford. *Production Executive*: Larry Cohen. *Production Designer*: Toby Carr Rafelson. *Film Editor*: Marcia Lucas.

Cast: Ellen Burstyn (Alice Hyatt), Kris Kristofferson (David), Alfred Lutter (Tommy), Billy Green Bush (Donald), Diane Ladd (Flo), Lelia Goldoni (Bea), Lane Bradbury (Rita), Vic Tayback (Mel), Jodie Foster (Audrey), Harvey Keitel (Ben), Valerie Curtin (Vera), Murray Moston (Jacobs), Harry Northup (Joe and Jim's Bartender), Mia Bendixsen (Alice, age 8), Ola Moore (Old Woman), Martin Brinton (Lenny), Dean Casper (Chicken), Martin Scorsese, Larry Cohen (Patrons at Diner), Mardik Martin (Customer in Club).

Unit Production Manager: John G. Wilson. *Assistant Director*: Mike Moder. *Second Assistant Director*: Mike Kusley. *Sound Mixer*: Don Parker. *Script Supervisor*: Julie Pitkanen. *Makeup*: Bob Westmoreland. *Hair Stylist*: Lola "Skip" McNalley.

M.P.A.A. Rating: PG.

Running Time: 112 minutes.

Awards: Academy Award, Ellen Burstyn, Best Actress; Academy Award Nomination, Robert Getchell, Best Original Screenplay.

Home Video: Warner Bros. cassette and laserdisc.

Synopsis: Suddenly widowed, Alice Hyatt sets out with her son Tommy to live her dream of being a singer. Unable to find singing jobs, she resorts to waitressing in a coffee shop. There she meets David, a rancher, who eventually proposes marriage. Alice finds romantic happiness, but refuses to give up on her dream of a singing career.

Commentary: See Chapter One.

SCORSESE: There was this whole thing in the 1970s of trying to "understand" the women's movement. I remember we had some criticism from some feminist groups because Alice winds up going with a man at the end. I just thought she'd decided she'd, you know . . . just like to have a man!

ITALIANAMERICAN

A National Communications Foundation Production.

Director: Martin Scorsese. *Scenario*: Martin Scorsese, Mardik Martin, Larry Cohen. *Producers*: Saul Rubin, Elaine Attias. *Cinematography (16mm)*: Alex Hirschfeld. *Editor*: Bertram Lovitt.

Cast: Catherine Scorsese, Charles Scorsese, Martin Scorsese.

Running Time: 45 minutes

Home Video: Voyager laserdisc, "Three by Scorsese" (which also includes *American Boy: A Profile of Steven Prince*, and *The Big Shave*.

Description: In the living room of their Elizabeth Street apartment, Scorsese's parents, Charles and Catherine, discuss their childhood and the history of their families. They touch on many aspects of the Italian-American immigrant experience in the process.

Commentary: Scorsese's most ingratiating film, this heartfelt tribute to his parents is also a serious attempt to understand his family history. Scorsese is extremely attentive to the nuances of his parents' remarks, and his responsibility in presenting those nuances to viewers. There is even a minidrama when Scorsese follows his mother into the kitchen to find out why she is so upset with what his father said about their past.

TAXI DRIVER

Columbia, a Division of Columbia Pictures Industries, Inc. Presents a Bill/Phillips Production.

Director: Martin Scorsese. *Screenplay*: Paul Schrader. *Producers*: Michael Phillips and Julia Phillips. *Cinematography*: Michael Chapman. *Supervising Film Editor*: Marcia Lucas. *Film Editors*: Tom Rolf, A.C.E., Melvin Shapiro. *Music*: Bernard Herrmann.

Cast: Robert De Niro (Travis Bickle), Jodie Foster (Iris), Cybill Shepherd (Betsy), Harvey Keitel (Sport/Matthew), Albert Brooks (Tom), Peter Boyle (Wizard), Leonard Harris (Sen. Charles Palantine), Diahnne Abbott (Concession Girl), Steven Prince (Andy, the Gun Salesman), Frank Adu (Angry Black Man), Victor Argo (Melio), Victor Magnotta (Secret Service Photographer), Murray Moston (Iris's Timekeeper), Harry Northup (Doughboy), Peter Savage (the John), Robert Shields (Palantine's Aide), Robert Utt (Campaign Worker), Martin Scorsese (Passenger Watching Silhouette).

Special Make-up: Dick Smith. *Visual Consultant*: David Nichols. *Creative Consultant*: Sandra Weintraub. *Associate Producer*: Phillip M. Goldfarb. *Art Director*: Charles Rosen. *Camera Operator*: Fred Schuler. *Assistant Cameramen*: Alex Hirshfeld, Bill Johnson, Ron Zarilla. *Second Unit Camera*: Michael Zingale. *Assistant Director*: Peter R. Scoppa. *2nd Assistant Directors*: Ralph Singleton, William Eustace. *Script Supervisor*: Kay Chapin. *Set Decorator*: Herbert Mulligan. *Property Master*: Les Bloom. *Special Effects*: Tony Parmelee. *Scenic Artist*: Cosmo Sorice. *Costume Designer*: Ruth Morley. *Wardrobe*: Al Craine. *Make-up*: Irving Buchman. *Hairdresser*: Mona Orr. *Supervising Sound Effects*: Frank E. Warner. *Sound Effects Editors*: Sam Gemette, Jim Fritch, David Hourton, Gordon Davidson. *Assistant Editors*: George Trirogoff, William Weber. *Assistant to the Director*: Amy Jones. *Songs*: "Too Late For the Sky," written and performed by Jackson Browne; "Hold Me Close," by Keith Addis and Bernard Herrmann. *Re-recording Supervisor*: Tex Rudloff. *Special Publicity*: Marion Billings.
Dedication: Our Gratitude and Respect to Bernard Herrmann, June 29, 1911–December 24, 1975.
M.P.A.A. Rating: R.
Running Time: 113 minutes.
Awards: Palme D'Or (Grand Prize) 1976 Cannes Film Festival; Academy Award nominations for Best Picture, Best Actor (Robert De Niro), and Best Supporting Actress (Jodie Foster.)
Home Video: RCA/Columbia cassette and Criterion Collection laserdiscs (CAV and CLV formats.)

Synopsis: Cabdriver Travis Bickle, a Vietnam veteran with a tenuous hold on reality, is both attracted to and repulsed by the seamy New York City. Obsessed with Betsy, a campaign worker for presidential candidate Charles Palantine, the lonely cabbie asks her for a date. It ends in disaster when he takes her to a porno movie. Travis next turns his attention to Iris, a teenage prostitute he wants to rescue from the streets. He also makes an abortive attempt at shooting Palantine at a political rally. In the wake of this failure he goes after Iris's pimp Sport, whom he kills, along with several other pimps, in a bloody shootout. Iris is returned to her family and the newspapers hail Travis as a hero.

Commentary: See Chapter Three.

Scorsese made a cameo appearance in this action comedy directed by Paul Bartel for Roger Corman's New World Pictures. Corman, Francis Ford Coppola, and Jonathan Demme also made guest appearances.

NEW YORK, NEW YORK

A United Artists Release. A Robert Chartoff–Irwin Winkler Production.

Director: Martin Scorsese. *Screenplay*: Earl Mac Rauch and Mardik Martin. *Story*: Earl Mac Rauch. *Producers*: Irwin Winkler and Robert Chartoff. *Associate Producer*: Gene Kirkwood. *Cinematography*: Laszlo Kovacs, A.S.C. *Supervising Film Editors*: Irving Lerner, Marcia Lucas. *Film Editors*: Tom Rolf, A.C.E., B. Lovitt. *Production Design*: Boris Leven.

Cast: Liza Minnelli (Francine Evans), Robert De Niro (Jimmy Doyle), Lionel Stander (Tony Harwell), Barry Primus (Paul Wilson), Mary Kay Place (Bernice), Georgie Auld (Frankie Harte), George Memmoli (Nicky), Dick Miller (Palm Club owner), Murray Moston (Horace Morris), Lenny Gaines (Artie Kirks), Clarence Clemons (Cecil Powell), Kathy McGinnis (Ellen Flannery), Norman Palmer (Desk Clerk), Adam David Winkler (Jimmy Doyle, Jr.), Dimitri Logothetis (Desk Clerk), Frank Sivera (Eddie Di Muzio), Diahnne Abbott (Harlem Club Singer), Margo Winkler (Argumentative Woman), Steven Prince (Record Producer), Don Calfa (Gilbert), Bernie Kuby (Justice of the Peace), Selma Archerd (Wife of Justice of the Peace), Bill Baldwin (Announcer in Moonlit Terrace), Mary Lindsay (Hat Check Girl in Meadows), Jon Cutler (Musician in Frankie Harte Band), Nicky Blair (Cab Driver), Casey Kasem (d.j.), Sydney Guilaroff (Hairstylist), Peter Savage (Horace Morris' Assistant), Shera Danese (Doyle's Girl in Major Chord), Harry Northup (Alabama), Mardik Martin (Well Wisher in Moonlit Terrace), Larry Kert ("Happy Endings" Sequence).

Original Songs: "Theme From 'New York New York,'" "There Goes the Ball Game," "But the World Goes Round," "Happy Endings": John Kander and Fred Ebb. *Musical Supervisor and Conductor*: Ralph Burns. *Executive in Charge of Production*: Hal W. Polaire. *Choreographer*: Ron Field. *Production Consultant*: David Nichols. *Technical Consultant*: Georgie Auld. *Casting*: Lyn Stalmaster. *Supervising Sound Editor*: Kay Rose. *Music Editor*: William Saracino. *Costume Design*: Theadora Van Runkle. *Hair Designs for Liza Minnelli*: Sydney Guilaroff. *Art Director*: Harry R. Kemm. *First Assistant Director*: Melvin D. Dellar. *Second Assistant Director*: Michael Grillo. *Film Editor*: David Ramirez. *Assistant Film Editors*: Michael Ripps, Arthur W. Forney, Phylis Smith Althenhaus, Scott Burrow, Eric A. Sears, Michael Sheridan. *Camera Operator*: Robert Stevens. *First Assistant Camera*: Joseph E. Thibo. *Sound Mixer*: Lawrence Jost. *Make-Up Artist*: Michael Westmore. *Make-Up for Liza Minnelli*: Christina Smith. *Men's Costumers*: Richard Bruno, Michael Chavez. *Women's Costumers*: Margo Baxley, Frances K. Harrison. *Hair Stylists*: Mary Keats, June Miggins. *Set Decorators*: Robert Devestel, Ruby R. Levitt. *Special Effects*: Richard Albain. *Script Supervisor*: Hannah Scheel. *Saxophone Solos*: Georgie Auld. *"Billets Doux" performed by the* Hot Club of France Quintet. *M.P.A.A. Rating*: PG. *Running Time*: 136 minutes (1977 release), 163 minutes (1980 rerelease). *Home Video*: CBS/Fox tape and laserdisc (of the 163-minute version).

Synopsis: At a victory celebration marking the end of World War II, musician Jimmy Doyle meets singer Francine Evans. After a rocky start, a romance begins. When she gets a job touring with the Frankie Harte Band, Francine asks Jimmy to join her. On the road they get married. But the Big Band Era is coming to a close. Harte sells Jimmy the band, which continues to win bookings on the strength of Francine's singing. When she becomes pregnant and is forced to leave, the band falls apart, and their marriage begins to unravel. While Francine's career as a singer is on the rise, Jimmy is having difficulty finding work. His undisguised jealousy reaches a boiling point in a climactic fight between them that brings on her labor. She gives birth to a boy, but Jimmy leaves her. The story takes up again several years later when Francine is a successful film star. Jimmy, who has his own jazz club, comes to see the opening night of her new show. He asks to see her afterward. She agrees, but has second thoughts and doesn't keep the date.

Commentary: See Chapter Four

THE ACT

With a book by George Furth and songs by John Kander and Fred Ebb, *The Act* was Scorsese's first—and in all likelihood last—attempt at directing a Broadway musical. Conceived as a vehicle for Liza Minnelli, *The Act* (originally called *In Person*, then *Shine It On*) seemed a sequel to *New York, New York*. Like the film, it deals with the onstage and personal life of a musical comedy star much like the character Minnelli played in the film.

SCORSESE: I screened *Viaggio in Italia* at the Pacific Film Archives for George Furth. I wanted the show to be like it in a way—a kind of *Scenes From a Marriage* with music. Well, you can imagine how *that* went over. George was laughing. Cy Feuer, the producer, said, "Marty, why do you want to do this? Musical comedy is the hardest thing you can get involved in." Well, you know, it was a personal thing—wanting to work with Liza. But he was right. I think we did six weeks outside of New York in tryouts. I stayed with the show for about four or five weeks. Then I asked Gower Champion to come in and take over.

Just about everyone had a look at the show. I remember Michael Bennett coming down and saying to me, "Marty, you have to be captain of the ship." Well, I like to be quieter about things. People took that as indecision. When I would see the show each night, after things got rolling everything seemed fine. But each night of a show is slightly different, and I wanted it to be the same all the time. I left the show mainly because of the gossip about me and Liza and the bad reviews we got on the road. They were so biased. I thought the best thing I could do for her was to get out of it so they could bring the show to New York and people would be able to see it for itself.

The Act opened to generally cool notices, and ran for a season largely on the strength of Minnelli's drawing power. Controversy arose shortly after the show's opening when it was revealed that Minnelli, who had performed all but one of the show's numbers, lip-synched some of them to a prerecorded track.

THE LAST WALTZ

A United Artists Release

Director: Martin Scorsese. *Producer*: Robbie Robertson. *Executive Producer*: Jonathan Taplin. *Cinematography*: Michael Chapman. *Production Designer*: Boris Leven. *Editors*: Yeu-Bun Yee, Jan Roblee. *Concert Producer*: Bill Graham.

Cast: The Band (Rick Danko, Levon Helm, Garth Hudson, Richard Manuel, Robbie Robertson), Eric Clapton, Neil Diamond, Bob Dylan, Joni Mitchell, Neil Young, Emmylou Harris, Van Morrison, The Staples, Dr. John, Muddy Waters, Paul Butterfield, Ronnie Hawkins, Ringo Starr, Ron Wood, and Martin Scorsese.

Soundtrack Production: Rob Fraboni. *Concert Music Production*: John Simon. *Additional Directors of Photography*: Laszlo Kovacs, A.S.C., Vilmos Zsigmond, A.S.C., David Myers, Bobby Byrne, Michael Watkins, Hiro Narita. *Camera Operators*: Fred Schuler, Joe Marqutte, Ray J. De La Motte, Sean Doyle. *First Assistant Cameramen*: Hans Baumgartner, Dustin Blauvelt, Gary Boren, Lawrence Gruenberg, W. Steven Peterson, Anthony Rivetti, Tibor Sands, George Stevenson, Ted Sugiura, John Toll, Ronald Vargas. *Second Assistant Cameramen*: Charles Colegrove, Joseph Cosko, Jr., Alan Disler, Edward L. Rich. *Chief Technical Engineer*: Ed Anderson. *Music Editors*: Kenneth Wannberg and Robert Raff. *Sound Effects Editors*: Richard L. Oswald, Paul Laune. *Unit Production Manager*: Melvin D. Dellar. *Associate Producer*: Steven Prince. *Concert Line Producer*: L.A. Johnson. *Studio and Documentary Line Producer*: Frank Marshall. *Treatment and Creative Consultant*: Mardik Martin.

Filmed at Winterland Arena, San Francisco, MGM Studios, Culver City, Shangri-la Studios, Malibu.
Re-Recording: Goldwyn Studios. *Lenses and Panaflex Cameras*: Panavision. *Lighting Equipment*: Pattim Services. *Color Filters*: Lee Filters, Ltd. *Production Facilities*: Metro-Goldwyn-Mayer Studios. *Processing*: MGM Laboratories. *Prints*: Deluxe.

The Performances:

"Who Do You Love".................................Ronnie Hawkins
"Such a Night"... Dr. John
"Helpless"...Neil Young
"The Weight".. The Staples
"Dry Your Eyes".. Neil Diamond
"Coyote"..Joni Mitchell
"Mystery Train".. Paul Butterfield
"Mannish Boy"... Muddy Waters
"Further On Up the Road"....................... Eric Clapton
"Evangeline"...Emmylou Harris
"Caravan"... Van Morrison

"Forever Young" and

"Baby, Let Me Follow You Down"..............Bob Dylan

"I Shall Be Released"...................................Ringo Starr, Ron Wood, Ensemble.

Poems:

"Introduction to the Canterbury Tales"......Michael McClure

"Loud Prayer"...Lawrence Ferlinghetti

The Band: Rick Danko — bass, violin and vocal; Levon Helm — drums, mandolin, and vocal; Garth Hudson — organ, accordion, saxophone, and synthesizers; Richard Manuel — piano, keyboards, drums, and vocal; Robbie Robertson — lead guitar and vocal.

Songs: "Don't Do It," "Theme From 'The Last Waltz,'" "Up on Cripple Creek," "The Shape I'm In," "It Makes No Difference," "Stagefright," "The Weight," "Old Time Religion," "The Night They Drove Old Dixie Down," "Evangeline," "Genetic Method/Chest Fever," "Ophelia,""Sip the Wine," performed by Rick Danko.

M.P.A.A. Rating: PG.

Running Time: 117 minutes.

Home Video: MGM/UA cassettes and laserdiscs.

Synopsis: A documentary of the folk-rock group The Band's 1976 "farewell" concert at San Francisco's Winterland Theater. The film also contains interviews with Band members (chiefly Robbie Robertson) and musical sequences shot on the sound stages of MGM.

Commentary: Unlike every "rockumentary" up to that time, the film's concert sequences were shot in 35mm. Scorsese planned each camera movement as if he were shooting a conventional dramatic film. Robertson became a close friend and Scorsese collaborator, producing the music for *The King of Comedy* and *The Color of Money*. See also *Somewhere Down the Crazy River* (1988).

SCORSESE: Music has always been very important to me. When I was growing up, in my neighborhood, there was music everywhere. In the summer especially you would hear the record players and the juke boxes. They were always outside on the street. One was playing swing and another had ballads. Then somewhere else, say on the second floor, there was opera. It was like a series of miniconcerts. And certain pieces of music became related to certain activities — like killing rats. We had to kill them. They'd run after them with bats, and there would be music playing. Music to kill rats by!

AMERICAN BOY: A PROFILE OF STEVEN PRINCE

A New Empire Films/ Scorsese Films Production

Director: Martin Scorsese. *Scenario*: Mardik Martin, Julia Cameron. *Producer*: Bertram Lovitt. *Cinematography (16mm)*: Michael Chapman. *Editors*: Amy Jones, Bertram Lovitt.

Cast: Steven Prince, Martin Scorsese, George Memmoli, Mardik Martin, Julia Cameron, Kathi McGinnis.

Home Video: Voyager laserdisc, "Three by Scorsese" (which also includes *Italianamerican* and *The Big Shave*).

Synopsis: In the home of actor George Memmoli, Steven Prince discusses his past before an audience including Scorsese, Memmoli, and several of their friends.

Commentary: Steven Prince is the "black sheep" son of a well-spoken middle-class Jewish family (his uncle was William Morris Agency's legendary founder, Abe Lastfogel). Prince is a born monologist in the manner of Ondine (of Andy Warhol's *The Chelsea Girls*), with a touch of Lenny Bruce, and a delivery occasionally reminiscent of Jerry Lewis. He was a road manager for singer-songwriter Neil Diamond, worked as an assistant to Scorsese on *New York, New York*, and in *Taxi Driver* played the gun salesman who dealt dope on the side.

Prince's sometimes-funny, sometimes-horrific tales of drug-taking and life on society's dangerous margins bear comparison with the writings of such Beat Generation fringe types as Alexander Trocchi, Irving Rosenthal, and Herbert Huncke. To Scorsese, Prince plainly represents some of his darkest imaginings—Travis Bickle's kinder, gentler younger brother. His insistence that Prince keep his distance from him in the film's opening shot—in which they are shown floating in a hot tub together—is very telling in this regard.

American Boy, like *Italianamerican,* seems artless at first, a talking head interview. On closer inspection it is one of Scorsese's subtlest films. While the director seems to be involved in what Prince is saying, the hand signal he gives to the cameraman at one point betrays his total control of the situation. Scorsese's insistence that Prince retell several times the story of the last time he spoke with his father is an attempt at peeling away the layers of his subject's defense. While obviously not involved with Prince in the same way, Scorsese's efforts are comparable to Godard's inclusion of a take in *A Woman Is a Woman* where Anna Karina breaks down and cries.

RAGING BULL

A United Artists Release. A Robert Chartoff–Irwin Winkler Production

Director: Martin Scorsese. *Screenplay*: Paul Schrader and Mardik Martin. Based on the book *Raging Bull* by Jake La Motta with Joseph Carter and Peter Savage. *Producers*: Irwin Winkler and Robert Chartoff. *Produced in association with* Peter Savage. *Associate Producer*: Hal W. Polaire. *Cinematography*: Michael Chapman. *Film Editor*: Thelma Schoonmaker. *Sound Effects Supervising Editor*: Frank Warner. *Music*: Pietro Mascagni (excerpts from "Cavalleria Rusticana," "Guglielmo Ratcliff," and "Silvano").

Cast: Robert De Niro (Jake La Motta), Cathy Moriarty (Vickie La Motta), Joe Pesci (Joey), Frank Vincent (Salvy), Nicholas Colasanto (Tommy Como), Theresa Saldana (Lenore), Frank Adonis (Patsy), Mario Gallo (Mario), Frank Topham (Toppy) Lori Anne Flax (Irma), Joseph Bono (Guido), James V. Christy (Dr. Pinto), Bernie Allen (Comedian), Bill Mazer (Reporter), Bill Hanrahan (Eddie Eagan), Rita Bennett (Emma, Miss 48s), Mike Miles (Sparring Partner). *Reeves Fight*: Floyd Anderson (Jimmy Reeves), Gene Lebell (Ring Announcer), Harold Valan (Himself-Referee), Victor Magnotta (Fighting Soldier). *Pool*: Michael Badalucco (Soda Fountain Clerk). *Webster Hall Dance*: Thomas Beansy Lobasso (Beansy), Paul Forrest (Monsignor), Peter Petrella (Johnny), Sal Serafino Tomassetti (Bouncer Outside). *First Robinson Fight*: Johnny Barnes (Sugar Ray Robinson), John Thomas (Robinson's Trainer), Kenny Davis (Referee), Paul Carmello (Announcer). *Second Robinson Fight*: Jimmy Lennon (Himself - Announcer), Bobby Rings (Referee). *Copacabana #1*: Charles Scorsese

(Charlie), Linda Artuso (Janet), Mardik Martin (Waiter), Geraldine Smith (Girl #1), Maryjane Lauria (Girl #2). *Janiro Fight*: Kevin Mahon (Tony Janiro), Angelo Lamonea (Cornerman), Chuck Hicks (Cornerman), Martin Denkin (Referee), Shay Duffin (Ring Announcer). *Copacabana #2*: Peter Savage (Jackie Curtie), Daniel P. Conte (Detroit Promoter), Joe Malanga (Bodyguard), Sabine Turco, Jr. (Bouncer #1), Steve Orlando (Bouncer #2), Silvio Garcia, Jr. (Bouncer #3), Robert Uricola (Man Outside Cab), Andrea Orlando (Woman in Cab), John Arceri (Maitre d').

Debonair Social Club: Joseph A. Morale (Man at Table #1), James Dimodica (Man at Table #2). *Fox Fight*: Eddie Mustafa Muhammad (Billy Fox), "Sweet" Dick Whittington (Announcer), Jack Lotz (Himself - Referee), Walt Larue (Cornerman #1), Peter Fain (Cornerman #2), Kevin Breslin (Crowd Voice). *Cerdan Fight*: Louis Raftis (Marcel Cerdan), Frank Shain (Frank Shain — Announcer), Corey Wallace (Joe Louis), Fritzie Higgins (Woman With Voice), Gene Alla Poe (Audie Murphy), George Latka (Referee), Fred Dennis (Cornerman #1), Robert B. Loring (Cornerman #2). *Dauthuille Fight*: Johnny Turner (Laurent Dauthuille), Don Dunphy (Don Dunphy — Radio Announcer), Jimmy Lennon (Ring Announcer), Vern De Paul (Vern — Dauthuille's Trainer), Chuck Hassett (Referee), Gil Perkins (Cornerman #1), Gene Borkan (Cornerman #2), Ken Richards (Reporter at Phonebooth). *Third Robinson Fight*: Count Billy Varga (Ring Announcer), Harvey Parry (Referee). *Miami Club*: D.J. Blair (State Attorney Bronson), Laura James (Mrs. Bronson), Richard McMurray (J.R.), Thomas Murphy (J.R.'s Friend), Mary Albee (Underage I.D. girl), Lisa Katz (Woman with I.D. girl), Martin Scorsese (Barbizon Stagehand).

Production Designer in New York/ Visual Consultant in Los Angeles: Gene Rudolf. *Art Directors in Los Angeles*: Alan Manser, Kirk Axtell. *Art Director in New York*: Sheldon Haber. *Costume Designers*: Richard Bruno, John Boxer. *Production Manager*: James D. Brubaker. *First Assistant Director*: Allan Wertheim, Jerry Grandey. *Second Assistant Directors*: Joan Feinstein, Elie Cohn, Robert Barth. *Makeup Created by* Michael Westmore. *Camera Operators*: Joe Marquette, Eddie Gold. *First Assistant Cameraman*: Dustin Blauvelt, Ed Ramirez. *Second Assistant Cameramen*: Richard Fee, Bruce McCallum. *Sound Mixers*: Les Lazarowitz, Michael Evje. *Script Supervisor*: Hannah Scheel. *Set Decorators*: Fred Weiler, Phil Abramson. *Set Dresser*: Jack Mortellaro. *Property Masters*: Emily Ferry, Tom Saccio. *Scenic Artist*: Eugene Powell. *Costumers*: Bill Loger, Andrea Weaver, Betty M. Nowell, Marilyn Putnam, Dean Skipworth. *Hairstylists*: Jean Burt Reilly, Verne Caruso, Mary Keats, Mona Orr. *Makeup Artists*: Frank Westmore, Mike Maggi. *Special Effects*: Raymond Klein, Max E. Wood. *Boxing Technical Advisor*: Al Silvani. *Technical Advisor*: Frank Topham. *Assistant to Mr. Scorsese*: Donna Gigliotti. Assistants to Mr. De Niro: Johanne Todd, Shawn Slovo. *Production Assistants*: Tim Athan, Bill Chartoff, Jean De Niro, June Guterman, Mary Hickey, Janice Peroni, Mark Rubin, Steve Schottenfield, David Ticotin, Rachel Ticotin, Charles Winkler. *Sound Effects Editors*: William J. Wylie, Chester Slomka, Gary Gerlich. *Assistant Sound Effects Editor*: Victoria Martin. *Publicist*: Marion Billings. *Prints by Technicolor. Excerpts from the screenplay* "On the Waterfront" by Budd Schulberg. *Excerpts from the soundtrack of* "Of Mice and Men" (1939) with Lon Chaney, Jr., Burgess Meredith and Charles Bickford.(*Music by* Aaron Copeland. *Produced and Directed by* Lewis Milestone.) Jake La Motta screening material and the voice of Ted Husing announcing the actual La Motta-Robinson fight (February 14, 1951) provided by The Big Fights, Inc.

Songs: "At Last," by Mack Gordon and Harry Warren; "A New Kind of Love," by Sammy Fain, Irving Kahal, and Pierre Norman; "Webster Hall," by Garth Hudson; "Stonelli Fiorentini," by and performed by Carlo Buti; "Scapricciatiello (Infatuation)," performed by Renato Carosone; "Turi Giuliano," by S. Bella and O. Strano, performed by Orazio Strano; "Cow Cow Boogie," by Gene DePaul and Benny Carter, performed by Ella Fitzgerald and the Ink Spots; "Whispering

Grass," by Doris Fisher and Fred Fisher, performed by the Ink Spots; "Stone Cold Dead in the Market," performed by Ella Fitzgerald and Louis Jordan; "Till Then," performed by the Mills Brothers; "Big Noise From Winnetka," performed by Bob Crosby and the Bobcats; "Heartaches," performed by Ted Weems; "Do I Worry," performed by the Ink Spots; "Two O'Clock Jump," performed by Harry James; "Drum Boogie," performed by Gene Krupa; "All or Nothing at All," performed by Harry James; "Blue Velvet," performed by Tony Bennett; "Flash," performed by Harry James; "Jersey Bounce," performed by Benny Goodman; "Come Fly With Me" and "Mona Lisa," performed by Nat King Cole; "I Ain't Got Nobody," performed by Louis Prima and Keely Smith; "Nao Tenho Lagrimas," performed by Patricio Teixeira; "Prisoner of Love," performed by Perry Como; "Prisoner of Love," performed by Russ Columbo; "Frenesi," performed by Artie Shaw; "My Reverie," performed by Larry Clinton and his Orchestra; "Just One More Chance"; "That's My Desire," performed by Frankie Laine; "Bye Bye Baby," performed by Marilyn Monroe; "Lonely Nights," performed by the Hearts; "Tell the Truth," performed by Ray Charles.

Dedication: Remembering Haig P. Manoogian, Teacher

May 23, 1916 – May 26, 1980

With love and resolution, Marty.

M.P.A.A. Rating: R.

Running Time: 128 minutes.

Awards: Academy Award, Robert De Niro, Best Actor; Academy Award, Thelma Schoonmaker, Best Film Editing; Academy Award Nominations: Best Picture, Irwin Winkler and Robert Chartoff, producers; Best Director, Martin Scorsese; Best Supporting Actor, Joe Pesci, Best Supporting Actress, Cathy Moriarty; Best Cinematography, Michael Chapman; Best Sound, Donald O. Mitchell, Bill Nicholson, David J. Kimball, Les Lazarowitz.

Home Video: CBS/Fox cassette, Criterion Collection laserdisc (CAV format.)

Synopsis: This film is an examination of aspects of twenty-three years in the life of former middleweight boxing champion Jake La Motta. It begins with a brief scene set in 1964 with the former boxer rehearsing his nightclub act, and flashes back to his 1941 bout with Jimmy Reeves. Highlights of many of La Motta's most important fights are shown, but the film centers on La Motta's relationship with his brother and manager, Joey, and his tumultuous marriage to his second wife, Vickie.

While he continues to win fights, Jake confesses to Joey his ambivalence about his career. He is obsessed with the notion that Vickie might be unfaithful to him, specifically with a lieutenant of Tommy Como, a mobster eager to profit from Jake's career. Hoping to win the championship, Jake capitulates to Como's demand that he throw a fight. Jake is briefly banned from the ring, but his career continues, he gets a shot at the championship, and wins. Jake's paranoia over Vickie continues to grow, culminating with the accusation that she has slept with his brother Joey. Joey severs all ties with Jake.

Some years later in Miami, Jake has grown fat and out of boxing shape. He has retired from the ring and opened a night club. When he unwittingly serves a minor at the club, the police arrest him on a morals charge. Vickie files for divorce. After serving time in prison, La Motta is reduced to being a standup comic at sleazy night spots. One evening he spots Joey on the street and attempts a reconciliation. The film ends as it began, with La Motta in his dressing room reciting Brando's speech from *On the Waterfront*: "I coulda been a contender instead of a bum, which is what I am."

Commentary: See Chapter Two.

IL PAP'OCCHIO (In the Pope's Eye)

Scorsese played the small part of a television director in this Italian-made comedy. Directed by Renzo Arbore, and starring Roberto Begnini and Isabella Rossellini, this light topical satire concerns a pope who starts a television station in order to attract young people to the church. Shortly after its Italian premiere, the film was briefly banned as "an offense to the state of religion" (shades of *The Last Temptation of Christ*). When a court lifted the ban, the film became an Italian box office hit. It has never been released in the United States.

THE KING OF COMEDY

Arnon Milchan Presents a Twentieth-Century Fox Release

Director: Martin Scorsese. *Executive Producer*: Robert Greenhut. *Producer*: Arnon Milchan. *Screenplay*: Paul D. Zimmerman. *Cinematography*: Fred Schuler. *Production Designer*: Boris Leven. *Production Supervisor and Editor*: Thelma Schoonmaker.

Cast: Robert De Niro (Rupert Pupkin), Jerry Lewis (Jerry Langford), Diahnne Abbott (Rita), Sandra Bernhard (Masha), Shelley Hack (Cathy Long), Margo Winkler (Receptionist), Fred De Cordova (Bert Thomas) Ed Herlihy (Himself), Lou Brown (Band Leader), Catherine Scorsese (Rupert's Mother), Kim Chan (Jonno), Tony Randall (Himself), Dr. Joyce Brothers (Herself), Victor Borge (Himself), Mounted Photograph (Liza Minnelli), Martin Scorsese (TV Director), Cathy Scorsese (Dolores), Chuck L. Low (Man in Chinese Restaurant), George Kapp (Mystery Guest), Ralph Monaco (Raymond Wirtz), Rob-Jamere Wess (Security Guard #1), Audrey Dummett (Cook), June Prud'homme (Audrey), Edgar J. Scherick (Wilson Crockett), Thomas M. Tolan (Gerrity), Ray Dittrich (Giardello), Richard Dioguardi (Captain Burke), Jay Julien (Langford's Lawyer), Harry Ufland (Langford's Agent), Scotty Bloch (Crockett's Secretary), Leslie Levinson (Roberta Posner), Alan Potashnick, Michael Kolba, Robert Colston, Ramon Rodriguez, Chuck Coop, Sel Vitella (Men at Telephone Booth), Loretta Tupper, Peter Potulski, Vinnie Gonzales (Stage Door Fans), Mick Jones, Joe Strummer, Paul Simmion, Kosmo Vynil, Ellen Foley, Pearl Harbour, Gaby Salter, Jerry Baxter-Worman, Dom Letts (Street Scum), Matt Russo (Cabbie), Thelma Lee (Woman in Telephone Booth), Whitey Ryan (Stage Door Guard), Doc Lawless (Chauffeur), Marta Heflin (Autograph Seeker), Katherine Wallach (Autograph Seeker) Charlie Kaleina (Autograph Seeker), Richard Baratz (Caricaturist), Jim Lyness (Ticket Taker), Bill Minkin (McCabe), Diane Rachell (McCabe's Wife), Dennis Mulligan, Tony Devon, Peter Fain, Michael F. Stodden, Jerry Murphy (Plainclothesmen), Jimmy Raitt (Stage Manager), Charles Scorsese (First Man at Bar), Mardik Martin (Second Man at Bar), William Jorgensen, Marvin Scott, Chuck Stevens, William Littauer (Voices of Newsmen), Jeff David (Announcer).

Casting: Cis Corman. *Music Production*: Robbie Robertson. *Associate Producer*: Robert F. Colesberry. *First Assistant Director*: Scott Maitland. *Second Assistant Director*: Lewis Gould. *Supervising Sound Editor*: Frank Warner. *Set*

Decorators: George DeTitta, Sr., Daniel Robert. *Art Directors*: Edward Pisoni, Lawrence Miller. *Script Supervisor*: Robert O. Hodes. *Camera Operator*: Dick Mingalone. *First Assistant Camera*: Sandy Brooke. *Sound Mixer*: Les Lazarowitz. *Scenic Artist*: Edward Garzero. *Property Master*: Jimmy Raitt. *Set Dresser*: David Weinman. *Costume Supervisor*: William Loger. *Hair Design*: Lyn Quiyou. *Make-Up Artist*: Philip Goldblatt. *First Assistant Editor*: Richard Candib. *Unit Manager*: Ezra Swerdlow. *Post-Production Supervisor*: Barbara De Fina. *Post-Production Coordinator*: Holly Huckins. *Music Consultant*: Mark Del Costello. *Color by* Technicolor. *Prints by* DeLuxe.

M.P.A.A. Rating: PG.

Running Time: 108 minutes.

Home Video: RCA/Columbia, Tape and Laserdisc.

Synopsis: Aspiring standup comic Rupert Pupkin saves his idol, television talk-show host Jerry Langford, from a mob of his obsessed fans. An obsessive fan himself, Pupkin makes a pitch to appear on Langford's show; Langford tells Pupkin to call his office. Spurred by fantasies of success, Pupkin is brought low by the unenthusiastic response to his act by Langford's staff. Langford further rejects Pupkin when he tries to crash a weekend at the star's home (with unsuspecting girlfriend Rita in tow). With the help of Masha, another obsessed Langford fan, Pupkin kidnaps his idol. The ransom is a chance to perform his monologue on the show. Pupkin appears and becomes an instant media celebrity.

Commentary: See Chapters Two and Four.

SCORSESE: I love Jerry's film *Smorgasbord*, especially for that first sequence in the psychiatrist's office, where everything is so slippery he can't stand up. It's a perfect visual representation of your mind slipping away from you. When I was eleven years old I used to see Jerry at the Paramount Theater. And then, there I was on *The King of Comedy*, working with him!

PAVLOVA — A WOMAN FOR ALL TIME

Scorsese plays Metropolitan Opera House director Gatti Cassaza in this British-Russian coproduction about the life of legendary ballerina Anna Pavlova. Director Emil Loutiano objected to the significantly shorter "western version" that *Pavlova*'s Anglo-Cypriote producer, Frixos Constantine, made under the supervison of Michael Powell. He claimed it violated the Anglo-Soviet agreement that "specifically and authoritatively states that the film is to be made in one single version for all world sales." No version of *Pavlova* has been released in the United States to date.

THE LAST TEMPTATION OF CHRIST (aborted production)

In 1971, director Sidney Lumet announced plans for a film version of Nikos Kazantzakis's controversial novel from a script by Off-Broadway playwright Seymour Simckes (author of *Seven Days of Mourning*). "I suppose you could say it's a dramatization of how a man pushes himself to extremes he was never capable of," said Lumet of the project in an interview with *The New York Times*. "Judas emerges as a strong man, a sort of hero, if you will...We'll start shooting in Israel perhaps in September." The production never went before the cameras.

In February 1983, Scorsese traveled to Israel to begin preproduction on his film of *The Last Temptation of Christ* for Paramount Pictures. Scripted by Paul Schrader, with a budget of $12–15 million, the film was to star Aidan Quinn as Jesus, with Harvey Keitel as Judas, Barbara Hershey as Mary Magdalene, and Sting as Pontius Pilate. One year later, and just weeks prior to shooting, Paramount cancelled the film, in response to a letter-writing campaign waged by many of the same forces that would oppose the film's 1989 production for Universal Pictures.

A chief complaint of the protestors was that Scorsese intended to portray Christ as homosexual. Ironically, this very notion was taken up in earnest in 1990 by gay British filmmaker Derek Jarman in *The Garden*, in which two homosexual lovers enact the Passion of Christ.

Many of the costumes designed for the aborted *Last Temptation* were reportedly used in a less controversial Paramount production, *King David*, directed by Bruce Beresford and starring Richard Gere.

AFTER HOURS

The Geffen Company Presents a Double Play Production released through Warner Bros.

Director: Martin Scorsese. *Screenplay*: Joseph Minion. *Producers*: Amy Robinson, Griffin Dunne, Robert F. Colesberry. *Cinematography*: Michael Ballhaus. *Editor*: Thelma Schoonmaker. *Music*: Howard Shore. *Production Designer*: Jeffrey Townsend.

Cast: Griffin Dunne (Paul Hackett), Rosanna Arquette (Marcy), Verna Bloom (June), Thomas Chong (Pepe), Linda Fiorentino (Kiki), Teri Garr (Julie), John Heard (Tom the Bartender), Richard "Cheech" Marin (Neil), Catherine O'Hara (Gail), Dick Miller (Waiter), Will Patton (Horst), Robert Plunkett (Mark), Bronson Pinchot (Lloyd), Rocco Sisto (Coffee Shop Cashier), Larry Block (Taxi Driver), Victor Argo (Diner Cashier), Murray Moston (Subway Attendant), John P. Codiglia (Transit Cop), Clarke Evans (Neighbor #1), Victor Bumbalo (Neighbor #2), Bill Elverman (Neighbor #3), Joel Jason (Biker #1), Rand Carr (Biker #2), Clarence Felder (Bouncer), Henry Baker (Jett), Margo Winkler (Woman with Gun), Victor Magnotta (Dead Man), Robin Johnson (Punk Girl), Stephen J. Lim (Club Berlin Bartender), Frank Aquilino, Maree Catalano, Paula Raflo, Rockets Redglare (Angry Mob Members), Martin Scorsese (Man with Spotlight in Club Berlin).

Associate Producer: Deborah Schindler. *Casting*: Mary Colquhoun. *Costume Designer*: Rita Ryack. *Production Manager*: Michael Nozik. *First Assistant Director*: Stephen J. Lim. *Second Assistant Director*: Christopher Griffin. *Production Executive*: Nellie Nugiel. *Set Decorator*: Leslie Pope. *Art Director*: Stephen J. Lineweaver. *Location Manager*: Gary Weiner. *Script Supervisor*: Mary A. Kelly. *Production Coordinator*: Denise Pinckley. *Stunt Coordinator*: Harry Madsen *Property Master*: Tom Allen. *Set Dressers*: David Allen, Joel Aaron Blumenau. *Gaffer*: Stefan Czapsky. *Wardrobe Supervisor*: Deirdre Williams. *Wardrobe Assistants*: Paulette Aller Shelton, Charles Scorsese. *Supervising Sound Editor*: Skip Lievsay. *Music Editor*: Thomas Drescher. *Assistant Sound Editors*: Louis Bertini, Marissa Littlefield. *Publicity*: Marion Billings.

Music Credits: "Symphony in D-Major, K-73n, First Movement," by Wolfgang Amadeus Mozart, performed by the Academy of Ancient Music, Jaap Schroder, conductor; "Air Overture No. 3 in D," by Johann Sebastian Bach, performed by

Collegium Aureum; "En La Cueva," written and performed by Cuadro Flamenco; "Sevillanas," written and performed by Manitas DePlata; "You're Mine," by Johnnie Mitchell and Robert Carr, performed by Robert and Johnnie; "We Belong Together," by Robert Carr, Johnnie Mitchell, and Hy Weiss, performed by Robert and Johnnie; "Angel Baby," by Rose Hamlin, performed by Rosie and the Originals; "Last Train to Clarksville," by Bobby Hart and Tommy Boyce, performed by the Monkees; "Chelsea Morning," written and performed by Joni Mitchell; "I Don't Know Where I Stand," written and performed by Joni Mitchell; "Over the Mountain and Across the Sea," by Rex Garvin, performed by Johnnie and Joe; "One Summer Night," by Danny Webb, performed by the Danleers; "Pay to Cum," written and performed by The Bad Brains; "Is That All There Is?" written by Jerry Leiber and Mike Stoller, performed by Peggy Lee, arranged by Randy Newman.

M.P.A.A. Rating: R.

Running Time: 97 minutes.

Home Video: Warner Bros. cassette and laserdisc.

Synopsis: Paul Hackett, a lonely computer programmer, meets Marcy, a mysterious, attractive blonde, in a coffee shop and makes a date to meet her that evening at a loft in New York's SoHo area. Discovering she is emotionally unstable, he leaves. But having lost his money on the way downtown, he has no way to return home. A series of increasingly frustrating encounters occurs as he asks for help from a bartender, a waitress, and a number of passersby. Some try to help, but most either ignore or make light of his situation. He is chased by a mob who are convinced he is the burglar who has been preying on the neighborhood. Taking refuge in a nightclub, he meets a woman sculptor who hides him inside a plaster sculpture. The real burglars steal the sculpture, but it falls out of the truck in front of Paul's office. Still flecked with plaster, Paul enters and goes to his desk where his computer screen greets him with the words "Good morning, Paul."

Commentary: Eager to work again after Paramount's cancellation of *The Last Temptation of Christ*, Scorsese selected Joseph Minion's script, which began as an assignment for Yugoslavian filmmaker Dusan Makavejev's NYU screenwriting class. Reunited with Amy Robinson, his *Mean Streets* star-turned-producer, Scorsese decided to make *After Hours,* a low-budget film like those with which he began his career. The result is one of his sharpest and most inventive films, highlighted by beautifully detailed black comic performances, particularly those of Rosanna Arquette, Linda Fiorentino, Catherine O'Hara, and Teri Garr.

While the tone of *After Hours* is close to that of *The King of Comedy*, the visual style is much more elaborate. Rapid tracking shots — like the film's very first shot, which barrels across an office toward Paul — are frequently used. There are also a number of homages to favorite Scorsese films. A shot of keys being dropped from a loft window is a tribute to the falling pencil of *Peeping Tom*. The close-up of Paul ringing Marcy's bell, followed by lap dissolves of him climbing the stairs to her loft, is derived from George Stevens' *Shane.*. A close-up of Paul running with a key in his hand is from the climax of *Marnie*.

Minion's lightly satirical attack on yuppie smugness (exemplified by Paul) is a precursor for his less forgiving broadside, *Vampire's Kiss*, directed by Robert Bierman. The office building entranceway featured in *After Hours* is seen again in that 1989 release.

MIRROR MIRROR (episode of "Amazing Stories" television series)

An Amblin Production.

Director: Martin Scorsese. *Screenplay:* Joseph Minion from a story by Steven Spielberg. *Producer*: David E. Vogel. *Cinematography*: Robert Stevens. *Editor*: Joe Ann Fogle. *Music*: Michael Kamen. *Production Designer*: Rick Carter.

Cast: Sam Waterston (Jordan), Helen Shaver (Karen), Dick Cavett (Himself), Tim Robbins (Phantom), Dana Gladstone (Producer), Valerie Grear (Host), Michael C. Gwynne (Jail Attendant), Peter Iacangelo (Limo Driver), Jonathan Luria (Cameraman), Harry Northup (Security Guard), Glenn Scarpelli (Jeffrey Gelb), Jack Thibeau (Tough Guy).

Running Time: 24 minutes.
Home Video: *Amazing Stories—Book Four*, MCA Tape and laserdisc.

Synopsis: A successful horror film director is plagued by the recurring vision of a black-clad phantom whose reflection he sees in mirrors. While the director believes he's going insane, his girlfriend realizes that he is turning into this phantom himself.

Commentary: Scorsese teamed with screenwriter Minion once again for this episode of Steven Spielberg's much-ballyhooed, but ultimately unsuccessful fantasy anthology series. The principal setting, the director's elaborate, antiseptically clean modern home, is similar to Jerry Langford's penthouse in *The King of Comedy*. Also reminiscent of *King* is the devoted fan camped on the hero's doorstep. However, he is successful at chasing the fan away. The demonic absorption plot has its roots in a number of Edgar Allan Poe stories, and the Roger Corman films adapted from them. But the treatment is rather rushed, as if Scorsese had filmed an idea not fully developed. The film clip used to illustrate the hero's work is from the 1966 Hammer Studios horror film *Plague of the Zombies*, directed by John Gilling.

THE COLOR OF MONEY

Touchstone Pictures Presents in Association with Silver Screen Partners II. A Martin Scorsese Picture.

Director: Martin Scorsese. *Screenplay*: Richard Price, based upon the novel by Walter Tevis. *Producers*: Irving Axelrad, Barbara De Fina. *Cinematography*: Michael Ballhaus. *Editor*: Thelma Schoonmaker. *Production Designer*: Boris Leven. *Music*: Robbie Robertson.

Cast: Paul Newman (Eddie Felson), Tom Cruise (Vincent), Mary Elizabeth Mastrantonio (Carmen), Helen Shaver (Janelle), John Turturro (Julian), Bill Cobbs (Orvis), Robert Agins (Earl at Chalkies), Alvin Anastasia (Kennedy), Randall Arney (Child World Customer #1), Elizabeth Bracco (Diane at Bar), Vito D'Ambrosio (Lou in Child World), Ron Dean (Guy in Crowd), Lisa Dodson (Child World Customer #2), Donald A. Feeney (Referee #1), Paul Geier ("Two Brothers and a Stranger" Player), Carey Goldenberg (Congratulating Spectator), Joe Guastaferro (Chuck the Bartender), Paul Herman (Player in Casino Bar), Mark Jarvis (guy at Janelle's), Lawrence Linn (Congratulating Spectator), Keith McCready (Grady Seasons),

Jimmy Mataya (Julian's friend in Green Room), Grady Mathews (Dud), Carol Messing (Casino Bar Band Singer/ Julian's Flirt), Iggy Pop (Skinny Player on Road), Richard Price (Guy Who Calls Dud), Charles Scorsese (High Roller #1), Forest Whitaker (Amos), Zoe (Dog Walkby).

Costume Designer: Richard Bruno. *Casting*: Gretchen Rennell. *Stunt Coordinator*: Rick LeFevour. *Stunts*: Eddie Fernandez, Stacy Logan, Richard M. Wilkie. *Production Manager/ Associate Producer*: Dodie Foster. *First Assistant Director*: Joseph Reidy. *Set Decorator*: Karen A. O'Hara. *First Assistant Editor*: James Y. Kwei. *Supervising Sound Editor*: Skip Lievsay. *Music Editor*: Todd Kasow. *Assistant Music Editor*: Bob Nichols. *Re-Recording Mixer*: Tom Fleischman, Sound One Corp. *Camera Operator*: Frank M. Miller. *First Assistant Camera*: Donald C. Carlson. *Sound Mixer*: Glenn Williams. *Script Supervisor*: Sioux Richards. *Key Makeup Artist*: Monty Westmore. *Key Hair Stylist*: Kathe Muller Swanson. *Makeup Artist*: Lillian Toth. *Hair Stylist*: Brian J. Kossman. *Costume Supervisor*: William Loger. *Costumer*: Cheryl A. Weber. *Production Coordinator*: Elise Rohden. *Orchestrations*: Gil Evans. *Special Musical Participations*: Willie Dixon. *Additional Electronic Music Arrangements*: Gary Chang.

Songs: "Strangers in the Night," by Charles Singleton, Eddie Snyder and Bert Kaempfert; "I'll Never Smile Again," by Ruth Lowe; "Anema E Core," by Tito Manlio and Salve d'Esposito, English lyrics by Mann Curtis and Harry Akst; "The Day the Rains Came," by Pierre Delanoe and Gilbert Becaud, English lyrics by Carl Sigman; "The Girl From Ipanema," by Vinicius de Morales and Antonio Carlos Jobim, English lyrics by Norman Gimbel; "I'll Remember April," by Don Raye, Gene dePaul, and Pat Johnston, performed by Charlie Parker; "Feel Like Going Home," by Scott Kempner, performed by The Del Lords; "Va Pensiero" from "Nabucco," by Giuseppe Verdi; "Walk on the Wild Side," by Elmer Bernstein and Mack David, performed by Jimmy Smith; "Still a Fool," written and performed by Muddy Waters; "My Baby's in Love With Another Guy," by Lawrence Lucie and Herman Brightman, performed by Robert Palmer; "She's Fine — She's Mine," written and performed by Bo Diddley; "It's My Life Baby," by Don Robey and Ferdinand "Fats" Washington, performed by Eric Clapton and Big Town Playboys; "Who Owns This Place?" by Don Henley, Danny Kortchmar, and J. D. Souther, performed by Don Henley; "Let Yourself In for It," written and performed by Robert Palmer; "It's In the Way You Use It," by Eric Clapton and Robbie Robertson, performed by Eric Clapton; "Two Brothers and a Stranger," written and performed by Mark Knopfler; "Don't Tell Me Nothin'," by Willie Dixon and Robbie Robertson, performed by Willie Dixon; "Standing on the Edge," by Jerry Williams, performed by B.B. King; "One More Night," written and performed by Phil Collins; "Still the Night," by Sammy Llana, Kurt Neumann and Guy Hoffman, performed by Bodeans; "Werewolves of London," by Leroy Marivell, Robert Wachtel, and Warren Zevon, performed by Warren Zevon; "Out of Left Field," by Carl Oldham and Dan Penn, performed by Percy Sledge.

M.P.A.A. Rating: R.

Running Time: 119 minutes.

Awards: Academy Award, Paul Newman, Best Actor. Academy Award nomination: Mary Elizabeth Mastrantonio, Best Supporting Actress.

Home Video: Touchstone cassette and laserdisc.

Synoposis: Former pool player "Fast" Eddie Felson, now a successful liquor dealer, is drawn to the game again when he meets Vincent, a young nonprofessional with a natural talent for the game. Eddie convinces Vincent's girlfriend Carmen that he can mold the youth into a top-rank player. He takes the couple on the road to show them the fine points of the game. Vincent enjoys life in the pool halls, but he's very resistant to taking the older man's advice about playing —

specifically when to win and when it's smarter to lose. Frustrated with Vincent's attitude, Eddie resumes playing himself. When he's beaten by Amos, a skillful con artist half his age, Eddie tells Vincent that he has nothing further to teach him, and that he should go out on his own. After going their separate ways, Eddie, Vincent, and Carmen meet again at a major pool tournament in Atlantic City, where the two men resume their friendship.

Commentary: Scorsese's voice over the opening credits reading a commentary about pool ("for some players, luck is an art itself") is the most personal aspect of this slick, fast-moving, but essentially unsatisfying melodrama. A sequel to *The Hustler*, written and directed by Robert Rossen, Scorsese's film has none of the grit or anguish of that 1961 release, which also starred Paul Newman as Eddie Felson. Newman and Mastrantonio give excellent performances, and Scorsese makes the film consistently watchable with a virtuoso display of rapid camera movements, unusual shot framings, and inventive editing ideas. But *Color* lacks the dramatic conviction of Scorsese's best work. Eddie's decision to become a player again seems arbitrary, and the film goes slack in its last quarter.

ARMANI COMMERCIAL #1

Empori Armani Productions

Director/Scenario: Martin Scorsese. *Producer:* Barbara De Fina. *Cinematography (black and white):* Nestor Almendros.
Cast: Christophe Bouquin, Christina Marsilach.
Running Time: 30 seconds.

Synopsis: A boy and a girl sit on a bed in what appears to be a room of an Italian villa. She is teaching him Italian by pointing to the features of his face and repeating the words for them. The boy repeats a word and kisses her hand.

Commentary: Scorsese says he was taught what Italian he knows by much the same method as that shown in this commercial. Like numerous current fashion and fragrance ads, the commercial is designed to sell a mood associated with a product, rather than the product itself.

'ROUND MIDNIGHT

Scorsese appears as Goodley, the manager of the New York jazz club Birdland, in Bertrand Tavernier's *film á clef* about the friendship of legendary jazz pianist Bud Powell (played by legendary jazz saxophonist Dexter Gordon) and his devoted French admirer, Francis Paudras. Scorsese's part consists largely of a rapid-fire monologue about the pains and pleasures of living in New York.

1987

BAD

Optimum Productions

Director: Martin Scorsese. *Screenplay:* Richard Price. *Producers:* Quincy Jones, Barbara De Fina. *Cinematography:* Michael Chapman. *Editor:* Thelma Schoonmaker. *Choreography:* Michael Jackson, Gregg Burge, Jeffrey Daniel.

Cast: Michael Jackson (Daryl), Adam Nathan (Tip), Pedro Sanchez (Nelson), Wesley Snipes (Mini Max), Greg Holtz, Jr.

(Cowboy), Jaime Perry (Ski), Paul Calderon (dealer), Alberto Alejandrino (Hispanic Man), Horace Daily (Street Bum), Mark Foster (Crack Customer), Roberta Flack (Daryl's Mother).

Running Tme:16 minutes.

Synopsis: *Bad* was inspired by an actual incident in which an honors student became embroiled in urban gang activity. The music video begins as a black-and-white dramatic vignette about a prep school youth who, during his holidays, returns to his ghetto neighborhood. He is challenged by his childhood friends to prove that he is still as "bad" as he had been by robbing a passerby on the street. His refusal takes the form of a musical number shot in color.

Commentary: Designed as a followup to Jackson's wildly successful "long form" music video *Thriller* (directed by John Landis), *Bad* did not duplicate its success. Shown only once on network television, *Bad* was never released as a home video and has been seen only a handful of times on MTV. However, the color portion of the video has been shown frequently.

Scorsese pays homage in the opening sequence to *The Cool World*, Shirley Clarke's classic 1964 study of urban African-American teenagers. Jackson is shown riding a series of trains on which his white fellow passengers are gradually replaced by blacks. Though skillfully made, *Bad* suffers from the attempt to "say something" about ghetto life, and yet be "pure entertainment." Sharp-eyed viewers can spot Scorsese's face on the "Wanted" poster Michael Jackson rips from a subway wall during the musical number.

1988

SOMEWHERE DOWN THE CRAZY RIVER
Limelight Productions.

Director/Scenario: Martin Scorsese. *Producers*: Amanda Pirie, Tim Clawson. *Cinematography*: Mark Plummer. *Production Designer*: Marina Levikova.

Cast: Robbie Robertson, Sammy Bo Dean, Maria McKee.

Running Time: 4 1/2 minutes.

Synopsis: Following a few close-ups of guitars and drums, Robbie Robertson appears in silhouette against a white background. The lighting shifts to reveal his face and he speaks of a love affair that began on an evening when it was "too hot to sleep." As the video progresses, and Robertson sings, the background changes color to red, blue, and purple. Maria McKee appears in silhouette, and then dances into full view. Sammy Bo Dean wanders into the shot from time to time to repeat the refrain of Robertson's song. The video ends with Robertson embracing McKee, who kisses his chest as she tosses her hair back and forth.

Commentary: "Take a picture of this," Robertson says midway through the number. "The fields are empty. Abandoned '59 Chevy. Layin' in the back seat listenin' to Little Willie John. Yeah. That's when time stood still. Y'know I think I'm gonna go down to Madame X and let her read my mind. She said that voodoo stuff don't do nothin' for me."

Half story, half song, this sexual reverie is the most purely carnal film Scorsese has ever made. "One thing you gotta learn is not to be afraid of it," Robertson says.

THE LAST TEMPTATION OF CHRIST

A Universal Pictures and Cineplex Odeon Films Presentation.

Director: Martin Scorsese. *Screenplay*: Paul Schrader, *based on the novel by* Nikos Kazantzakis. *Producer*: Barbara De Fina. *Executive Producer*: Harry Ufland. *Cinematography*: Michael Ballhaus, A.S.C. *Editor*: Thelma Schoonmaker. *Production Designer*: John Beard. *Costume Designer*: Jean-Pierre Delifer. *Music*: Peter Gabriel.

Cast: Willem Dafoe (Jesus), Harvey Keitel (Judas), Paul Greco (Zealot), Steven Shill (Centurion), Verna Bloom (Mary, Mother of Jesus), Barbara Hershey (Mary Magdalene), Roberts Blossom (Aged Master), Barry Miller (Jeroboam), Gary Basaraba (Andrew, Apostle), Irvin Kershner (Zebedee), Victor Argo (Peter, Apostle), Michael Been (John, Apostle), Paul Herman (Phillip, Apostle), John Lurie (James, Apostle), Russell Case, Mary Seller, Donna Marie (People at Sermon), Leo Burmester (Nathaniel, Apostle), Mohamed Mabsout, Ahmed Nacir, Mokhtar Salouf, Mahamed Ait Fdil Ahmed (Other Apostles), Andre Gregory (John the Baptist), Peggy Gormley (Martha, Sister of Lazarus), Randy Danson (Mary, Sister of Lazarus), Robert Spafford (Man at Wedding), Doris Von Thury (Woman with Mary, Mother of Jesus), Tomas Arana (Lazarus), Alan Rosenberg (Thomas, Apostle), Del Russel (Moneychanger) Nehemiah Persoff (Rabbi), Donald Hodson (Saducee), Harry Dean Stanton, (Saul/Paul), Peter Berling (Beggar), David Bowie (Pontius Pilate), Julliette Caton (Girl Angel).

Casting: Cis Corman. *Production Manager*: Laura Fattori. *First Assistant Director*: Joseph Reidy. *Second Assistant Directors*: Fabio Jephcott, Ahmed Hatimi. *Art Director*: Andrew Sanders. *Set Decorator*: Giorgio Desideri. *Supervising Sound Editor*: Skip Lievsay. *Dialogue Supervisor*: Phillip Stockton. *Music Supervisor*: Tom Kasow. *Re-Recording Mixer*: Tom Fleischman. *Sound Editors*: Jeffrey Stern, Thomas A. Gulino, M. P. S. E.. *Foley Editors*: Eliza Paley, Gail Showalter, Steven Visscher. *Second Camera Operators*: David Slama, David Dunlap. *First Assistant Cameraman*: Florian Ballhaus. *Sound Mixer*: Amelio Verona. *Script Supervisor*: Rachel Griffiths. *Assistant Art Director*: John Frankish. *Assistant Set Decorator*: Alberto Tosto. *Prop Master*: Elio Altamura. *Wardrobe Supervisor*: Bona Nasalli Roca. *Makeup Supervisor*: Manlio Rocchetti. *Hair Supervisor*: Aldo Signoretti. Hairstylist: Mirella Ginnoto. *Special Effects Supervisor*: Dino Galliano. *Special Effects Technician*: Iginio Fiorentini. *Choreographer*: Lahcen Zinoune. *Stunt Coordinator*: Franco Salamon. *Unit Manager*: Marco Valerio Pugini. *Location Managers*: Antonio Gabrielli, Ahmed Darif. *Production Coordinator*: Gabriella Toro. Filmed Entirely on location in Morocco.

M.P.A.A. Rating: R

Running Time: 163 minutes.

Awards: Los Angeles Film Teachers Association Award to Martin Scorsese. Academy Award Nomination, Martin Scorsese, Best Director.

Synopsis: Plagued by blinding headaches, Jesus, a Nazarene carpenter, complains to his mother, Mary, that he is not sure whether God or Satan is trying to get a hold on him. His friend Judas is convinced that Jesus has the potential to be a political leader who can protect the Jews against Rome, and that he should stop building crosses for the them to crucify rebellious Jews. It is Mary Magdalene, a young woman who took up prostitution when Jesus spurned her love, who moves Jesus to change his course.

Jesus begins to preach and attract disciples. After meditating alone in the desert, where he is tempted by Satan in many forms, Jesus returns to spread his message more openly. Practicing miracles and alternating pleas for peace and brotherhood with calls to overthrow accepted laws, he raises the ire of the Jewish leadership. Telling Judas to betray him to the Romans in order to fulfill his mission, Jesus is arrested, tortured, and crucified as an enemy of the state.

While Jesus is on the cross, a young girl tells him that he has "done enough" and doesn't have to die. Taking him down from the cross, she leads him to Magdalene, whom he marries. Magdalene dies in a mysterious flash of blinding light. The young girl tells Jesus not to mourn, that "all women are one." He marries both Martha and Mary, and has children by them. On his deathbed, Jesus's disciples come to visit him. All are sad except Judas, who complains that the tumult that surrounds them would never have happened had Jesus died on the cross. Judas unmasks the young woman as Satan, and Jesus is on the cross again. What Satan had showed him was a vision — one last temptation — of life as an ordinary man. Jesus dies knowing his mission has been accomplished.

Commentary: See Chapter Three.

ARMANI COMMERCIAL #2
Emporio Armani Productions.

Director/Scenario: Martin Scorsese. *Producer*: Barbara De Fina. *Cinematography*: Michael Ballhaus. *Cast*: Jens Peter, Elisabetha Ranella.
Running Time: 30 seconds.

Synopsis: A woman angrily breaks into an apartment and is unknowingly observed by the man who apparantly lives there. She tosses things on the floor, and he starts to leave. She senses his presence and knocks over a bottle of perfume. A close-up of a splash of perfume onto a black surface fills the screen. The woman runs after the man but fails to catch him.

Commentary: Looking forward to many of the thematic ideas of *Life Lessons*, the deliberate dramatic overstatement of this commercial makes it something of a parody of others in its genre (e.g., Calvin Klein's *Obsession*) as well as a self-parody of Scorsese's love of sweeping camera movements and unusual visual angles.

 1989

LIFE LESSONS (episode of NEW YORK STORIES)
Touchstone Pictures presents a Jack Rollins and Charles H. Joffe Production.

Director: Martin Scorsese. *Screenplay*: Richard Price. *Producer*: Barbara De Fina. *Cinematography*: Nestor Almendros A.S.C. *Editor*: Thelma Schoonmaker. *Production Designer*: Kristi Zea.

Cast: Nick Nolte (Lionel Dobie), Rosanna Arquette (Paulette), Patrick O'Neal (Phillip Fowler), Phil Harper (Businessman), Kenneth J. McGregor, David Cryer, Paul Geier (Suits), Jesse Borrego (Reuben Toro), Gregorij von Leitis (Kurt Bloom), Steve Buscemi (Gregory Stark), Lo Nardo (Woman at Blind Alley), Peter Gabriel (Himself), Mark Boone, Jr. (Hank), Illeana Douglas (Paulette's Friend), Paul Mougey (Guy at Blind Alley), Deborah Harry (Girl at Blind Alley), Paul Herman, Victor Argo (Cops), Victor Trull (Maitre d'), Richard Price (Artist at Opening), Brigitte Bako (Young Woman).

Stunt Coordinator: Danny Aiello, III. *Costume Designer*: John Dunn. *Production Manager*: Bruce S. Pustin. *First Assistant Director*: Joseph Reidy. *Production Coordinator*: Alesandra Cuomo. *Script Supervisor*: Martha Pinson. *Art Director*: Wray Steven Graham. *Set Decorator*: Nina F. Ramsey. *Set Dresser*: Dave Weinman. *Camera Operator*: Tony Jannelli. *Still Photographer*: Brian Hamil. *Property Master*: James Mazzola. *Sound Recordist*: Frank Graziadei. *Makeup Artist*: Allen Weisinger. *Hairstylist*: Milton Buras. *First Assistant Editor*: Geraldine Peroni. *Supervising Sound Editor*: Skip Lievsay. *Dialogue Editor*: Jeffrey Stern. *Sound Editors*: Bruce Pross, Tony Martinez.

Songs: "Whiter Shade of Pale," by Keith Reid and Gary Brooker, performed by Procol Harum; "Politician," by Jack Bruce and Peter Brown, performed by Cream; "The Right Time," by Nappy Brown, Ozzie Cadena, and Lew Herman, performed by Ray Charles; "Like a Rolling Stone," by Bob Dylan, performed by Bob Dylan and The Band; "It Could Happen to You," by Johnny Burke and Jimmy Van Heusen; "That Old Black Magic," by Johnny Mercer and Harold Arlen; "Stella by Starlight," by Ned Washington and Victor Young; "Conquistador," by Keith Reid and Gary Brooker, performed by Procol Harum; "Nessun Dorma" (from *Turandot*) by Giacomo Puccini, performed by Mario Del Monaco with the Chorus and Orchestra of the Academia Di Santa Cecilia, Rome, conducted by Alberto Erede; "Sex Kick," by Nick Christian Sayer, performed by Transvision Vamp; "What Is This Thing Called Love?" by Cole Porter, performed by The Hot Club of France with Django Reinhardt and Stephane Grappelli; "Bolero De Django," performed by The Hot Club of France with Django Reinhardt and Stephane Grappelli.

Principal Painting: Chuck Connelley, courtesy of the Lennon/Weinberg Gallery. *Paulette's Artwork*: Susan Hambleton, courtesy of TrabiaMacAffee Gallery. *Performance Piece written and performed by* Steve Buscemi.

Running Time: 44 minutes.

Home Video: Touchstone cassette and laserdisc.

Synopsis: Painter Lionel Dobie is less concerned about his one-man show than he is by the fact that Paulette, his assistant and girlfriend, is leaving him.

Frustrated by her lack of success as a painter, and smarting from an unsuccessful fling with a self-obsessed performance artist, Paulette has decided to move back home. Lionel is desperate to hold on to her and begs her to stay, promising that she can live her own life.

At a party, Lionel is jealous of the attention another artist shows Paulette and she realizes he can't be taken at his word. The inevitable break comes after Lionel picks a fight with the performance artist. At the party celebrating the opening of Lionel's show, the painter meets a young woman who may come to take Paulette's place.

Commentary: See Chapter Four.

MADE IN MILAN

Emporio Armani Productions. Mercurio Cinematografica SRL.

Director: Martin Scorsese. *Scenario*: Jay Cocks. *Producer*: Barbara De Fina. *Cinematography*: Nestor Almendros. *Music*: Howard Shore. *Editor*: Thelma Schoonmaker. "Japanese Drums" performed by Kitaro. Photographs of farmers taken from book *Immagini del Mondo Popolare Silano Nel Primi Decenne de Secolo*. *Photographer*: Saverio Marra.

Running Time: 20 minutes.

Synopsis: Fashion designer Giorgio Armani discusses the city of Milan, his family history, and his ideas about fashion as he prepares for a show.

Commentary: Scorsese uses the occasion of this promotional film to try out a number of visual and technical ideas. The opening shot, in which the camera moves across the roof of Milan Cathedral, is among the most beautiful he has ever executed. Noteworthy, too, is a fashion show sequence shot against a neutral backdrop. Scorsese moves the camera slightly to the right as the models walk down the runway and exit to the left of the screen. As a result, it seems as if the models' feet aren't touching the ground. In another playful moment, a model is followed down a hallway. Picking up a video camera, he turns and films Scorsese and his crew — revealed in the next shot. A shot of Armani observing his fashion show from backstage is an homage to a similar scene in *The Red Shoes*.

GOODFELLAS

Warner Bros. presents an Irwin Winkler Production

Director: Martin Scorsese. *Screenplay*: Nicholas Pileggi and Martin Scorsese, *based on the book* "Wiseguy" by Nicholas Pileggi. *Producer*: Irwin Winkler. *Executive Producer*: Barbara De Fina. *Cinematography*: Michael Ballhaus, A.C.E. *Film Editor*: Thelma Schoonmaker, A.C.E. *Production Designer*: Kristi Zea.

Cast: Robert De Niro (James Conway), Ray Liotta (Henry Hill), Joe Pesci (Tommy De Vito), Lorraine Bracco (Karen Hill), Paul Sorvino (Paul Cicero), Frank Sivero (Frankie Carbone), Tony Darrow (Sonny Bunz), Mike Starr (Frenchy), Frank Vincent (Billy Batts), Chuck Low (Morrie Kessler), Frank DiLeo (Tuddy Cicero), Henny Youngman (Himself), Gina Mastrogiacomo (Janice Rossi), Catherine Scorsese (Tommy's Mother), Charles Scorsese (Vinnie), Suzanne Shepherd (Karen's Mother), Debi Mazar (Sandy), Margo Winkler (Belle Kessler), Welker White (Lois Bird), Jerry Vale (Himself), Julie Garfield (Mickey Conway), Christopher Serrone (Young Henry), Elaine Kagan (Henry's Mother), Beau Starr (Henry's Father), Kevin Corrigan (Michael Hill), Michael Imperioli (Spider), Robbie Vinton (Bobbie Vinton), John Williams (Johnny Roastbeef). Cicero's 50's Crew: Daniel P. Conte (Dr. Dan), Tony Conforti (Tony), Frank Pellegrino (Johnny Dio), Ronald Maccone (Ronnie), Tony Sirico (Tony Stacks). Joseph D'Onofrio (Young Tommy), Steve Forleo (City Detective #1), Richard Dioguardi (City Detective #2), Frank Adonis (Anthony Stabile), John Manca (Nicky Eyes), Joseph Bono (Mikey Franzese), Katherine Wallach (Diane), Mark Evan Jacobs (Bruce), Angela Pietropinto (Cicero's Wife), Marianne Leone

(Tuddy's Wife), Marie Michaels (Mrs. Carbone), Lo Nardo (Frenchy's wife). Women at cosmetics party: Melissa Prophet (Angie), Illena Douglas (Rosie), Susan Varon (Susan). Elizabeth Whitcraft (Tommy's Girlfriend at Copa), Clem Caserta (Joe Buddha), Samuel L. Jackson (Stacks Edwards), Fran McGee (Johnny Roastbeef's Wife), Paul Herman (Dealer), Edward McDonald (Himself), Edward Hayes (Defense Attorney), Daniela Barbosa (Young Henry's Sister #1), Gina Mattia (Young Henry's Sister #2), Joel Calendrillo (Young Henry's Older Brother), Anthony Valentin (Young Michael), Edward D. Murphy (Liquor Cop #1), Peter Hock (Mailman), Erasmus C. Alfano (Barbecue Wiseguy), John DiBenedetto (Bleeding Man); Manny Alfaro (Gambling Doorman), Thomas Lowry (Hijacked Driver), Margaret Smith (School Guard), Richard Mullally (Cop #1), Frank Albanese (Mob Lawyer), Paul McIssac (Judge 1956), Bob Golub (Truck Driver at Diner), Louis Eppolito (Fat Andy), Tony Lip (Frankie the Wop), Mikey Black (Freddie No Nose), Peter Cicale (Pete the Killer), Anthony Powers (Jimmy Two Times), Vinny Pastore (Man with Coatrack), Anthony Alessandro, Victor Colicchio (Henry's 60's Crew), Mike Contessa, Paul Suriano (Cicero's 60's Crew), Paul Mougey (Terriorized Waiter), Norman Barbera (Bouncer), Anthony Polemeni (Copa Captain), James Quattrochi (Henry Greeter #1), Laurence Sacco (Henry Greeter #2), Dino Laudicina (Henry Greeter #3), Thomas E. Camuti (Mr. Tony Hood #1), Andrew Scudiero (Mr. Tony Hood #2), Irving Welzer (Copa Announcer), Jesse Kirtzman (Beach Club Waiter), Russell Halley (Bruce's Brother #1), Spencer Bradley (Bruce's Brother #2), Bob Altman (Karen's Dad), Joanna Bennett (Marie #1), Gayle Lewis (Marie #2), Gaetano Lisi (Paul #3), Luke Walter (Truck driver), Ed Deacy (Detective Deacy), Larry Silvestri (Detective Silvestri), Johnny Cha Cha Ciarcia (Batts' Crew #2), Vito Picone (Vito), Janis Corsair (Vito's Girlfriend), Frank Aquilino (Batts' Crew #2), Lisa Dapolito (Lisa), Michael Calamdrino (Godfather at Table), Vito Antuofermo (Prizefighter), Vito Balsamo, Peter Fain, Vinnie Gallo, Gaetano LoGiudice, Garry Blackwood (Henry's 70's Crew), Nicole Burdette (Carbone's Girlfriend), Stella Kietel (Henry's Older Child, Judy), Dominique DeVito (Henry's Baby, Ruth), Michaelangelo Graziano (Bar Patron), Paula Gallo (Janice's Girlfriend #1), Nadine Kay (Janice's Girlfriend #2), Tony Ellis (Bridal Shop Owner), Peter Onorati (Florida Bookie), Jamie DeRoy (Bookie's Sister), Joel Blake (Judge-1971), H. Clay Dear (Security Guard w/Lobsters), Thomas Hewson (Drug Buyer), Gene Canfield (Prison Guard in Booth), Marguax Guerard (Judy Hill at 10 years); Violet Gaynor (Ruth Hill at 8 years), Tobin Bell (Parole Officer), Berlinda Tolbert (Stack's Girlfriend), Nancy Ellen Cassaro (Joe Buddha's Wife), Adam Wandt (Kid), Joseph P. Gioco (Garbageman), Isiah Whitlock Jr. (Doctor), Alyson Jones (Judy Hill at 13 years), Ruby Gaynor (Ruth Hill at 11 years), Richard "Bo" Dietel (Arresting Narc), Nick Giangiulio, Don Picard, Peter Bucossi, Norm Douglass, Paul Bucossi, Tony Guida, Mike Russo, Roy Farfel, Janet Paparazzo, Alex Stevens, Phil Neilson (Stuntpersons).

Casting: Ellen Lewis. *Associate Producer*: Bruce Pustin. *Unit Production Manager*: Bruce Pustin. *First Assistant Director*: Joseph Reidy. *Second Assistant Director*: Vebe Borge. *Costume Designer*: Richard Bruno. *Titles*: Elaine and Saul Bass. *Second Unit Director*: Joseph Reidy. *Art Director*: Maher Ahmad. *Set Decorator*: Les Bloom. *Editor*: James Kwei. *First Assistant Editor*: David Leonard. *Script Supervisor*: Sheila Paige. *Music Editor*: Christopher Brooks. *Supervising Sound Editor*: Skip Lievsay. *Supervising Dialogue Editor*: Philip Stockton. *Dialogue Editors*: Marissa Littlefield, Fred Rosenberg, Jeff Stern, Bruce Kitzmeyer. *Production Sound Mixer*: James Sabat. *Sound Recordist*: Frank Graziadei. *Camera Operator*: David Dunlap. *First Assistant Cameraman*: Florian Ballhaus. *Makeup Artists*: Allen Weisinger, Carl Fullerton. *Hairstylists*: Bill Farley, Alan D'Angerio. *Mr. De Niro's Makeup and Hair*: Ilona Herman. *Chief Lighting Technician*: Jerry DeBlau.

Songs: "Rags to Riches" by Jerry Ross and Richard Adler, performed by Tony Bennett; "Can't We Be Sweethearts" by Morris Levy and Herb Cox, performed by The Cleftones; "Hearts of Stone" by Eddie Ray and Rudy Jackson, performed by

Otis Williams and The Charms; "Sincerely" by Harvey Fuqua and Alan Freed, performed by The Moonglows; "Firenze Sogna" by Cesarini, performed by Giuseppe di Stefano; "Speedo" by Esther Navarro, performed by The Cadillacs; "Parlami d'Amore Mariu" by Enrico Neri and C.A. Bixio, performed by Giuseppe di Steffano; "Stardust" by Hoagy Carmichael and Mitchell Parrish, performed by Billy Ward and His Dominoes; "This World We Live In (Il Cielo in Una Stanza)" by Toang, Mogal and Ray, performed by Mina; "Playboy" by Brian Holland, Robert Bateman, and William Stevenson, performed by The Marvellettes; "It's Not for Me to Say" by Robert Allen and Al Stillman, performed by Johnny Mathis; "I Will Follow Him" by Norman Gimbel, Arthur Altman, J.W. Stole and Del Roma, performed by Betty Curtis; "Then He Kissed Me" by Phil Spector, Ellie Greenwich and Jeff Barry, performed by The Crystals; "Look in My Eyes" by Richard Barrett, performed by The Chantels; "Roses Are Red" by Al Byron and Paul Evans, performed by Bobby Vinton; "Life Is But a Dream" by Raul Cita and Harvey Weiss, performed by The Harptones; "Leader of the Pack" by George Morton, Jeff Barry and Ellie Greenwich, performed by the Shangri-Las; "Toot Toot Tootsie Goodbye" by Ernie Erdman, Ted Fiorito, and Gus Kahn; "Happy Birthday to You" by Mildred J. Hill and Patty S. Hill; "Ain't That a Kick in the Head" by Sammy Cahn and Jimmy Van Heusen, performed by Dean Martin; "He's Sure the Boy I Love" by Barry Mann and Cynthia Weil, performed by The Crystals; "Atlantis" by Donovan Leitch, performed by Donovan; "Pretend You Don't See Her" by Steve Allen, performed by Jerry Vale; "Remember (Walkin' in the Sand)" by George Morton, performed by The Shangri-Las; "Baby I Love You" by Ronny Shannon, performed by Aretha Franklin; "Beyond the Sea" by Jack Lawrence and Charles Trenet, performed by Bobby Darin; "The Boulevard of Broken Dreams" by Al Dubin and Harry Warren, performed by Tony Bennett; "Gimme Shelter" by Mick Jagger and Keith Richards, performed by The Rolling Stones; "Wives and Lovers" by Burt Bacharach and Hal David, performed by Jack Jones; "Monkey Man" by Mick Jagger and Keith Richards, performed by The Rolling Stones; "Frosty the Snowman" by Steven Nelson and Jack Rollins, performed by The Ronettes; "Christmas (Baby Please Come Home)" by Phil Spector, Ellie Greenwich, and Jeff Barry, performed by Darlene Love; "The Bells of St. Marys" by Douglas Furber and Emmett Adams, performed by The Drifters; "Unchained Melody" by Hy Zaret and Alex North, performed by Vito and the Salutations; "Danny Boy" by Frederic E. Weatherly; "Sunshine of Your Love" by Jack Bruce, Peter Brown, and Eric Clapton, performed by Cream; "Layla" by Eric Clapton and Jim Gordon, performed by Derek and the Dominos; "Jump Into the Fire" composed and performed by Harry Nilsson; "Memo From Turner" by Mick Jagger and Keith Richards, performed by The Rolling Stones; "The Magic Bus" by Peter Townshend, performed by The Who; "What Is Life" composed and performed by George Harrison; "Mannish Boy" by McKinley Morganfield, Mel London, and Elias McDaniel, performed by Muddy Waters; "My Way" by Claude Francois, Jacques Revaux, and Paul Anka, performed by Sid Vicious.

M.P.A.A. Rating: R.

Running Time: 146 minutes.

Awards: Academy Award, Joe Pesci, for Best Supporting Actor. Nominations: Best Picture, Best Director (Martin Scorsese), Best Screenplay Adaptation (Nicholas Pleggi, Martin Scorsese), Best Supporting Actress (Lorraine Bracco), Best Editing (Thelma Schoonmaker).

Home Video: Warner Bros. cassette and laserdisc.

Synopsis: A film adapatation of Nicholas Pileggi's nonfiction biography of mobster Henry Hill, from his youth to his recruitment into the government's witness protection program. Consisting of a series of brief scenes narrated by Hill, the film explores the specifics of mob life (on the streets and in prison) and Hill's relationships with his wife, Karen, his mistresses, Janice and Sandy, and fellow mobsters James Conway and Tommy DeVito.

DeVito's cold-blooded murder of a "made" (i.e. Mafia-protected) mobster eventually leads to his own death.

Conway masterminds a multimillion dollar airport heist, but ends up killing all his partners in its aftermath. Hill's fear that he and his wife are next on Conway's hit list inspires his "singing" to the authorities.

SCORSESE: I cowrote the script with Nick Pileggi because you can literally *see* it all in the book: cut to the keys flying into his hands, cut to the shoes and move up to show his new clothes. It's all in the editing, except for the dialogue scenes. In a way *GoodFellas* ended up being already done in my head and on paper so that shooting seemed an afterthought. I kept thinking, "Why couldn't they do it themselves without me?" It was all there on paper.

THE GRIFTERS

A Miramax Films Release.

Director: Stephen Frears. *Screenplay*: Donald Westlake, *based on the novel* by Jim Thompson. *Producers*: Martin Scorsese, Robert Harris, James Painten. *Executive Producer*: Barbara De Fina. *Co-Producer*: Peggy Rajski. *Cinematography*: Oliver Stapleton. *Editor*: Mike Audsley.

Cast: Anjelica Huston (Lily Dillon), John Cusack (Roy Dillon), Annette Bening (Myra Langtry), Pat Hingle (Bobo Justus), Henry Jones (Simms), Michael Laskin (Irv), Eddie Jones (Mints), J.T. Walsh (Cole), Charles Napier (Hebbing), Jan Munroe (Guy at Bar), Stephen Tobolowsky (Jeweler), Richard Holden (Cop), Xander Berkeley (Lt. Pierson), Michael Greene (Dealer), Jason Ronard (Shill), John Drew Barrymore (Roper), Sandy Baron (Doctor), Lou Hancock (Nurse), Juliet Landau (Lili, ages 19-22), Bradley Pierce (Roy, age 5), Gailard Sartain (Joe), Noelle Harling (Carol), Ivette Soler (Maid), Ashton Buzamat (Roy, age 8), Jack McGee (Clerk), Ron Campbell (Second Clerk), Steve Buscemi (Kaggs), Paul Adelstein (Soldier #1), Jeremy Piven (Soldier #2), Gregory Sporlader (Soldier #3), David Sinaiko (Soldier #4), Jeff Perry (Drunk), Micole Mercurio (Waitress), Jonathan Gries (Drunk's Friend), Sy Richardson (Cab Driver), Frances Bay (Arizona Motel Clerk), Teresa Gilmore Cappa (Vickie, the Receptionist), Billy Ray Sharkey (G-man #1), Jimmy Noonan (Bartender), John Gillespie (Bartender/stunt), Elizabeth Ann Feeley (Receptionist #2), Trisha King (Beachgoer #1), Robert J. Wees (Racetrack Announcer), Martin Scorsese (Narrator).

Casting: Juliet Taylor, Vickie Thomas. *Casting Associate*: Jory Weitz. *Production Designer*: Dennis Casner. *Art Director*: Leslie McDonald. *Set Designer*: Gershon Ginsberg. *Set Director*: Nancy Haigh. *Production Manager*: Llewellyn Wells. *First Assistant Director*: Stephen Buck. *Assistant Editor*: Julie Fainer. *Production Coordinator*: Kathleen Courtney. *Script Supervisor*: Mary Cybulski. *Production Assistants*: Brian Jochum, Peter Nunnery. *Stunt Coordinators*: Gary Jansen, John Gillespie. *Lead Man*: Robert Greenfield. *Key Set Dresser*: Tinker Linville. *Scenic Artist*: Michael Diagle. *Prop Master*: Doug Fox. *Still Photographer*: Suzanne Hanover. *Sound Mixer*: John Sutton. *Costume Designer*: Richard Hornung. *Assistant Designer*: Mark Bridges. *Hairstylist*: Sydney Cornell. *Makeup*: Juliet Hewett.
Awards: New York Film Critics Association, Los Angeles Film Critics Association, and National Society of Film Critics, Anjelica Huston, Best Actress. Academy Award Nominations: Anjelica Huston, Best Actress; Annette Bening, Best Supporting Actress; Stephen Frears, Best Director; Donald Westlake, Best Adapted Screenplay.
M.P.A.A. Rating: R.
Running Time: 119 minutes.
Home Video: cassette.

Synopsis: When smalltime con man Roy Dillon lands in the hospital, his mother, Lily, comes to his aid. Roy is wary of his mother, who works for professional gambler Bobo Justus by placing large bets in order to influence the odds at racetracks. In return, Lily is wary of Roy's girlfriend Myra, a con woman who wants to involve Roy in a big-time job.

Myra attempts to murder Lily, but the older woman outsmarts her, kills her, and assumes Myra's identity to start a new life with money stolen from Bobo. Roy refuses to go along with her, and in a struggle is accidentally killed.

Commentary: Scorsese's first film as a producer is an adaptation of "hardboiled" novelist Jim Thompson's darkly cynical character study of smalltime con artists. It is the sort of film that always interested Scorsese as a moviegoer. As a movie*maker*, however, Scorsese has a rather different relationship with the elements *The Grifters* entails. While a story about small and big time con artists conning one another might have attracted his interest as a director (i.e., his love of characters living on the margins of society), it is highlighted by other aspects that he, in all likelihood, would not have been comfortable in dealing with (particularly the quasi-incestuous mother-son relationship between Huston and Cuzack). Having directed such off-beat projects as *Bloody Kids, My Beautiful Laundrette*, and *Sammy and Rosie Get Laid*, Stephen Frears has little difficulty coming to grips with the Thompson story. Being British, Frears regards it all from the coolly distanced perspective of an outsider. This, coupled with the film's odd mixture of time frames (it appears to be taking place in both the Los Angeles of the 1950s *and* today), gives *The Grifters* its special flavor.

AKIRA KUROSAWA'S DREAMS

Scorsese appears as Van Gogh in the fifth sequence of writer-director Akira Kurosawa's fanciful retelling of some of his own dreams. Much like the White Rabbit in *Alice in Wonderland*, Scorsese's Van Gogh tells the film's narrator he has no time to talk, but must paint his canvases instead. The film is in Japanese, but Scorsese's Van Gogh speaks in English.

SCORSESE: Kurosawa said he wanted me in the part because of the way I acted in 1980 when I went before him to plead my case to put him on the list of supporters for my color film stock preservation effort. He said he remembered my "intensity." He only gave me ten minutes, and you know, I talk *fast*!

 1991

GUILTY BY SUSPICION

Scorsese plays Joe Lesser, a character modeled in part on director Joseph Losey, in this drama of the Hollywood Red Scare era, written and directed by longtime Scorsese producer Irwin Winkler.

CAPE FEAR

Universal Pictures. Amblin Entertainment in association with Cappa Films and Tribeca Productions.

Director: Martin Scorsese. *Screenplay*: Wesley Strick, *based on a screenplay by* James R. Webb and the novel *The Executioners by* John D. MacDonald. *Producer*: Barbara De Fina. *Executive Producers*: Kathleen Kennedy and Frank

Marshall. *Cinematography*: Freddie Francis. Bernard Herrmann's *original score adapted, arranged and conducted by* Elmer Bernstein. *Editor*: Thelma Schoonmaker. *Production Designer*: Henry Bumstead.

Cast: Robert De Niro (Max Cady), Nick Nolte (Sam Bowden), Jessica Lange (Leigh Bowden), Juliette Lewis (Danielle Bowden), Joe Don Baker (Claude Kersek), Robert Mitchum (Lieutenant Elgart), Gregory Peck (Lee Heller), Martin Balsam (Judge), Illeana Douglas (Lori Davis), Fred Dalton Thompson (Tom Broadbent), Zully Montero (Graciella), Craig Henne, Forest Burton, Edgar Allan Poe IV, Rod Ball, W. Paul Bodie (Prisoners), Joel Kolker, Antoni Corone (Correction Officers), Tamara Jones (Ice Cream Cashier), Domenica Scorsese (Danny's Girlfriend),Catherine Scorsese, Charles Scorsese (Fruit Stand Customers).

Costume Designer: Rita Ryack. *Casting*: Ellen Lewis. *Unit Production Manager*: Deborah Lee. *First Assistant Director*: Joe Reidy. *Camera Operator*: Gordon Hayman. *Art Director*: Jack G. Taylor, Jr. *Set Decorator*: Alan Hicks. *Production Sound Mixer*: Tod Maitland. *Supervising Sound Editor*: Skip Lievsay. *Supervising Dialogue Editor*: Philip Stockton. *Re-Recording Mixer*: Tom Fleischman. *Post Production Supervisor*: Margery Mailman. *First Assistant Editor*: Cara Silverman. *Music Scoring Mixer*: Shawn Murphy. *Orchestration*: Emilie A. Bernstein. *Music Consultant*: Christopher Palmer. *Music Editor*: Kathy Durning - Triad Music, Inc. *Orchestra Conductor*: Emile Charlap. *Dialogue Editor*: Marissa Littlefield. *Sound Effects Recordist*: Andy Aaron. *Mr. De Niro's Makeup and Hair*: Ilona Herman. *Mr. Nolte's Makeup and Hair*: Edouard Henriques III. *Ms. Lange's Makeup*: Dorothy Pearl. *Ms. Lange's Hairstylist*: Lydell Quiyou. *First Assistant Camera*: William McConnell. *Production Coordinator*: Celia Randolph. *Assistant Production Coordinator*: Lisa Maniscalco. *Script Supervisor*: Corey B. Yugler. *Lead Set Dresser*: Kevin Oates. *Set Dressers*: Michael Calabrese, Robert Crowley, Eric Helfritz, Richard Howarth, Theodore Pappas, J. Randy Peterson. *Propmaster*: Richard Adee. *Propman*: Gary Dunham. *Miniature Special Effects Supervisor*: Derek Meddings. *Miniature Special Effects filmed at the Magic Camera Company, Producer*: Roger Lofting. *Director of Photography*: Paul Wilson. *Art Director*: Jose Granell. *Production Manager*: Susie Ford. *First Camera Operator*: John Morgan. *Matte Painting and Special Optical Effects*: Syd Dutton and Bill Taylor, A.S.C. of Illusion Arts. *Technical Coordinator*: Douglas Merrifield. *Extras Casting*: Ellen Jacoby Casting International.

Songs: "Tipitina," written by Alice Byrd, performed by Professor Longhair; "Patience," written and performed by Guns N' Roses; "Per Te D'Immenso Giubilo," from "Lucia di Lammermoor" by Gaetano Donizetti; "Do Right Woman - Do Right Man," written by Dan Penn and Chips Moman, performed ny Aretha Franklin; *Video Clips*: "The Bog," performed by Bigod 20; "Been Caught Stealing," performed by Jane's Addiction; "The Creature From the Black Leather Lagoon," performed by The Cramps. *Film Clips*: *Problem Child* and *All That Heaven Allows,* courtesy of Universal Pictures. Filmed in Panavision. Color by Technicolor. Dolby Stereo.

Academy Award Nominations: Robert De Niro, Best Actor; Juliette Lewis, Best Supporting Actress.

M.P.A.A. Rating: R.

Running Time: 127 minutes.

Synopsis: Convicted rapist Max Cady leaves prison after fourteen years. Having learned that Sam Bowden, the public defender assigned to his case, withheld evidence that might have set him free, Cady is determined to have revenge. Bowden, now a prosperous lawyer, has troubles of his own—a rebellious teenage daughter Danielle, and his wife, Leigh, still resentful over his sexual infidelity that nearly ended their marriage. Armed with these facts, Cady subtly sets the Bowmans against one another and makes threats on the family. Sam is unable to keep Cady at bay legally (or illegally). After Cady murders Bowman's housekeeper and a detective Bowman hired to protect him, the lawyer and his family escape to their vacation houseboat in Cape Fear. Cady follows, and in the film's climax battles with Sam and his family as a storm rages. The boat is destroyed in the storm and Cady drowns, but the shaken family survives.

Commentary: Though it's not sexually graphic by today's standards the original 1962 version of *Cape Fear* directed by J. Lee Thompson, was considered the most daringly "adult" of the psychological thrillers of its era. This was due principally to the film's dwelling on the possibility that Max Cady (played by Robert Mitchum) would rape Bowden's (Gregory Peck) wife and daughter (Polly Bergen and Lori Martin). In this equally controversial remake, Scorsese downplays rape as a threat in favor of psychological seduction. In the film's most famous scene, De Niro's Cady, pretending to be a drama teacher, confronts Danielle (Lewis) in a deserted classroom. Instead of attacking her — as we in the audience expect — he simply talks to her, preying on her curiousity about sex and her mistrust and resentment of her parents.

While containing several scenes of physical violence (the attack on the legal assistant played by Illeana Douglas, the murders of the housekeeper and the detective), Scorsese's *Cape Fear* achieves its greatest impact through suspense. Evoking both Hitchcock (there are homages to *Vertigo*, *Psycho*, *Marnie* and *The Birds*) and the lush melodramas of the late fifties and early sixties (particularly Vincente Minnelli films like *Some Came Running* and *Two Weeks in Another Town*), *Cape Fear* is both a thriller in its own right and a comment on the thriller form. By casting Gregory Peck, Robert Mitchum, and Martin Balsam in cameo parts, and using Bernard Herrmann's score from the 1962 version, Scorsese makes plain his desire to keep faith with Hollywood's past. But, by making a popular genre film, he demonstrates to the current Hollywood establishment that he is not an ivory-tower artist.

SCORSESE: I'd read different scripts. Bob [De Niro] asked me to do it a few times, and Steve [Spielberg] did a few times. Then Stephen Frears got involved and Donald Westlake did a script. They asked me to come down for a reading. Kevin Kline, Demi Moore and a bunch of people read. It was kind of nice, but it was the same script [as the original film]. I started to get bored halfway through. So Steve said, "Well, if you don't like the script you can always change it." I said, "Oh!"

1992

THE AGE OF INNOCENCE
A Columbia Pictures Release.

Director: Martin Scorsese. *Producer:* Barbara De Fina. *Screenplay:* Martin Scorsese and Jay Cocks, adapted from the novel by Edith Wharton. *Cinematography:* Michael Ballhaus. *Film Editor:* Thelma Schoonmaker. *Production Designer:* Dante Feretti. *Visual Consultant:* Robin Standefer. *Casting:* Ellen Lewis. *Costume Designer:* Gabriella Pescucci. *Assistant Director:* Joseph Reidy.

Cast: Daniel Day Lewis (Newland Archer), Michelle Pfeiffer (Ellen Olenska), Winona Ryder (May Welland), Miriam Margolyes (Mrs. Mingott), Richard E. Grant (Larry Lefferts), Alec McGowan (Silerton Jackson), Geraldine Chaplin ((Mrs.

Welland), Mary Beth Hurt (Regina Beaufort), Stuart Wilson (Julius Beaufort), Sian Phillips (Mrs. Archer), Caroline Farina (Janie), Michael Gough (Henry van der Luyden), Alexis Smith (Louisa van der Luyden), Norman Lloyd (Ledder Blair), Jonathan Pryce (Riviere), Domenica Scorsese (Katie Blinker), Robert Sean Leonard (Ted), Cristina Pronzati (Italian Maid), Joanne Woodward (Narrator).

Synopsis: Adapted by Scorsese and Jay Cocks from Edith Wharton's novel (filmed in 1924 under the same title and again in 1934 by RKO as a vehicle for John Boles and Irene Dunn, this romance is set in New York high society of the 1870s. It tells of Newland Archer (Daniel Day Lewis), a fashionable man about town, who, on the eve of his wedding, falls in love with his married cousin. Counseling her not to go ahead with her plans for a divorce, he goes ahead with his marriage— knowing that his true feelings have been compromised. Years later, after his children are grown and his wife has died, he gets another chance to meet his lost love, but passes it by.

Mad Dog and Glory

Written by longtime Scorsese collaborator Richard Price, this Scorsese/De Fina production, directed by John McNaughton, concerns a mild-mannered police detective ironically nicknamed Mad Dog (Robert De Niro). He inadvertently saves the life of a Chicago loan shark (Bill Murray), and is offered the favors of a woman called Glory (Uma Thurman).

FUTURE PROJECTS:

Mine

A musical biography of the life of composer George Gershwin, this Irwin Winkler production has been in the planning stages for nearly a decade at Warner Bros. Paul Schrader wrote a script dealing with the high points of Gershwin's life in an episodic fashion and bracketing each episode with musical production numbers. This approach to the Gershwin story was put aside in favor a new one by John Guare.

Scorsese: Paul Schrader's script was wonderful. It had all sorts of interesting things in it. But I looked at it and said, "Is there anything for me to direct?" It was all *there* like *Mishima*. Guare's approach is about the people that surround Gershwin. The title comes from the song "Mine." It expresses how the people around him feel: "He belongs to me!" "No, he belongs to me!" So when he dies there's this void in their lives. It's about how a genius's life affects all the others who live in his shadow.

Silence

Based on a novel by Shusaku Endo, this is a tale of a Portuguese priest living in seventeenth-century Japan, a time of religious persecution. Like the missionaries who have come before him, the priest realizes that by practicing Christianity he is risking an almost certain death. If he recants his beliefs, he may be able to survive.

Scorsese: I think the Japanese director Shinoda made a version of the story twenty years ago. But that doesn't really stop me, because I think it's a great story. I have a feeling it should be done really quickly, like eight weeks. I don't feel I want to do it next, being so close to *Last Temptation*. I feel I want to have some fun and do costume drama, a musical, and then *Silence*.

The Gangs of New York

Scorsese has been interested for over a decade in fashioning a film based on Herbert Asbury's classic study of the turn-of-the-century urban underworld.

Scorsese: It has to be constructed on paper before any money can be spent on it. We did a draft of it last year, Jay Cocks and I. We're going to try to do another and see if that works. If not, we'll get somebody else to work on it, and hopefully Universal and Alberto Grimaldi will want to make it sometime over the next few years. It's a big picture, and in today's Hollywood you have to be very careful about how much you spend on certain stories, certain themes. For us, *The Gangs of New York* is the beginning of the gangster film overlapping with the end of the western.

THE NEIGHBORHOOD

SCORSESE: This is a project that Nicholas Pileggi and I are working on. It's going to be on an epic scale, examining three generations of an Italian family in America, starting from way back when the family was in Sicily. It will show the change that moves from generation to generation; the change from Italian to Italian-American to American. A lot of the stories in the film will involve things that actually happened in my family, stories my parents told me over the years — like the ones in *Italianamerican*. The film will be about trying to keep a family together, which is a hard thing when you're living in a situation where the influence of the underworld is all around you. People tried to lead honorable lives while still having to deal with crime.

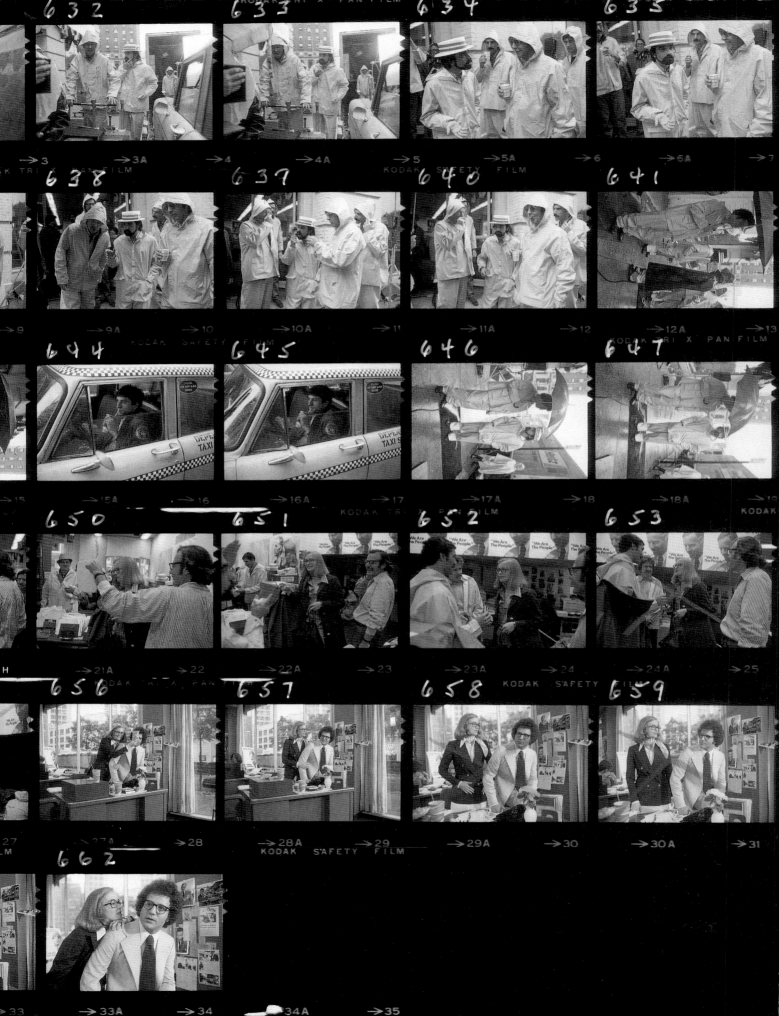

Index

THE END